Lights in the Darkness

Lights in the Darkness

Exploring Catholic Themes in Twelve Extraordinary Films

Phillip M. Thompson

CASCADE *Books* · Eugene, Oregon

LIGHTS IN THE DARKNESS
Exploring Catholic Themes in Twelve Extraordinary Films

Copyright © 2017 Phillip M. Thompson. All rights reserved. Except for brief quotations in critical publications or reviews, no part of this book may be reproduced in any manner without prior written permission from the publisher. Write: Permissions, Wipf and Stock Publishers, 199 W. 8th Ave., Suite 3, Eugene, OR 97401.

Cascade Books
An Imprint of Wipf and Stock Publishers
199 W. 8th Ave., Suite 3
Eugene, OR 97401

www.wipfandstock.com

PAPERBACK ISBN: 978-1-4982-9508-6
HARDCOVER ISBN: 978-1-4982-9510-9
EBOOK ISBN: 978-1-4982-9509-3

Cataloguing-in-Publication data:

Names: Thompson, Phillip M.

Title: Lights in the darkness : exploring Catholic themes in twelve extraordinary films / Phillip M. Thompson.

Description: Eugene, OR: Cascade Books, 2017 | Includes bibliographical references and index.

Identifiers: ISBN 978-1-4982-9508-6 (paperback) | ISBN 978-1-4982-9510-9 (hardcover) | ISBN 978-1-4982-9509-3 (ebook)

Subjects: LCSH: Motion pictures—Religious aspects—Catholic Church | Film | Religion

Classification: PN1995.9. R4 T50 2017 (print) | PN1995.9. R4 T50 (ebook)

Manufactured in the U.S.A.   JUNE 30, 2017

I dedicate this book to my professor, Jean Bethke Elshtain of the University of Chicago, who used film in many of her classes. It was an honor to be mentored by such a special scholar.

The people who sit in darkness have seen a great light.

—MATT 4:16; ISA 9:2

Table of Contents

Preface ix
Acknowledgements xix
Introduction 1
  Catholic Themes
    Grace
    Sacramentality
    Conversion and Redemption
    Fortitude
    Pilgrimage
    The Common Good
    Justice
    Conscience
    Faith and Reason
    Wisdom
  A Spiritual Mosaic

Part I—Saints and Sinners
Chapter 1 *A Man for All Seasons* 19
Chapter 2 *The Flowers of Saint Francis* 29
Chapter 3 *The Mission* 38

Part II—Religious in the Modern World
Chapter 4 *Diary of a Country Priest* 51
Chapter 5 *Of Gods and Men* 60

Part III—The Common Good
Chapter 6 *Babette's Feast* 71
Chapter 7 *Spitfire Grill* 79

Table of Contents

Part IV—Justice and Human Dignity
Chapter 8 *Au Revoir Les Enfants* 89
Chapter 9 *Dead Man Walking* 98
Chapter 10 *Entertaining Angels* 110

Part V—Prophetic Warnings
Chapter 11 *Decalogue 1* 123
Chapter 12 *GATTACA* 133

Part VI—The Problems with Jesus Movies
Chapter 13 The Challenges of a Jesus Movie 149
    Challenge #1 Fully Human and Fully God
    Challenge #2 Jesus and His Gaps
    Challenge #3 Which Jesus?
    Challenge #4 Fault-Lines: The Role of Jews and Romans
    An Impossible Task

Part VII—Director's Cut
Chapter 14 Exploring the Lights 163

Appendix A: Movie Lists 169
Bibliography 175
Index/Subject Index 183
Scripture Index 190

Preface

When movies explore the complexity and depth of the human experience, they can be transformative. A number of years ago, I taught a class on law and ethics at Saint Edward's University in Austin, Texas. I showed my class *Decalogue 5—You Shall Not Kill,* a movie from the series on the Ten Commandments by the Polish director, Krzysztof Kieslowski. I was worried about how the students would respond to a film in Polish with English subtitles that had none of the glitz and glamor of American cinema. In fact, the film had quite an impact; the students were stunned. The artistry of the director, the skill of the actors, and the brilliance of the screenwriter had challenged their minds and moved their hearts. When the film was finished, they remained silently in their seats for several minutes.

With the help of the film, my students had entered into a dreary, dying communist world and met a young man, Jacek, charged with the apparently senseless and brutal murder of a taxi driver. As you follow his story, you witness the murder and proceed to the trial. Jacek suffers guilt and disillusionment from the death of his sister who was killed by a drunk young man on a tractor. Jacek had been drinking with the young man before he got on the tractor. Jacek is filled with shame and rage. Given the source of his rage, the balance of mercy and judgment at his trial is tipped in favor of punishing him but perhaps preserving his life. Nonetheless, the pitiless machinery of the state ignores the background story and discards the prisoner's life. In the end all that remains is pain. Alone after the trial, the defense attorney repeats in anguish, "I abhor it! I abhor it!"

So the content of *Decalogue 5* through the art of Kieslowski compelled my students to think carefully about the criminal justice system. What is justice—giving each person what is due them? What is relevant in the taking of a life by the state? The movie reminds the viewer that he or she has a responsibility for justice. The ideal of justice explored in this film is just one

Preface

of the theological themes analyzed in the book. This book will focus on the positive possibilities for such reflections by analyzing a number of Catholic themes in twelve special movies.

My analysis will employ a specific form of content analysis that Melanie Wright, author of *Religion and Film*, describes as one that applies "particular theological or doctrinal positions" in order to discover "God's presence in everything including the products of human culture—to look at how films raise and handle questions of meaning and in doing so prompt religious adherents to think about 'the spirit of the age.'"[1] My students, watching *Decalogue 1*, were brought to a moment of reflection on the spirit of their age—a century of unimaginable state-sponsored death.

The art of film builds on a long history of human visual content that has sought to express meaning. We see this in the drawings on the caves of Lascaux, located in what is today France, seventeen thousand years ago. Images have shaped religions through the millennia, but this reality has too often been ignored or undervalued in the scholarly world. Margaret Miles concluded in *Seeing and Believing, Religion and Values in the Movies* that "religious images have informed the religious lives of our antecedents far more pervasively and profoundly than our slender attention to them in the academic study of religion would acknowledge."[2]

Not everyone would encourage the exploration of this connection between visual images and the faith. Some religious critics might well ask of my book, "Are you not mixing Athens and Jerusalem, the profane and the sacred?" After all, the movie industry is often portrayed—and not without some justification—as antagonistic to the Catholic faith. Scott Derrickson, director of *The Exorcism of Emily Rose*, who is Christian but not Catholic, notes that media images of Catholics are often "unqualified portrayals of Catholics as sexually repressed killjoys, corrupt moneygrubbers, maddening hypocrites, fanatical criminals, medieval moralists, and predatory child rapists." For his examples, he cites George Carlin's scandalous Cardinal Glick in *Dogma*, Nicole Kidman's crazed Catholic mother in *The Others*, and John Standing's depraved Bishop Lilliman in *V for Vendetta*.[3]

Beyond a tendency to narrowly stereotype Catholicism, modern cinema often presents content problems in its espousal of mindless violence, sexuality, and crudity. My brother-in-law, Michael Zibilich, has a rule that

---

1. Wright, *Religion and Film*, 14.
2. Miles, *Seeing and Believing*, x.
3. Greydanus, "Is Hollywood Anti-Catholic?"

Preface

if something explodes in the first five minutes, he leaves the theater. He must have departed from many movies. Of course, there is nothing wrong on occasion with some adventure, escapism, or a bit of mindless pleasure, even with some explosions. Not all visual narratives have to be profoundly edifying. The novelist Walker Percy confessed that he enjoyed on occasion the secret pleasure of sitting in a motel room watching the television show, *The Incredible Hulk*.[4] There must be a limit to such pleasures, however, for we risk becoming mindless consumers absorbing endless amounts of visual cotton candy. The result is not surprising: brain decay. We risk sinking to what the monk and social critic Thomas Merton described as a "subnatural passivity" in which we accept a "vast, inhuman void, full of words, formulas, slogans, declarations, echoes, ideologies!" We become passive recipients prone to manipulation by slick and stimulating messaging as form trumps content. If we abandon serious thought in our culture, we risk becoming enthralled to "forces that are arbitrary, destructive, blind."[5] Concerns about the depth of visual content are especially pressing in the current screen age where the average adult American is in front of a screen for more than ten hours a day.[6]

Considering the negative potential in films, one temptation is to employ governmental censorship to remove the pernicious aspects. This remedy began with reaction to *The Kiss* in 1896, where two actors re-enacted a scene on film from their play, *The Widow Jones*, for less than a minute. One magazine decried this "beastly" film with two people "pasturing on each other's lips." The content became much more daring with subsequent movies that tackled issues like prostitution, venereal disease, and abortion. At the same time, movies were attracting large audiences with weekly attendance in Manhattan reaching one hundred thousand by 1910.[7]

The combination of high attendance and questionable content provoked a reaction. Censorship efforts became national with the creation of the National Board of Censorship of Motion Pictures in 1909—a voluntary agency that granted its seal of approval to 95 percent of the submitted films.

---

4. Leary, "Surviving His Own Bad Habits."

5. Merton, "Letter to Mr. L. Dickson," 168–69; Merton, *Conjectures of a Guilty Bystander*, 79.

6. Bauder, "Media use in America up a full hour over just last year." The exact number for media use is ten hours and thirty-nine minutes. This claim is based on a study of the Nielsen Company for the first three months of 2016. The number of hours in 2015 for the same time period was nine hours and thirty-nine minutes.

7. Walsh, *Sin and Censorship*, 4–7.

Preface

The regulation of movies was buttressed by the United States Supreme Court's unanimous decision to rule as constitutional a public board of censors in Ohio in *Mutual Film Corporation v. Industrial Commission of Ohio* in 1915.[8]

In 1930 the Motion Picture Producers and Distributors of America adopted a Motion Picture Production Code, sometimes referred as the "Cardinal's Code," because of the Catholic influence. The Production Code provided a single set of standards for judging film.[9] The code had limited impact until the formation of a movie watchdog in 1934, the Catholic Legion of Decency, that worked closely with the Production Code Administration to modify and block a wide array of films.[10]

This censorship regime began to crumble in the 1960s because of a national change in morals, a lessening of Church control, and a less compliant Hollywood leadership. The national consensus on what was vulgar or problematic was rapidly dissolving. The legality of censorship was challenged in the 1950s and 1960s by United States Supreme Court cases limiting First Amendment impingements on film. Governmental boards of censorship were eliminated. The movie industry abandoned the Production Code in 1968 and adopted the current rating system.[11]

With or without official censorship, Catholics still have to discern how to engage this influential new communication technology of the twentieth century. The Church gradually adopted a position of denouncing immoral content while concurrently recognizing the positive possibilities in film. In 1936 in the encyclical *Vigilanti Cura*, Pope Pius XI recognized in movies a very popular and powerful medium that could be dangerous, especially for the young when films "show life under a false light," "cloud ideals," and destroy "pure love" or "respect for marriage and affection for the family."[12] His successor, Pope Pius XII, also recognized the powerful capacity of films to locate the viewer in the perspective of an actor and to experience his or her feelings, emotions, and beliefs. In speaking to Italian filmmakers in 1955, Pius XII asked them to weigh carefully their responsibilities.

---

8. Jewett, "'A Capacity for Evil,'" 59–78; *Mutual Film Corporation v. Industrial Commission of Ohio*, 236 US 230 (1915).

9. Walsh, *Sin and Censorship*, 61.

10. Black, *The Catholic Crusade*, 4–5.

11. Ibid., 229–31.

12. Pius XI, *Vigilanti Cura*, n. 15–20.

Preface

> Don't you think it would be a good idea, if right from the beginning, you should take the honest evaluation of movies and the rejection of anything unworthy or degrading into your own hands in a special way? No one could make the charge of incompetence or undue interference if you, acting in a serious-minded way, with a maturity of judgment based on wise moral principles, should express disapproval of anything that was harmful to human dignity, to the good of individuals and society and especially to the young .... In place of senseless or degrading shows, give us good, noble, beautiful performances, which can be deeply moving, and even touch the heights of art without being disturbing and harmful.[13]

Today, governmental censorship and formal Church admonitions no longer have as much influence. Instead, individual Catholics must utilize their consciences and engage in a careful discernment. There are many movies that deserve a harsh critique and many more that should be labeled mindless if not per se harmful. We can find little in many movies to nurture our moral life. And yet there are some amazing pearls strewn amidst the chaff.

These pearls can appeal to another human desire—to seek deeper levels of meaning. Our restless hearts cannot ignore those deep transcendent yearnings, the realm of what the theologian Paul Tillich labeled "ultimate concerns."[14] There is something compelling in the human journey that often compels people to explore the realm of "ultimate concerns" such as the meaning of despair and hope, sin and salvation, and life and death. If a film fully explores human life, it will touch on such "ultimate concerns" and will inevitably explore some of the themes in this book.

Given the aforementioned possibilities and challenges, I would propose a dialogue paradigm with film that is a good faith effort to explore common ground and to bear faithful, but not rigidly hostile, witness to any differences. As Saint Thomas Aquinas noted, "We must love them both, those whose opinion we share and those whose opinions we reject. For both have labored in the search for truth and both have helped us in the finding of it." Aquinas was not a closet relativist with his charitable approach. He noted that we should seek positions with greater validity. He followed the aforementioned quote with, "Yet we must 'be persuaded by the

---

13. Pius XII, "Technical Advances and the Power of Movies," 235–36.
14. Tillich, "The Lost Dimension in Religion," 29, 76–79.

more certain,' i.e. we must follow the opinion of those who have attained the truth with greater certitude."[15]

In this dialogue paradigm, an open engagement and prophetic witness are held together in a constructive tension. In his thoughtful letter to George Coyne on religion and science, Saint John Paul II stated that we should proceed in a form of dialogue that he labeled "critical openness," and I think this ideal can be applied more broadly to an engagement of the Church with culture and its art forms like film. With "critical openness," we can approach films seeking to balance a prophetic criticism of any ethical problems with an appreciation for their insights and artistry. This engagement should operate in a spirit of charity that seeks opportunities for understanding and mutual enrichment. For example, Saint John XXIII's open engagement with culture sparked the atheist, Marxist, and homosexual Pier Pasolini, to produce *The Gospel According to Saint Matthew*. Critical openness permits us to adopt, as Saint John Paul II observed, "a growing critical openness towards people of different cultures and backgrounds, different competencies and viewpoints." And what is our alternative? We either approach such a dialogue with "depth and nuance or with a shallowness that debases the Gospel and leaves us ashamed before history."[16] A dialogue with film that has depth and nuance has much to offer our spiritually parched age.[17]

There are some propitious signs such as a renewed interest in biblical movies that may bode well for such a dialogue. In 2014, Hollywood released *Noah* and *Exodus*. This renewed interest is a bit of a mixed blessing. On the positive side, *Noah* has some good acting and rather amazing special effects like the flood scene. In another aspect, however, the film is like a cross between the Bible and *Transformers*. Rock figures, who are the descendants of fallen angels or Nephilim, morph from boulders into rock-throwing giants on the side of Noah. In the Bible, they are not rock monsters and do not side with Noah.[18] Moreover, the film is also lacking in artistic merit. The movie critic Matt Zoller Seitz correctly summarizes

---

15. Aquinas, *Commentary on Aristotle's Metaphysics*, 12:9, no. 2566.
16. On Pier Pasolini and John XXIII see Criterion Collection, "The Gospel According to Saint Matthew."; John Paul II, "Letter to George V. Coyne."
17. See Barbour, *Religion in an Age of Science*, 27–28; Haught, *Science and Religion*, 17–21.
18. Gen 6:4.

Preface

the film as "an immense, weird, ungainly, often laughably overwrought and silly movie."[19]

The movie *Exodus* offers another cinematic glimpse into a heroic biblical episode. *Exodus* portrays with proper depth the intensity of Moses, the tenderness of the marital and familial bonds, and the terrible plight of the Hebrew slaves. Still, there are some curious aspects. The plot eliminates the many confrontations of Moses with Pharaoh and the prophet's initial insecurities regarding his ability to speak for his people. Moses is also portrayed as more modern superhero and warrior than biblical prophet. This superhero aspect is appealing to our culture, but it ignores much of the richness of the biblical story.

Despite the considerable flaws of *Noah* and *Exodus* that distort the biblical narratives, practical considerations favoring the continuing of the resurgence of biblical films include a potentially large audience, the films not requiring purchasing rights to the stories, and their dramatic story lines. Perhaps the most compelling reason is a simple one. As Jonathan Bock, president of Grace Hill Media, a marketing firm that has helped several Hollywood studios target religious audiences notes, "Hollywood has the best storytellers. And the Bible has the best stories."[20]

A connection to Hollywood, while not without potential problems, could prove beneficial for religions in a society in which many people are abandoning their religious affiliations. The largest religious affiliation for incoming freshman students at universities in the United States as of 2015 was none at 27.5 percent. The percentage of students with no specific religious affiliation has doubled since 2000.[21] These students are not indifferent to transcendent possibilities. Many are spiritual but not religious, meaning they do not adhere to the creed of a specific denomination or religion, but 69 percent of the unaffiliated believe in God.[22] Films can provide an invaluable venue for engagement between seekers and religions. Many people are longing for serious faith-based films and an equally serious reflection and critique of such films. Hence, I wrote this book, in part, to provide a nexus for such a dialogue. I have selected films in this book with religious themes

19. Seitz, "Noah."
20. Orden, "Hollywood's New Bible Stories," D 1–2.
21. Higher Education Research Institute at UCLA, *The American Freshman: National Norms Fall 2015*, 22. To get the doubling since 2000 compare the 2015 report with the chart on nones in the Higher Education Research Institute at UCLA, *The American Freshman: National Norms for Fall 2003*, 8.
22. Pew Research Religion and Public Life Project, "Nones on the Rise."

Preface

in movies that are not biblical. In everyday life and not just in the Bible, there are many seeds of spiritual possibility that we can fruitfully explore.

I suspect that this book will raise another question: why focus on Catholic themes? I think honesty in advertising requires me to confess that a significant portion of the content of the selected movies demonstrate themes of critical importance to Catholics such as sacramentality.[23] More importantly, I define and examine these themes in ways that are derived from my Catholic faith.

Of course you do not have to be Catholic to benefit from these films. Anyone who is interested in ultimate questions about the human condition may find these films of interest. It is worth noting that a majority of directors and screenwriters for these films were not Catholic, and quite a few were without any formal religious affiliation.[24] In addition, the selected movies examine the enormous complexity and richness of the human condition with considerable artistry and nuanced story lines. Because of their artistry, these films exhibit greater subtlety and depth than in many movies made by and for Christians.[25]

Sometimes, the dramatic and multilayered stories happen in explicitly Catholic contexts with characters who are saints recognized by the Church and Catholic priests, brothers, or religious sisters as in *A Man for All Seasons*, *The Flowers of St. Francis*, *Dead Man Walking*, *The Mission*, *Of Gods and Men*, and *Diary of a Country Priest*. Religious are less prominent, but the Catholic cultural aspect remains prominent in the iron curtain-era Poland of *Decalogue 1* and the Second World War France of *Au Revoir Les Enfants*. Still, I did not select only films with professed religious or explicitly Catholic cultures. There are no Catholic religious in the Protestant village of *Babette's Feast*, in the Gilead Maine of *Spitfire Grill*, or the science fiction future of *GATTACA*. What is Catholic in these films is how themes such as the operation of grace, redemption, the common good, and the sacramental dimensions of life shape these narratives. Finally, a unifying feature in all of the selected films is the assumption that life is a gift—a divine blessing that humanity may honor or squander.

23. When the title of a book hides a unequivocal denominational commitment by the author, this can justifiably lead to charges of intentional obfuscation. See Polk, "Review of *Christians in the Movies*."

24. I have not selected films by these worthy Catholic or raised as Catholic directors: Martin Scorsese, Alfred Hitchcock, Frank Capra, John Ford, Francis Coppola, and Brian de Palma. For their many worthy contributions, see Blake, *AfterImage*.

25. Parham, "Why Do Heathens Make the Best Films?"

Preface

Let me now share some additional aspects of my selection process. The number of potential selections was enormous, and it was not easy to winnow the field. My criteria included artistic excellence and the presence of profound spiritual themes. Most importantly, the films had to challenge my mind, touch my heart, and move my soul. Others may, with much justification, offer a very different list. To suggest some other movies, I have included in Appendix A: Movie Lists at the end of the book a list of movies from the Vatican Office of Social Communications, the *National Catholic Register*, and a Catholic movie expert, Richard Leonard, SJ. These lists will provide hundreds of additional movies that are worthy of your consideration.

Having explained my selection process, let me suggest some general questions for each of the twelve movies presented in this book.

- How do the movies help you to reflect on God, creation, and humanity?
- What spiritual themes are introduced?
- What is revealed about life as a pilgrimage?
- How do the sacramental themes such as God's grace operate in and through the world?
- What are the challenges of living ethically in a fallen world?

At the end of each chapter, I provide specific questions that will help you to explore each movie. In answering these questions, you will hopefully discover some insights on what it means to be fully human. In our brief moment of time, we experience love and hate, joy and loss, faith and despair. We need art to explore these opposing yet related realities and the many other dramatic aspects of human life in order to assist our innate human search for meaning.

So, what do we gain by viewing these twelve movies? These movies are presented as vehicles for a special journey, a pilgrimage into the mystery of God's creation. The Catholic writer Flannery O'Connor thought of mystery as an inexhaustible spiritual dimension that continually unlocked new possibilities about love, friendship, holiness, suffering, forgiveness, redemption, and death.[26] Hopefully, this book and the movies I have selected will provide some helpful guidance and illuminate your pilgrim's journey into the mystery.

---

26. O'Connor, *Mystery and Manners*, 79.

Acknowledgements

This book owes a profound debt of gratitude to Dr. Jean Bethke Elshtain, an amazing teacher and mentor for me at the University of Chicago Divinity School. Listening to her in class was a special experience. Her wry humor, considerable patience, and passionate commitment to the realm of ideas illuminated her classes. She also combined a warm, down-to-earth personality with razor-sharp capacities for parsing concepts and theories. Most importantly, she was wise—a virtue in short supply in any age. Finally, she had a special sense of how to integrate the best of human culture into her thought and classes. This included documentaries like *The Lynchburg Story* and films like *Blade Runner*.

I would be remiss if I did not thank my wife, Beth, and son, William. They both inspire me every day. In selecting the movies, I was thinking in part about the best movies I could give to William that would strengthen his faith and engage his intellect.

I also wish to thank those who reviewed chapters of the book and offered very helpful suggestions. This would include Dr. Pauline Albert, Mary Alma Durrett, Dr. Patty Kubus, and Ginia Taylor. I also benefited from student answers to questions on the movies in this book on an assignment on the film chapters that would include Daniel Busichio, Raekwon Malik, Clare Fogarty, Hannah Mallen, Yura Jang, Nasir Sayani, and Natasha Trepel.

Introduction

For God loves nothing so much as the one who dwells with Wisdom. For she is fairer than the sun and surpasses every constellation of the stars.

—WIS 7:28–29

IT WAS THE EVENING of March 28, 2012. Timothy Radcliffe, OP, the former Master of the Dominican order, strode slowly to a podium in the Glenn Memorial Church at Emory University in Atlanta, Georgia. His white habit was matched by his grey hair that was arranged somewhat haphazardly on his head. With an avuncular delivery, Radcliffe displayed his usual combination of dry wit and spiritual insight. His topic was "The Christian Imagination and the Contemporary Search for Wisdom." He began by talking of a recent "amazing" movie, *Of Gods and Men,* about a Trappist monastery in Algeria in the 1990s. Radcliffe had viewed the film with an atheist friend in London.

For Radcliffe, the film disclosed several important lessons about how a religion can engage contemporary culture. He observed that the Christian faith is powerful because it is based on finding "the universal in particular people." The particular people in *Of Gods and Men* were eight Trappist monks in Tibherine, Algeria who were caught in a civil war in the 1990s. Despite threats to their lives, the monks made a difficult decision to not abandon their monastery and to continue serving their local community. Once made, the decision was fatal. The film ends with the monks being marched by their captors into the fog and their deaths. Radcliffe argued, however, that you could not view their last moments as a defeat. The monks were still helping one another; they were true to their mission of being present to each other in charity to the very end. The film illustrated how they made the right decision through a careful discernment rooted in their monastic values of community, faith, and love.

Radcliffe ended his talk by noting that *Of Gods and Men* is also important because humanity needs stories that provide meaning and guidance. The abbot Christian de Chergé wrote a final letter read at the end of the film in which he forgave his killer and expressed a desire to meet him in heaven as "good thieves in paradise if it please God, Father of us both." Radcliffe concluded, "That's the victory: tender words in the face of violence." The movie is thus critical for our age, because it reveals that "God is here and that is what we must show people."[1]

Radcliffe's lecture discloses how movies are an art form with the power to transform, but why are films capable of such inspiration and connection? After all, the process of watching a movie in a theater often begins in a rather unremarkable fashion. As you pass through the preliminary on-screen petitions for food, silence, and upcoming attractions, the audience is buzzing with the usual chitchat. Then *it* begins. The lights are dimmed. The rustling of voices recedes. The moviegoer is swiftly drawn into another reality. We are placed in a world. The cinematography utilizes natural scenery, sets, props, actors, costumes, and lighting to present the director's vision of a specific location and moment in time. The first few minutes of the film are critical for setting a tone and raising and beginning to answer some key questions: Where am I? What is happening? Where is this going? The form and content reveal whether the film is a drama, a comedy, a love story, or an adventure.

The experience of the impact of a movie on our imaginations has always fascinated me. My first memory of a movie was *Mary Poppins*.[2] I went for my sixth birthday. I can still remember the pure joy of that day. The movie immediately drew my imagination into a very different world. Here was joy, wonder, and unapologetic fun. The film even had Dick Van Dyke dancing with animated penguins. Of course, why not?

In my teenage years, I was often attracted to movies with strong male characters in outrageous adventures. I enjoyed the cool, detached vengeance of Clint Eastwood in the *Dirty Harry* movies. "Go ahead, make

---

1. Radcliffe, "The Christian Imagination and the Contemporary Search for Wisdom."
2. I was one of those children that benefited from the book becoming a movie. So I was intrigued by the background story outlined in *Saving Mr. Banks*. I saw *Mary Poppins* at the Cherokee Theatre on Peachtree Road in Atlanta, Georgia.

INTRODUCTION

my day." Or, if I was in a slightly more refined escapist mood, there was always Sean Connery as James Bond. "Shaken, not stirred." With Bond, James Bond, good versus evil was packaged in very elaborate and stylized confrontations.

Turning to more serious films I viewed in my teenage years, there was another category of films—movies with meaning. These films of meaning raised questions that still resonate with me on many levels and have shaped my thought and growth as an adult. I was drawn to movies that captured the struggle of an individual caught in the middle of sublime historical forces.[3] Hence, I enjoyed the epic tale of Russia spinning into revolutionary chaos in *Dr. Zhivago*. The film presented the historical forces that capsized the life of a good man, the poet and doctor Yuri Zhivago. Who can forget the scenes of the steam train chugging through a pitiless winter during the Russian Revolution? From the train, Zhivago witnessed a village destroyed by the Communists for assisting White Revolutionaries. When the doctor had a chance encounter with the Communist general, Strelnikov, who ordered this destruction, Strelnikov warns that he had to make a point. Zhivago retorted, "Your point, their village." This scene displays how ideologies in seeking their lofty goals can justify many horrors. The Polish director Krzysztof Kieslowski, who lived under Communism, warned that we must be leery of ideologies that provide a "feeling of absolutely knowing," because "the next minute its Army boots. It always ends up like that."[4] For Catholics, lethal force may be necessary in a just war,[5] but lethal force is inherently dangerous because violence is too often based in an ideology or driven by fear. Such violence may override any humane impulses.

The dangers unleashed by fear were also part of my youth. As a young white Southerner, I was both chastened and uplifted by the film version of *To Kill a Mockingbird*. Gregory Peck as Atticus Finch reminded me of my father. He was strong, kind, and thoughtful. Atticus fights for a black sharecropper who is falsely accused of raping a white woman. Atticus stands for justice—giving each person their due under the law—regardless of the contempt directed at him. Even though he loses the case through the

---

3. Perhaps this interest stemmed from my having listened to my father's stories of being in the Navy in the Second World War.

4. Stok, ed., *Kieslowski on Kieslowski*, 36.

5. The Catholic Church is currently in a vigorous internal debate about the merits of its just war and pacifist traditions. The central question is whether the Church's traditional acceptance of a just war theory is compatible with the Catholic tradition. Magliano, "Vatican Conference Urges Church to Abandon Just War Theory."

prejudice in the system, Atticus is unbowed as he leaves the courtroom. The segregated blacks in the upper gallery of the courtroom slowly begin to stand as Atticus prepares to leave the courtroom. Reverend Sykes tells Atticus' daughter, Scout, to stand, because "Your father's passing." I always tear up during this scene. It so powerfully evokes both the nobility and futility of Atticus's effort.

In *To Kill a Mockingbird*, otherwise good and decent people do terrible things. There were also good and decent people caught in the twisted reality of the Vietnam War in *The Deer Hunter*. The national divisions over the war in 1978 were still very raw. In the movie, the national trauma was symbolized in the story of several friends living blue-collar lives in industrial Pennsylvania. From a wedding and a final hunt for deer with friends, the film suddenly thrusts the audience and the main characters into the jungles of Vietnam. The traumas from their captivity leave profound scars. There are physical and mental losses that cannot be replaced or healed. The trio of young friends cannot return to their earlier lives. The movie ends with a singing of "God Bless America" after the funeral of their friend Nick. The pain and loss in this scene is etched on every face as they sing with hope battling despair. After viewing the film, I could not sleep much that night. The anguish in this movie was intense; a rinsing sadness washed over me. I never looked at the Vietnam War or the experience of those who served in a war in the same way again.

I also learned from the movies that there was another path—a way of redemption, simplicity, and love. At the age of thirteen, I viewed a captivating movie about Saint Francis, *Brother Sun, Sister Moon*. It is a 1960s kind of movie full of florid music, odd dress, and a complete rejection by Francis of worldly success. At the heart of the story is a young man wounded by war who rejects the false values of his society to follow the example of Jesus. Francis confronts his family and the bishop in the town square.

> I want to be . . . to be happy. I want to live like the birds in the sky. I want to experience the freedom and the purity that they experience. The rest is of no use to me. No use. Believe me. If the purpose of life is this loveless toil we fill our days with, then it's not for me. There must be something better. There has to be. Man is . . . a spirit. He has a soul. And that, that is what I want to recapture, my soul. I want to live. I want to live in the fields. Stride over hills. Climb trees, swim rivers. I want to feel the firm grasp of the earth beneath my feet without shoes, without possessions, without those shadows we call our servants. I want to be a beggar. Yes. Yes, a

Introduction

beggar. Christ was a beggar, and his holy apostles were beggars. I want to be as, as free as they are.

The simple and joyful love of Saint Francis resonated with me. After viewing the movie, I was ready to become a mendicant, which would have been quite a shock to my family. I rapidly dropped this thought and returned to my familiar life, but it was remarkable how this movie evoked such a powerful spiritual response. When I viewed this movie again recently, I was no longer that earnest young boy. The poetry and the dancing in nature seemed a bit romantic and were a little harder to accept as a more skeptical adult. Still, the display of the Franciscan values of simplicity, poverty, and service to others provided important lessons for me.

Catholic Themes

By recalling the impact of several films of my youth, I hopefully have made the case that movies can provoke and nurture moments of serious reflection and even spiritual enrichment.[6] I contend that the films I have selected for this book can also provide insights through their expression of Catholic themes. Let us examine some of these key themes.

Grace

At the center of the Christian experience is how grace—God's special gift of himself—operates in the world. This gift appears in many forms in these movies. Grace comes via encounters with others in critical moments, the gift of praising God in adversity, and using available tools and gifts to do God's will to the best of a character's abilities. Saint Francis in *The Flowers of Saint Francis* and his band of friars beg and scrounge even in the cold rain, but they remain aware of God's living presence in their encounters with people or nature. At the end of the movie, Saint Francis is trying to decide which direction the groups of friars should take to spread the word. At a crossroads, he invokes a children's game and has them spin around until they fall and whatever direction their bodies are pointing that is where they should journey to do God's will. This scene recalls Matthew 18:3: "Truly, I say to you, unless you turn and become like children, you will never enter

---

6. In my suggestion that academic development and personal growth are intimately connected, this book shares common ground with feminist theory. Ortiz, "Women, Theology and Film."

the kingdom of heaven." Childlike faith and trust invites grace into their lives.

Sacramentality

For Catholics, God is intimately connected to the world. The Latin word, *sacramentum*, means "a presence of the sacred." The Catholic writer, Pierre Teilhard de Chardin, SJ, contended that God is "not remote from us. He is at the point of my pen, my pick, my paint-brush, my needle—and my heart and my thoughts."[7] Material entities can accommodate sublime spiritual realities and meanings. In the Church, God's grace is invoked and operative in sacraments like the water of baptism and healing ointment for the anointing of the sick. This mediation is most powerfully present in the Eucharist, where we are given the real presence of the body and blood of Christ.[8]

The sacramentality of the Eucharist is referenced in the meal at the center of *Babette's Feast* that brings the healing power of grace into many lives. Forgiveness and reconciliation become possible through Babette's sacrifice and a transforming meal made to honor and reward a community of believers. God's grace is also present in *The Flowers of Saint Francis* in the divine aspect of creation that moves Saint Francis to reflect on God's abundant generosity. We are introduced to the presence of the sacred when the narrator reads from Saint Francis's "Canticle of Brother Sun and Sister Moon" over the opening credits:

> Praise be to you, O Lord, for Brother Fire,
> With whom you light up the night
> And who is beautiful and playful, robust and strong.
> Praise be to you, O Lord, for Sister and Mother Earth,
> who sustains, governs and brings forth the various fruits
> with their colorful flowers and leaves.

---

7. Teilhard de Chardin, *Hymn of the Universe*, 84.

8. One of the most startling examples of a sacramental reality in a film is in *Song of Bernadette*, about the young Bernadette Soubirous, who discovered the healing water of Lourdes. She eats plants and rubs her face with mud at the direction of the Virgin Mary. This is a bit shocking to the villagers, who mock her until it leads to the discovery of healing waters at this location.

INTRODUCTION

Conversion and Redemption

The presence of grace in the world encounters resistance in human beings who are fallen. As a result, we are all too capable of wronging others and ourselves. Fortunately, each human being is also made in the image and likeness of God, and hence no person is beyond divine grace and love. There is good in every person written on his or her heart.[9] The choices we make between good and evil are a source of much of the drama of human life, because we can dedicate our wills to very different paths. At some point in the trajectory of our choices, we may experience a conversion[10] or turning of our wills from evil to good. In *The Mission*, Robert De Niro's character, Captain Mendoza, is a Spanish slave trader in South America in the eighteenth century who kills his brother in a jealous rage. He is lost in total despair when a Jesuit priest, Father Gabriel—played by Jeremy Irons—challenges him to do penance by dragging his heavy armor and swords across streams and mountains on a trip to a remote mission of the Guarani Indians in what is today South America. At the mission, he is met by the indigenous people he had tormented and enslaved. They confront him and threaten to kill him. After some tense moments, they laugh and embrace Mendoza as he collapses in tears. Mendoza is redeemed and becomes a Jesuit priest.

Fortitude

There is another path requiring grace. It is the path of persistence in faith, a form of fortitude even in the face of many obstacles. *Diary of a Country Priest* offers a very stark glimpse at the suffering of a young priest in a remote village in France between the world wars. The young curé, whose name is not given to us, is suffering physically from what we will learn is stomach cancer. He suffers from many petty, cruel acts directed at him from most of the local population, from the poor to the local nobility. He wins a conversion of the countess, but he is blamed for her death rather than praised for her conversion. The young priest, like Jesus, is ridiculed and scorned; his noble intentions are misread or rejected at almost every turn. He leaves behind the mocking of the town to seek medical treatment, but instead he confronts the perils of his wavering faith and his impending

---

9. Rom 2:14–15.
10. Conversion is derived from the Latin word *conversio*, meaning "to turn."

death. In the end, he perseveres in his faith despite his many sufferings. His last words, "All is grace."

While the young curé in *Diary of a Country Priest* seeks the fortitude to hold onto his faith, the young atheist professor in *Decalogue 1* needs fortitude to reject total despair and seek some meaning in the seemingly senseless death of his young son, Pawel, who falls through the ice while skating on an apartment complex pond. The professor visits a partially constructed church at night and stares at an icon of the Madonna. He is sitting in agony before the altar and places a block of frozen holy water against his forehead. Pain and suffering have led the professor to at least wonder about how his rational mind can connect to the spiritual reality present in the water and represented by the Madonna. Will he receive the grace necessary to maintain his fortitude and complete his spiritual journey? We are given the question, but not the answer.

Pilgrimage

Grace, sacramentality, conversion, redemption, and fortitude are essential in the pilgrimage of humanity towards a spiritual home. We see the pilgrimage theme in the *homo viator* (man on the way) of Saint Augustine and the circle of creation emanating from God and returning to God in Saint Thomas Aquinas's *Summa Theologica*. In our lives, we too are on a journey—a special voyage of discovery in which we seek the source and meaning of our lives. The idea of a special revelatory journey is present in the science fiction film *GATTACA*, in which the protagonist, Vincent Freeman, dreams of voyaging into space. Vincent is blocked by the fact that he is a "natural," a person who was not created as perfectly as possible with genetic modifications. He has biological imperfections such as a weak heart that would block his selection. Through his persistence and some subterfuge, he is able to mask his genetic disadvantages. Vincent's success indicates that a human life, even in a future of genetically manufactured perfection, cannot be reduced to DNA. In the end, Vincent becomes freed of earthly limitations and becomes a cosmic pilgrim full of hope heading into the heavens.

Introduction

The Common Good

The motif of pilgrimage and spiritual movement often operates in the context of a community. As part of a community, we must occasionally sacrifice our personal interests for the common good. The common good was defined by Saint John XXIII as "the sum total of conditions of social living, whereby persons are enabled more fully and readily to achieve their own perfection."[11]

Babette Hersant is the former Parisian chef in *Babette's Feast*. She uses a sum of money she has received from winning a lottery not for her own benefit but to make a special meal for her adopted community. She makes this dinner in honor of two sisters who have given so much to others. Her sacrifice binds the community together through mutual love and support. Because of the presence of the sacred at Babette's meal, the community witnesses the forgiveness of old grudges, the renewal of marital bonds, and the joyous celebration of their faith.

In *Of Gods and Men*, a group of French Trappist monks in 1990s Algeria confront a terrible choice. They can remain and be servants to the nearby Muslim village where they assist the people with issues ranging from governmental red tape to medical care or they can leave because of threats from the Muslim radicals against all foreigners. Are they their brother's keeper in this situation? It is a difficult question to answer, but they ultimately choose the common good over their personal self-interest. The social life of their community is more important than their personal interests and fears.

Justice

The Catholic ideal of justice is based on the principle that human dignity recognizes the intrinsic value of every person. Every person was made by and for God and is owed a foundational level of respect. Respecting others gives glory to God. Nonetheless, people often wrestle with or question the right way to show justice and mercy to the people they encounter. Is it just for the monks in *Of Gods and Men* to leave the monastery or to stay there? What is due the Guarani tribe in *The Mission*? What is due the young Jewish boy hidden in a Catholic school in occupied France in *Au Revoir Les Enfants*? What if the person in question is the leper that Saint Francis

---

11. John XXIII, *Mater et Magistra*, n. 65.

encounters in the *The Flowers of St. Francis*? What if the person in question is a heinous murderer and rapist like Patrick Sonnier in *Dead Man Walking*? In order to give to each person what is due them, the scales of justice must balance judgment and mercy in making its decisions. Such decisions require a careful discernment.

Conscience

Closely connected to justice is the ideal of conscience, which is our internal guide to making ethical decisions. As it states in the Second Vatican Council's Pastoral Constitution, *Gaudium et Spes*, "Conscience is the most secret core and sanctuary of a man." Formed in the Church tradition and alone with God, a man detects in his conscience "a law which he does not impose upon himself, but which holds him to obedience. Always summoning him to love good and avoid evil, the voice of conscience when necessary speaks to his heart: do this, shun that. For man has in his heart a law written by God."[12] A conscience must often weigh competing ethical principles. Sir Thomas More as Chancellor of England in *A Man for All Seasons* examined his conscience in a world where loyalties shifted like the winds. When King Henry VIII decided to renounce his marriage in defiance of the papacy, the obligation of loyalty to the king as well as self-interest convinced most of the leadership of England to join him. Thomas More, in defiance of his friend the king and most of his peers, affirmed his first loyalty to God and his representative on earth the Pope. As he says in the final scene of *A Man for All Seasons*, as he is about to be beheaded, "I am the King's good servant, but God's first."

Faith and Reason

For Catholics, as Saint John Paul II concluded, "faith and reason are like the two wings on which the human spirit rises to the contemplation of truth."[13] Faith and reason are essential to the flourishing of human life. If we only follow faith, we can become superstitious. If we rely solely on our reason, we can become jaded, materialistic, and utilitarian. Relying solely on human reason, *GATTACA* provides a warning that we may try to manufacture our offspring and succumb to a false genetic determinism.

12. *Gaudium et Spes*, n.16.
13. John Paul II, *Fides et Ratio*, n.1.

Introduction

We may also be prideful if we rely solely on our reason. *Decalogue 1* is based on the First Commandment, "I am the Lord thy God, thou shalt have no other Gods."[14] The professor in the film, Krzysztof, relies too much on his computer and its calculations. This is a form of idolatry, an excessive valuing of human reason and technology. Based on his calculations, the professor lets his son, Pawel, skate on a nearby pond where he drowns due to an unforeseen thinning of the ice. The viewer is reminded that human beings cannot calculate or analyze their way to the perfect life. The movie is also a reminder that we are ultimately not in total control of our lives or their termination.

Wisdom

Ultimately, these films highlight a virtue useful in evaluating all of the other themes. The virtue of wisdom allows a person to do the right thing in the right way at the right time. As we are reminded in the book of Ecclesiastes, "There is an appointed time for everything. And there is a time for every event under heaven; A time to give birth and a time to die; A time to plant and a time to uproot what is planted; A time to kill and a time to heal; A time to tear down and a time to build up."[15] We need all relevant resources to thoughtfully determine the best course. When Thomas More is confronted with the marriage of King Henry VIII, he does not seek martyrdom. He uses his reason to find a way to be true to his spiritual obligations while not providing an excuse for the king to execute him. For example, his silence on the issue of the king's remarriage does not affirm the king's error, but it also protects him, for a while, from his execution for being a traitor. Like Jesus' commandment to the apostles, he is trying to be "as innocent as a dove and as wise as a serpent" because he is "a sheep among wolves."[16]

There are many forms of wisdom. It is wisdom to know our limits as we see in *Decalogue 1* and to proceed stealthily, as in *GATTACA*. There is also wisdom in seeing beyond the surface and aiding the wounded Percy in *The Spitfire Grill*. Hannah, the owner of the grill, could have easily dismissed the young woman who had been in prison, but wisely withholds too quick a judgment and eventually understands her pain and is the recipient of her many graces.

14. Exod 20:3.
15. Eccl 3:1–2.
16. Matt 10:16.

A Spiritual Mosaic

Returning to my criteria, I have also selected the twelve films highlighted in this book, because they have considerable artistic merit. The twenty-eight film awards granted to these movies confirm their artistic merit. Here is a list:

    Academy Awards (13):
      Best Actor
      Best Actress (3)
      Best Art Direction
      Best Cinematography
      Best Film
      Best Foreign Film (2)
      Best Screenplay (2)
      Best Supporting Actor
      Best Supporting Actress
    Bodil Award—Best European Award
    Cannes Film Festival—Grand Prize
    Cannes Film Festival—Palme D'or,
    Cesar Awards—Best Film
    Chicago Film Critics—Best Foreign Film
    Golden Globe Award—Best Original Score
    Golden Lion Award—Venice Film Festival
    London Critics Circle Film Festival—ALFS Award
    National Board of Review—Best Foreign Film
    Screen Guild—Best Actor and Best Actress
    Sundance Film Festival—Audience Award
    Venice Film Festival—Best Cinematography
    Venice Film Festival—FIPRESCI Award
    Venice Film Festival—International Award,
    Venice Film Festival—Prix Louis Delluc

Having selected films with Catholic themes and artistic merits, the movies are organized in a rough historical chronology from Saint Francis to the future society of *GATTACA*. I have also placed each film within various categories according to certain common elements. The first grouping of three movies is Part I—Saints and Sinners. One reason that Christianity is difficult is because it demands a life that is not always aligned with current social, political, or cultural values. This is why Thomas More defies his king,

Introduction

Saint Francis defies the expectations of his society, and the Jesuits defy the papal nuncio in *The Mission*.

The path of spiritual integrity is not much easier in the modern world in the second section of movies about contemporary Catholic religious in Part II. How can a religious be an imitation of Christ in a dangerous and fallen world? The young priest in *Diary of a Country Priest* in a rural village of a superficially Catholic France finds much hostility and barrenness. In the Muslim Algeria in *Of Gods and Men*, the Trappist monks are caught in a conflict of obligations. Their problem is not from the village where they are beloved and needed, but from the external military forces of the government and the rebels who want to impose political claims on them. How do they remain true to their religious commitments, to one another, to their community, and ultimately to God? In the end they choose the common good of continuing their mission in Tibherine.

How do lay people or those who are not consecrated religious discover a deeper meaning by promoting the common good in community? In Part III in the movies, *Babette's Feast* and *The Spitfire Grill*, there is a quest for community beyond our isolated selves. The world is filled with forces that block these connections. In *Babette's Feast*, set in late nineteenth-century Denmark, we learn how Babette, a French political refugee and formerly a famous cook in Paris, has worked as the servant of two pious sisters for many years. She wins the lottery in France and with her winnings decides to prepare a gourmet meal for her Protestant community. The meal, which is initially viewed as a waste and perhaps even pagan by the community, is an act of charity that transforms the lives of the attendees and facilitates the mending of many broken relationships. Similarly, in *The Spitfire Grill*, an owner of a cafe in a town in Maine takes in another kind of exile, a former female prisoner, Percy Talbot. As in *Babette's Feast*, there is fear of the outsider and deep divisions in the town. The community begins to heal because of the life and death of Percy, who drowns trying to protect a homeless veteran hiding in the forest. Here again, selfless giving can renew our common humanity.

Our common humanity is also a basis for the next set of movies dealing with justice, in Part IV. Justice is about giving each person what is due them by respecting their human dignity since they are made in the image and likeness of God. In *Au Revoir Les Enfants*, the movie is set in occupied France in the Second World War where there is a cat-and-mouse game between collaborators with the Nazis and those trying to resist the

Nazi pestilence. A young schoolboy at a Catholic school run by Carthusian priests eventually realizes that a new classmate is Jewish. He keeps the secret, but the friend and the French priests protecting him are betrayed. How do we think of justice in such a deformed moral universe where evil is in control and betrayal is often the reward for those who resist?

We know the innocent Jewish boy in *Au Revoir Les Enfants* does not deserve his death, but is the death penalty a just punishment that should be part of the American criminal justice system? When we first meet Patrick Sonnier in *Dead Man Walking*, he is an unrepentant sadist on death row. It is not easy to see any glimmers of humanity in Sonnier until late in the movie. Yet, the movie explores the idea that the death penalty is brutish and inhumane at its core, because it can dehumanize everyone involved in the process. In *Entertaining Angels*, there is the question of social justice for other kinds of outcasts. What do we owe the disabled, the poor, and the mentally unstable? Dorothy Day in this film responds to Jesus' command to feeds the poor and clothe the naked. For her questioning of a world that allows such suffering, she is often disparaged or under suspicion.

Now, turning to the Christian life in the modern world in Part V—Prophetic Warnings, the films raise important ethical issues about the advances of technology and science. In *Decalogue 1*, a prideful reliance on reason and technologies has fateful consequences leading to the death of a young boy. Any human calculation is susceptible to weakness, contingency, and error. Removing God from the equation makes us susceptible to failure because of our hubris. In *GATTACA*, humanity goes one step further. Procreation has become reproduction. Salvation is now a form of eugenics—a quest to perfect our species through our biological technologies. Salvation is not possible through genetic engineering. We are still subject to the imperfections of our choices. This is the case with the actual Jerome Morrow, the donor of genetically perfect blood and urine, for the deceptive Vincent Freeman, who is pretending to be Jerome at a space agency. Jerome received a silver medal in swimming and was so disappointed that he crippled himself by stepping in front of a car. Ironically, his striving for perfection leads only to a wheelchair and eventually suicide. *GATTACA* is a prescient warning that we are more than our genetic code and that the drive to perfect the human species may forfeit part of our humanity.

Finally, I have included a chapter on movies about Jesus because it is an obvious and perhaps problematic omission in my selection of movies. After all, Jesus is the primary source of Catholic theology, ethics, and life

INTRODUCTION

instruction, and what Catholic themes would not be found in his life? The problem is that Jesus films confront a particularly unresolvable problem in portraying a person whose nature is fully divine and fully human. Nonetheless, there are a number of fine movies that capture aspects of Jesus that have many merits, but they all fall a little short, and it is inevitably so given the difficulty of the task.

How to View These Movies

A final word on how to use this book. The movies vary in their form and complexity, so start with films that fit your interests and tastes. There is much to choose from. Some are adventures with broad popular appeal like *A Man for All Seasons*, *The Mission*, and *GATTACA*. On the other end of the spectrum, there are esoteric films, especially some of the European films like *The Flowers of Saint Francis*, *Diary of a Country Priest*, and *Decalogue 1*. Most of the films fall between the highly popular and the esoteric and are readily accessible for a wide range of viewers.

Once you choose, please note that at the beginning of each chapter is some information on the movie including the director, screenwriter, and awards. This information will highlight the artistic sources and merits of the film. Then, there is a list of key values in the movie. These lists are illustrative and not exhaustive. The hope is that the list of values will help the reader to search for and discover deeper ethical and spiritual meanings. Similarly, I have also included biblical quotations at the beginning of each movie chapter. These quotations are intended to ground the chapter in a biblical reference.

There are questions at the end of each chapter to ponder while watching the movie. These questions will also assist in the analysis of these films and hopefully lead to other inquiries that enrich your viewing experience. My advice is to watch the movie first and just enjoy it. Then, after this first viewing, think about what you found valuable or problematic. Before a second viewing, consider the Catholic themes in the movies outlined in the introduction, and then read the chapter on the selected movie and the questions at the end.

It is often worthwhile to watch these movies with others. I attended a seminar at Dartmouth College on the ethical, legal, and social implications of the Human Genome Project. We spent an afternoon discussing the movie *GATTACA*, and I was amazed at how much I had missed in the movie. Such communal activity can be a source of much pleasure and insight. Finally, at the very end of each chapter, I have placed several additional resources that will provide supplementary materials that may help to extend and deepen your reflections.

PART I

Saints and Sinners

chapter 1

A Man for All Seasons (1966) (G)

Director: Fred Zinnemann
Screenplay: Robert Bolt[1]
Awards: Academy Award—Best Film, Best Actor, Best Supporting Actor, Best Supporting Actress, Best Screenplay
Values: conscience, faith, fortitude, integrity, justice, wisdom, faith, and reason

What profit is there for one to gain the whole world and forfeit his life?
—MARK 8:36

The very title, *A Man for all Seasons*, suggests that Saint Thomas More's (1478–1535) integrity remained intact in all circumstances. In stormy or sunny days, he held to his moral compass that steadily guided his course. Erasmus of Rotterdam, a leading humanist and contemporary, described More as one "whose soul was more pure than any snow, whose genius was such that England never had and never again will have its like."[2] In the early twentieth century, the famous writer G. K. Chesterton proclaimed:

---

1. Fred Zinnemann directed many fine films including *High Noon, From Here to Eternity, The Day of the Jackal*, and *Julia*. Robert Bolt also wrote the screenplays for *Lawrence of Arabia, Doctor Zhivago*, and *The Mission*.
2. Zupan, *Philosophy for Breakfast*, 46.

"Thomas More is more important at this moment than at any moment since his death, even perhaps the great moment of his dying; but he is not quite so important as he will be in about a hundred years' time. He may come to be counted the greatest Englishman, or at least the greatest historical character in English history. For he was above all things historic; he represented at once a type, a turning point and an ultimate destiny."[3] Praise for More extends beyond Catholicism. The Anglican minister and satirist Jonathan Swift declared More "a person of the greatest virtue this kingdom ever produced."[4] Given these descriptions of More, it is perhaps not surprising that *The New York Times* review of the Academy Award-winning movie proclaimed it a "picture that inspires admiration, courage and thought."[5]

For a movie about a Catholic saint, it may surprise the reader that an agnostic, Robert Bolt, wrote the screenplay, and a Jewish filmmaker, Fred Zinnemann, directed the film. Bolt is subtle and depicts how More was highly respected by many, including King Henry VIII, for his wit, knowledge, diplomatic skills, and virtues. This is why Henry VIII made him Chancellor of England, the highest position in the government. There was an intractable problem, however, that ruined the relationship of king and counselor. The king desired to divorce his wife, Catherine of Aragon, who had not produced a male heir. Henry had already received a papal dispensation to marry Catherine because she was his brother's widow. Now, the king wanted the papacy to disregard its earlier dispensation because it was invalid, as he related to More, since it was a violation of Leviticus's prohibition of marrying the wife of your brother.[6] Although Henry VIII was declared by Pope Leo X in 1521 to be the *Fidei Defensor* or Defender of the Faith for his writings and his actions against the Reformation, the king's ultimate sense of duty was not to his faith but to his dynasty. This was partly a matter of pride, but it was also essential to avoid the chaos of dynastic wars that had plagued previous centuries in England. So Henry decided to remarry even though the Pope did not grant an annulment of his marriage

---

3. Chesterton, *The Fame of Blessed Thomas More*, 63.
4. Clark and Odell, *A Study of American and English Writers*, 3.
5. Crowther, "A Sturdy Conscience, a Steadfast Heart."
6. Lev 20:21: "If a man takes his brother's wife, it is severe defilement and he has disgraced his brother; they shall be childless." See also Lev 18:16. More notes for his king that Leviticus is contradicted by Deut 25:5: "When brothers live together and one of them dies without a son, the widow of the deceased shall not marry anyone outside the family; but her husband's brother shall come to her, marrying her and performing the duty of a brother-in-law." Henry VIII found Deuteronomy ambiguous.

A Man for All Seasons (1966) (G)

to Catherine.[7] The king retaliated by nationalizing the English Church, confiscating Church lands, and declaring himself the supreme head of the English Church.[8] The Pope then excommunicated Henry VIII.

Although he readily acknowledged the failings of the institutional Church and its need for reform, More ultimately judged Henry's actions to be a denial of the Pope's office as the apostolic successor of Saint Peter. More resigned his position as chancellor and refused to openly declare his opinions on the king's actions, instead remaining silent, which prevented him (at least for a while) from being executed because silence in the English law of this era was construed as indicating approval of the king's actions.[9] Nonetheless, Henry eventually imprisoned More in the Tower of London, and he was interrogated at all hours of the day and night. Finally, More was betrayed by a former student he had mentored, Richard Rich, who lied about what More said to him in a conversation regarding the king's authority. More was convicted and beheaded. His head was displayed on a pike on London Bridge. Like Jesus', More's life ended in disgrace and calumny in the eyes of most of his countrymen.

The legacy of Thomas More did not remain in infamy. His reputation was revived in numerous books and, of course, this movie. In *A Man for All Seasons*, the plot sticks closely to the historical events of More's life, and some of the dialogue in his interrogation and trial is taken verbatim from historical sources. We learn that Saint Thomas More was a courageous witness to his faith; he was firmly guided by his religious conscience,

---

7. The pope hesitated on the issue of the marriage. He was in a difficult position. Henry VIII was one of his most loyal allies, but the nephew of Catherine of Aragon was the king of Spain, Charles V, who was furious about the proposed divorce and had troops in Italy. Soldiers of Charles V had cruelly sacked Rome in 1527 so his threats had to be taken seriously by the pope.

8. The Supremacy Act of 1534 passed by Parliament which More would not sign declared in part that "kings of this realm, shall be taken, accepted, and reputed the only supreme head in earth of the Church of England, called *Anglicana Ecclesia;* and shall have and enjoy, annexed and united to the imperial crown of this realm, as well the title and style thereof, as all honours, dignities, pre-eminences, jurisdictions, privileges, authorities, immunities, profits, and commodities to the said dignity of supreme head of the same Church belonging and appertaining; and that our said sovereign lord, his heirs and successors, kings of this realm, shall have full power and authority from time to time to visit, repress, redress, reform, order, correct, restrain, and amend all such errors, heresies, abuses, offences, contempts, and enormities . . ." King Henry VIII, *The Supremacy Act 1534.*

9. The Latin maxim in English law used by More in this context, *qui tacet consentire*, means "silence gives consent."

not by self-interest. In one of the film's first scenes, he travels downriver to meet Cardinal Woolsey, the Chancellor of England, a realist played with a wonderful world-weary irony by Orson Welles. In the first words of their meeting, we detect the strength of More's character as he verbally spars with the cardinal. Woolsey presses More on why he was the only one to oppose him at the King's Council that morning and suggests that More was a "fool." More retorts, "Thank God there is only one fool on the Council." When asked his reasons, More declares, "I thought your grace was wrong."

In an interesting reversal of what we might expect to be their roles, the cardinal in this conversation is a pragmatist while More leans on faith and principle. Woolsey urges More to remove his "horrible moral squint" and see "facts flat on." More counters with an offer to pray for a son for the king. The cardinal urges a more temporal approach, including pressure on Rome and a threat to Church lands and freedoms. More cannot support this path; the king in matters of faith is not superior to his Holiness in Rome. More warns, "When statesmen forsake their own private consciences for the sake of their public duties, they lead their country by a short route to chaos." As he is leaving, the cardinal teases his colleague, "More, you might have made a fine cleric." The witty counter: "Like you, your grace." Advantage More.

More's integrity, grounded in principles of the faith and the sound judgment of his conscience, is the moral compass that guides him through political, religious, and personal turbulence. When his daughter, Meg, begs him to take the oath on the supremacy of the monarch over the Church but to not mean it, he responds that the oath was to God and "When a man takes an oath, he's holding his own self in his own hands like water and if he opens his fingers then he needn't hope to find himself again."

When he glanced at his peers, More must have observed that they were rapidly modifying their principles to keep their lands, offices, and most importantly their heads. One example is the self-interest of Richard Rich, whose lie insured More's death in exchange for his being made Attorney General of Wales. His fate sealed by Rich's betrayal, More slyly observes to the courtroom and Rich, "Why Richard, it profits a man nothing to give his soul for the whole world. But for Wales?"

The aristocracy of England, in general, are not much better. They have malleable principles. More chides his friend, the Duke of Norfolk, that "The nobility of England, My Lord, would have snored through the Sermon on the Mount, but you'll labor like scholars over a bulldog's pedigree." They then have this exchange over the difference between the obligations of friendship and faith.

A Man for All Seasons (1966) (G)

The Duke of Norfolk: Oh, confound all this. I'm not a scholar, I don't know whether the marriage was lawful or not but dammit, Thomas, look at these names! Why can't you do as I did and come with us, for fellowship!

Sir Thomas More: And when we die, and you are sent to heaven for doing your conscience, and I am sent to hell for not doing mine, will you come with me, for fellowship?

His enemies and even his old friend, Henry VIII, recognize More's unique integrity. The king knows the base motives of many of his followers, but he realizes that More is different, and most importantly that he is known throughout England to be honest.

Sir Thomas More: Then, why does your Grace need my poor support?

King Henry VIII: Because you're honest . . . and what is more to the purpose, you're known to be honest. There are those like Norfolk who follow me because I wear the crown; and those like Master Cromwell who follow me because they are jackals with sharp teeth and I'm their tiger; there's a mass that follows me because it follows anything that moves. And, then there's you.

While the nobility is opportunistic, More recognizes that religious zealots have a different issue in their intense but shifting spiritual loyalties. As for his future son-in-law William Roper's adamant but constantly mutating views for and against the Reformation, More counsels, "Now, listen, Will, two years ago you were a passionate churchman. Now, you're a passionate Lutheran. We must just pray that when your head's finished turning, your face is to the front again."

More preserves his integrity while navigating between those who are confused idealists like his son-in-law, and those who are crass utilitarians like the nobles and Richard Rich. He will use his reason and his cunning on behalf of staying alive as long as he does not violate his religious conscience. He desires to remain with his family, if possible. He confides to his daughter, Meg, that he will not seek a martyr's death.

> Listen, Meg, God made the angels to show Him splendor, as He made animals for innocence, and plants for their simplicity. But Man He made to serve Him wittily, in the tangle of his mind. If He suffers us to come to such a case that there is no escaping, then we may stand to our tackle as best we can, and, yes, Meg, then we can

clamor like champions, if we have the spittle for it. But it's God's part, not our own, to bring ourselves to such a pass. Our natural business lies in escaping. If I can take the oath, I will.

More's sense of integrity and justice extends to his official duties as a judge. He will give each person what he or she is due under the law. When he receives a petition and an attempted bribe from a woman whose daughter is to appear before him in court, he smiles benignly and declares, "I will give your daughter what I would give my own, a fair judgment, quickly." Moreover, he will not manipulate the law in order to attack those who might threaten him. When his family wants him to arrest Richard Rich because he is a spy and a threat, More responds, "There is no law against that." When his son-in-law Roper implores him to arrest Rich under God's law if there is not a human one, More quips, "Then let God arrest him." More provides a lesson for any age responding in fear to a chaotic political or military situation. We must not abandon the rule of law because of fear.

William Roper: So, now you give the Devil the benefit of law!

Sir Thomas More: Yes! What would you do? Cut a great road through the law to get after the Devil?

William Roper: Yes, I'd cut down every law in England to do that!

Sir Thomas More: Oh? And when the last law was down, and the Devil turned 'round on you, where would you hide, Roper, the laws all being flat? This country is planted thick with laws, from coast to coast, man's laws, not God's! And if you cut them down, and you're just the man to do it, do you really think you could stand upright in the winds that would blow then? Yes, I'd give the Devil benefit of law, for my own safety's sake!

Constantly interrogated at all hours and imprisoned during the last year of his life, More suffered horribly but remained true to his principles. In the interrogation scenes, he serves "God wittily in the tangles of his mind" in a number of verbal jousts.

At an Interrogation

Sir Thomas More: You threaten like a dockside bully.

Thomas Cromwell: How should I threaten?

A Man for All Seasons (1966) (G)

Sir Thomas More, who pauses for a second: Like a minister of state. With justice.

Thomas Cromwell: Oh, justice is what you're threatened with.

Sir Thomas More: Then, I am not threatened.

At His Trial

Duke of Norfolk: Your life lies in your own hands, Thomas, as it always has.

Sir Thomas More: Is that so, My Lord? Then, I'll keep a good grip on it.

The wit of Thomas More is refreshing and a lost art in our age of bombast and cynicism. More's wit also reveals a balanced perspective on life. He certainly knows the fallen aspect of our natures. This is the source of much of his mirth and wit. He recognizes all too well the swiftly turning passions of William Roper, the unquestioning loyalty of the Duke of Norfolk, the conniving of the civil servant, Thomas Cromwell, and the desire for status and power of Richard Rich.

Meg, his well-educated and thoughtful daughter, best understands his thought. It was to her that he turned to remove his chain of office as chancellor from his shoulders. She does this knowing that his true self is not his office. Earlier in the film referring to the question of who was Cardinal Woolsey, his wife, Alice More, dismisses the cardinal as "a butcher's son" and then More reminds her, "Chancellor of England." Meg queries her parents, "That's his office, what's the man?" And Meg thus raises a major point of the movie: what are we in the final analysis? Are we just our jobs and our wealth, or is there something more, something eternal in us?

Not only in his description in the movie of Meg's education as "a fine and delicate commodity," but in many other ways Thomas More appreciated and encouraged learning. He was High Steward for Cambridge and Oxford universities. He was one of the most learned men of Europe, a humanist who was immensely well-read in Greek and Roman sources.

A Man for All Seasons presents another lesson on learning. More realizes early in the movie that Richard Rich will be too easily lured at court into temptation by bribes and promises of power. For these reasons, he refuses to provide Richard a position at court, but he does offer a teaching position. As one who left the halls of political and legal power to become a teacher, I am always moved by More's advice to Rich.

Sir Thomas More: Why not be a teacher? You'd be a fine teacher, perhaps a great one.

Richard Rich: If I was, who would know it?

Sir Thomas More: You; your pupils; your friends; God. Not a bad public that.

More's final trial is a charade; the fix is in and Rich's fabricated story insures More's death. Still, More is not defenseless. Early on during his trial, More reminds everyone what is at stake. True, the tribunal charges him with a penalty that will bring his death, but the prisoner warns the audience that "death, even for kings he comes." By this quip, he reminds everyone there that their actions have consequences beyond their brief mortality.

Once his fate is sealed by Rich, More scolds his persecutors and defends the principle that insures his execution.

> Since the Court has determined to condemn me, God knoweth how, I will now discharge my mind concerning the indictment and the king's title. The indictment is grounded in an act of Parliament, which is directly repugnant to the law of God, and his Holy Church, the Supreme Government of which no temporal person may by any law presume to take upon him. This was granted by the mouth of our Savior, Christ himself, to Saint Peter and the Bishops of Rome whilst He lived and was personally present here on earth. It is, therefore, insufficient in law to charge any Christian to obey it. And more to this, the immunity of the Church is promised both in Magna Carta and in the king's own coronation oath.[10] [Cromwell crows that More is "malicious."] ... Not so. I am the king's true subject, and I pray for him and all the realm. I do none harm. I say none harm. I think none harm. And if this be not enough to keep a man alive, then in good faith, I long not to live. Nevertheless, it is

---

10. The *Magna Carta* states "In the first place we grant to God and confirm by this our present charter for ourselves and our heirs in perpetuity that the English Church is to be free and to have all its rights fully and its liberties entirely." On the Coronation Oath, More is probably referring to these words: "Sire will you grant and keep and by your oath confirm to the people of England the laws and customs given to them by the previous just and god-fearing kings, your ancestors, and especially the laws, customs, and liberties granted to the clergy and people by the glorious king, the sainted Edward your predecessor." "I grant and promise them."

A Man for All Seasons (1966) (G)

not for the supremacy that you have sought my blood, but because I would not bend to the marriage!"

So Thomas More's fate is sealed. He fasts and prays the last six days of his life. He was taken from the Tower of London to Tower's Hill to be executed. He wore a grey cape and had a beard, unlike in the movie. At his execution, as the movie records, his comments were brief and he indicated that he was the king's good servant but God's first. He then calmly accepted his fate, certain that God would not deny one "so blithe to go to him."

A Man for All Seasons is a superb film with beautiful cinematography and majestic music that chronicles the life of a saint—a person of heroic virtue—who did what most people in his day or ours cannot do, and that was to defy power and to suffer and die for a principle. More gave his last full measure to follow his God and his Church. Some critics have noted that when he was chancellor, there were six persons executed for their Protestant faith. More's exact role in these deaths is a matter of dispute, so what do we make of this charge? Saint John Paul II, when honoring him by making him patron saint of statesmen and politicians in October 2000, concluded, "It can be said that he [More] demonstrated in a singular way the value of a moral conscience . . . even if, in his actions against heretics, he reflected the limits of the culture of his time."[11] Moreover, it is worth noting that the Church of England added him in 1980 to their calendar of saints and heroes of the Christian church.[12]

So, we recognize in *A Man for All Seasons* a saint—a man of heroic virtue—who was in part a product of his culture, but also a figure with many spiritual and personal virtues such as courage, learning, and integrity that made him a man for all seasons. In the Catholic Church, he is the patron saint of lawyers, statesmen, and politicians, but anyone viewing this movie will recognize a humane leader, a man willing to die for his convictions. When Thomas More was canonized and became a saint in 1935, Pope Pius XI observed, "When he saw the doctrines of the Church were gravely endangered, he knew how to despise resolutely the flattery of human respect, how to resist, in accordance with his duty, the supreme head of the State when there was question of things commanded by God and the Church . . . nor could the tears of his wife and children make him swerve from the

---

11. John Paul II, *Proclaiming Saint Thomas More Patron Saint of Statesmen and Politicians.*
12. The Church of England, "Holy Days."

path of truth and virtue. In that terrible hour of trial, he raised his eyes to heaven, and proved himself a bright example of Christian fortitude."[13]

Questions

1) Are we "God's servant first," like More, or do we owe primary allegiance to idols like power, fame, or money?

2) What does Thomas More's statement that we are "to serve God wittily in the tangle of his mind" mean to you?

3) Thomas More says to his son-in-law Roper, "We must just pray that when your head's finished turning, your face is to the front again." Are we as a culture or individuals constantly spinning around in our beliefs? Why?

4) More notes to the Duke of Norfolk that the "nobility of England would have snored through the Sermon on the Mount." Why was this true? Are we any different?

5) Does Thomas More provide an example for our age? Why?

Resources

Crowther, Bosley. "A Sturdy Conscience, a Steadfast Heart: 'A Man for All Seasons' Opens at Fine Arts Paul Scofield Excels in Film by Zinnemann." *The New York Times* (December 13, 1966). http://www.nytimes.com/movie/review?res=9B02EED8153C E43BBC4B52DFB467838D679EDE&module=Search&mabReward=relbias%3Ar% 2C%7B%221%22%3A%22RI%3A8%22%7D.

Gaffney, Edward McGlynn, Jr. "Principled Resignation of Thomas More." *Loyola Los Angeles Law Review* 31 (1997–1998) 63–78.

Leonard, Richard. *Movies That Matter: Reading Film through the Lens of Faith.* Chicago: Loyola Press, 2006, 7–9.

---

13. Pius XI, "On the Occasion of the Papal Mass in St. Peter's for the Canonization of St. Thomas More."

chapter 2

The Flowers of Saint Francis (1950) (NR)

Director: Roberto Rossellini

Screenplay: Roberto Rossellini and Frederico Fellini

Award: Vatican Office of Social Communication, Forty-Five Best Films

Values: humility, community, compassion, mercy, peace, empathy, and solidarity

Rather, God chose the foolish of the world to shame the wise, and God chose the weak of the world to shame the strong, and God chose the lowly and despised of the world, those who count for nothing, to reduce to nothing those who are something, so that no human being might boast before God.

—1 COR 1:27–29

With the advent of Pope Francis, there has been a heightened interest in Saint Francis of Assisi (1182–1226). Saint Francis is one of the most popular figures in the history of Christianity. He is seen as an icon of environmentalism, interfaith dialogue, and concern for the poor, but he was also medieval in his extreme fasting, penances, struggles with the devil, and stigmata. His writings were so few that to research Francis one has to rely on subsequent recollections, often written seventy-five years or more after his death, that offered very dramatic accounts of his life. Rossellini's film was based loosely on such stories from *The Little Flowers of St. Francis* and *The Life of Brother Juniper.*

The film is set after Pope Innocent III approved of Francis's movement as long as he and his followers were tonsured. In the film, Francis is living outside of Assisi at the chapel known as the Portiuncula.[1] We are presented a series of brief glimpses, ten scenes or flowers, of Francis in his early years with his followers. The scenes are short vignettes that teach lessons about the spiritual life. There is no seamless narrative uniting these scenes.

Francis and his band of followers are living very simply, imitating Christ. In their enthusiastic daily existence, they flit across the land like a flock of merry geese following their leader. The influential film critic André Bazin wondered if the "little brothers of Francis seem to have no better way of glorifying God than to run races."[2] Such behavior was shocking and stirring in Francis's day, the high middle ages, a world awash in both grinding poverty and growing trade and wealth as exemplified by his merchant father. Turning to the trauma of postwar Italy, Rossellini believed that Francis offered the demoralized country an alternative vision of innocence, fraternity, peace, and joy.[3] This vision was offered in a stark and realistic portrait. Rossellini declared that, "Even imagining what St. Francis might be like as a man, I never abandoned reality, either as regards the events . . . or in other visual aspect. . . . What I have tried to do in this film is to show a new side of St. Francis, but not one that lies outside of reality: to show a Saint Francis who is humanly and artistically credible in every sense."[4]

The film is not easy for a modern audience. It is in black and white and has none of the slickness or special effects so common in current films. The film is shot in the neorealist style of postwar Italy in poor or nondescript locations. The activities recorded are generally not dramatic as they focus on the daily life of the brothers. The camera angles and lighting are very simple and natural. The editing of scenes is minimal. We are placed in the

---

1. The Portiuncula chapel is officially called "Our Lady of the Angels." This area was known for people allegedly hearing the sounds of angels singing. Portiuncula is the little area of land on which the chapel was built by the Benedictines. The chapel was allegedly built by Pope Liberius between 352–366 CE. It had fallen into disrepair by the time of Francis. He rebuilt the chapel.

2. Bazin, *What is Cinema?*, vol. 2, 100.

3. In the preface to the American edition, a narrator discusses how the film is placed in the context of the challenges of its time.

4. Rossellini, *My Method*, 37.

The Flowers of Saint Francis (1950) (NR)

position of another member of Francis's flock of eleven followers. The film captures simple responses to events—not stylized acting. To this end, Rossellini, who often employed non-actors in his films, selected Saint Francis and most of his followers from a local Franciscan monastery. There is also one beggar from the local village, Peparuolo, who plays an elderly and befuddled man who becomes a friar. The friars wear plain tunics and live amidst the elements, often walking barefoot even in the cold rain and mud.

Why this simple approach to making this film? In some senses, the filmmaking parallels the simplicity of Francis in its austerity.[5] Some rather awkward organ music and a written description precede each scene harkening back to silent movies. The narrative structure is nonlinear. Each vignette or story seems to be unique and largely disconnected. The development of characters is somewhat limited. Rossellini told an audience in the early 1960s that his goal in the film was to "affirm everything that stood against slyness and cunning. In other words, I believed then and still believe that simplicity is a powerful weapon.... The innocent one will always defeat the evil one. I am absolutely convinced of this."[6]

By using this neorealist approach, Rossellini can highlight the spontaneous and free character of the friars. Their actions imitate Jesus, not the broader world. They attempt to love and follow God every minute. This effort is not stylized; it can be awkward, funny, and even a bit absurd. The absurd in the real reflects how the movie was a collaborative effort between Rossellini, the realist, and the screenwriter, Frederico Fellini, who would soon thereafter become famous for his surrealist style. The result was that the film presents a kind of divine madness. The original Italian name for the film was "Francis, God's Jester." Such a jester or holy fool often stands against the perceived wisdom of his world. From its earliest days, Christianity has challenged the powerful and the learned through simplicity and humility. Freed from social concerns, a holy fool can flaunt social conventions through extreme actions, humor, and associating with outcasts. The actions of the holy fool promote humility, critique the false values of the broader society, and reach those who could not be reached in any other way.[7] The impact is dramatic as Saint Francis's meek and simple faith conquers many hearts.

5. For a comparison of the austerity of the film and St. Francis, see Ponder, "O Great God, Humility and Camera Movement in Roberto Rossellini's 'The Flowers of St. Francis,'" 1–32.

6. Brunette, *Roberto Rossellini*, 131.

7 Ware, "The Holy Fool as Prophet and Apostle," 7–15.

This humility allows Francis and his followers to offer an antidote to the claims of power in the movie represented by Nicolaio, the Tyrant of Viterbo, who requires an elaborate and ridiculous contraption to enter into or leave his armor. His armor is a symbol of man's aggression and pride; it attempts to make this little man appear imposing when he is in reality a small buffoon. In another scene, Francis witnesses a nobleman killing a robber. Francis asks the nobleman, "Is a bit of gold worth a man's life?" The noble in response gives some coins to Francis. Does the noble not understand that the point is that each human person is of infinite value in the love of God? Francis throws the coins down to the ground as if they were burning his hands and runs to the dead man.

Although there are some spiritually intense lessons, the film is not severe in its tone. For Rossellini, the key to capturing the Franciscan spirit is to "turn down all solemnity" for "St. Francis was always laughing at himself, because he was a silly, poor man."[8] The laughter is a sign of his humility—taking his faith but not himself seriously.

If there is a constant theme in the movie, it is becoming one's true self before God. This requires humility, and Francis rejects a dangerous pride that is the enemy of our relationship with other human beings and God. Pride focuses people on their desires and ambitions. In *The Flowers of St. Francis*, we learn the need for humility in the first scene. Francis and his small band of followers are returning from Rome having been granted the approval to live as penitents and preach the gospel by Pope Innocent III. They are walking in a cold rain on a muddy road in their bare feet. The rain pours on their tonsured heads. Their prospects are bleak on this blustery day. Undeterred, a number of the friars stop to discuss the best way to preach. One friar will reveal a secret about true peace and joy. Another friar wants to speak of the glory of faith and yet another of the need to battle for virtue. The friars are missing a fundamental Franciscan truth. Francis, in other scenes, battles against being ensnared in prideful rhetoric instead of engaging in charitable acts. In contrast Francis encourages his friars to "consider our vocation, to which God has mercifully called us, not only for our own good, but for the salvation of many. We are to go throughout the world, encouraging everyone, more by deed than by word."[9]

Actions must be based on a humble recognition of our own fallen nature. When Brother Juniper asks Francis why many follow him when he

---

8. Gallagher, *The Adventures of Roberto Rossellini*, 344.
9. Father Leo et al., *Legend of Three Companions, Life of Saint Francis of Assisi*, n. 36.

The Flowers of Saint Francis (1950) (NR)

is "neither handsome, nor great, nor noble," Francis explains, "God found no more humble creature on earth. Because he saw among sinners no one more vile than me. So that men would see that every virtue and good comes from him. Glory be to God forever."

Francis is attuned to viewing the world as a good creation inhabited by a fallen humanity. The operation of God's grace in such a world is reflected in the honesty and modesty of these poor brothers. The role of human beings in this good creation is to praise God, to seek to help others, and to live in peace and compassion. Later in the first scene, Francis and his friars arrive at the comfort of the hut they have built only to be chased from it by a man who has occupied it. The friars submit and do not resist his threat, but move on. Francis expresses his joy outside the hut because they have given shelter to a person. This is charity in action. Once again, Francis wants charitable actions more than sermons.

The Franciscan brothers in the movie are like the apostles in that they have great virtues but also very human failings. Still, there is a commitment to the common good—the good of one another and their neighbors. They share everything; they give much of what they have to the poor. Twice, Brother Juniper literally gives the clothes off his back to the poor. When they are leaving at the end of the movie to preach, they offer the gifts they have received to the less fortunate. The friars thus promote the common good of the community by imitating Jesus and offering charity to a fallen world.

Once again humility is at the heart of Francis's charism. With Franciscan humility, the friars do not think less of themselves but of themselves less. Franciscans are directed to living in solidarity with others. Numerous times in the film, we see a suffering Francis with his head in his hands. For example, he makes this gesture when he believes that he has been too harsh on his friars by making them sit in the rain. He asks a brother friar to step on his neck and mouth, and rock back and forth three times as a penance. The brother refuses and tells Francis that his answer can be seen in their faces and their joy in following him.

In another vignette, Francis is praying with his head in his hands one night, but he is interrupted by a clanking noise. It is a leper walking with a cowbell to warn of his condition. Francis is overwhelmed by the pain of yet another discarded person like the robber and places his face in his hands. He then arises and walks to the side of the leper and gazes at him, but when the leper returns his gaze, Francis looks down and the leper continues walking.

He is scared and at a loss. Francis then walks up and grabs his arm, but the leper releases it and continues walking. Behind the leper, Francis reaches out as if wondering how to connect to the leper. He then runs in front of the leper again and hugs him, putting his head against the poor man. As the leper leaves, Francis falls to the ground weeping with his head in his hands. This is an important epiphany for Francis. He had hated the smell of lepers, and his embrace is a victory over his false self. He realizes that he can serve everyone, and this realization grounds his compassion.[10] The American director Martin Scorsese aptly summarizes this scene: "Francis' lack of self in that scene never fails to move me—the way he feels the suffering of another human being so completely that he allows it to enter into him and inhabit his own soul. I've never seen another film that deals with this basic question of compassion so eloquently."[11]

So the pain of human life provokes a charitable response in Francis. Charity was also required within the community. In a subsequent scene, the ever-stumbling Brother Juniper cooks all of the food in a huge pot so he will not have to cook for a long time and can leave to preach. Told of this action that did not make sense, in part I suspect because they have no place to keep the soup from spoiling, Francis rubs his face with his hands, indicating a mixture of frustration and amusement. The discipline imposed on Juniper seeks to teach a lesson in humility. Saint Francis grants Juniper's desire by letting him preach, but orders him to begin every sermon with, "I talk and talk and yet accomplish little."

The lesson that holy actions for others are preferable to pious words is one that Juniper does not learn easily. Set free to preach, Juniper first tries to preach to a group of school children from a bridge, but a nearby waterfall muffles his words. He then walks into the camp of Nicolaio, the tyrant who is besieging Viterbo. He tries to talk, but the soldiers in the camp instead use him for sport and throw him around like a rag doll. In the midst of this humiliation, Juniper finally understands that only actions of humility and peace will sway his tormentors. Taken to the tyrant, he is threatened with death on the suspicion that he is an assassin. The tyrant takes Juniper into his tent and stares at and threatens to strike the young Franciscan, but he cannot shake the wide-eyed innocence of his captive. Frustrated, the tyrant admits defeat, releases Juniper, and raises the siege.

---

10. Wolf, *The Poverty of Riches*, 9.
11. Scorsese, "A Personal Appreciation."

The Flowers of Saint Francis (1950) (NR)

As we learn from the example of Juniper, Francis is the leader, guide, and mentor of his community, but his yoke is light. In the film he often smiles when he makes a request, and there is always a sense that his commands are necessary and based in fraternal concern. Anyone willing to submit to the requirements of being a part of the friars is invited to join and is welcomed into a community of mutual concern. Giovanni, an elderly and confused villager, is made a friar after his family abandons him because the family wants a cow more than him. The brothers accept him as one of their own despite his confused actions and utterances. The different approaches of the family and the brothers raise the question of what we value in our world. Admittedly, Giovanni can be frustrating. He repeats almost everything Francis says. He places sticks in the pot of soup when Juniper tells him to put in all the food. Despite his eccentricities, Giovanni is loved for his earnest and simple faith. He always hugs Francis when he sees him. At the end of the film, when the friars are leaving to preach across Italy, Giovanni gives his cape, his sandals, and even his walking stick to the poor. Giovanni may be befuddled, but his heart has grasped the essentials of the Franciscan way. He strictly accepts Jesus's admonition in Matthew 10 when he sends out his apostles and orders them to take "no sack for the journey, or a second tunic, or sandals, or walking stick. The laborer deserves his keep."

Francis enjoys the beauty of the created world as an example of the generosity of God. He seeks to be at peace with nature. When Juniper let a fire be extinguished, Francis notes that Brother Fire needs wood and we must not be stingy with him. All beings and objects must work together for the greater glory of God. In another scene, surrounded by a flowering bush and birds singing, Francis is beginning the Lord's Prayer when a bird alights on his shoulder. He takes the bird gently from his shoulder, and cupping the bird in his hand confides, "My brother, you can praise God so easily, because you are free to fly through the air so pure. Now allow me some peace to sing his praises."

A sense of wonder permeates the world of Francis. When the friars are given some bells, they are overjoyed. On another occasion, Brother Giovanni proclaims that fire is beautiful. This sense of beauty and wonder stems from an appreciation for God's creation. The beauty of the world also provides for all. The friars are thus free to beg for much of their sustenance, and they often give to the poor what they do not immediately need. There is an abiding, innocent faith that God will provide, and that they should share equally with all. Francis tells Brother Juniper when he receives a cloak donated by Claire of Assisi that, "God does not abandon those who serve him." In this scene, I am reminded of Matthew 6:28–30, "And why are you worried about clothing? Observe how the lilies of the field grow; they do not toil nor do they spin; yet I say to you that not even Solomon in all his glory clothed himself like one of these. But if God so clothes the grass of the field, which is alive today and tomorrow is thrown into the furnace, will He not much more clothe you? You of little faith." Generosity fosters a keen sense of hospitality. When Saint Claire of Assisi is scheduled to arrive for a visit, the friars eagerly clean their spaces, cut their hair, and bring flowers so that she may walk on them. They wish to show respect and admiration for her holiness.

One of the most memorable scenes is towards the end of the movie. We learn that perfect joy exists while being beaten and thrown in the mud. Francis and Brother Leon are approaching a house, and Francis speculates about whether perfect happiness in imitating Christ in restoring sight to the blind, healing the crippled, casting out demons, restoring hearing to the deaf, bringing the dead back to life, speaking to angels, or knowing all of nature's secrets. Francis concludes that none of these are true joy. What to do? They must await an answer. It comes in the form of the irate owner who wants nothing to do with their request for alms. Eventually, the insistent friars "provoke" a beating, and they are pushed out of the house and into a field where each one is thrashed with a stick and falls in the mud. Covered in mud, the answer has been delivered. They have found true joy in suffering for the love of their Savior.

This movie is worth watching a number of times. It has for the modern audience some eccentricities, and it takes a while to become comfortable with its simple style. Upon its release in 1950, it was not a box office success. Rossellini, who was married, was mired in the scandal of his affair with the equally married Ingrid Bergman. The movie made less than thirteen thousand dollars in Italy. Nonetheless, with the passage of time, it has been reconsidered in a new light. Many film directors consider it a classic. The French director Francois Truffaut proclaimed it "the most beautiful film in the world." The American director Martin Scorsese declared, "I've never seen the life of a saint treated on film with so little solemnity and so much warmth."[12] The movie brings to life a very human portrait of an amazing saint and his followers. We glimpse holiness in everyday life. Rossellini

---

12. Ibid.

The Flowers of Saint Francis (1950) (NR)

allows us to see how "foolish" friars can live a life of sanctity, and by extension this applies to our world as well. We can also live simply, praise God, and have compassion for the least among us.

We should also live a life of holiness with joy in our heart. This sense of joy and celebration extends to modern-day Franciscans. When Rossellini asked the Franciscans, who were his actors, what gift he could give them for being in the film, the friars consulted the local town, and they decided on fireworks. A magnificent fireworks display was their reward. Such is the luminous legacy of Saint Francis and this movie, which captures the spontaneous joy of those who believe in a good creation and creator. This movie reminds us how a small and simple life remains a light for millions.

Questions

1) The friars express their joy openly in their singing and running. Have we as adults lost our sense of this joy in life—this freedom to praise God and live happily?

2) Do we express our solidarity with the poor like Francis, connecting with the marginalized, or do we feel reluctance to engage those who are different? Is our connection to the poor a kind of detached sympathy or can we really connect with them in a deep empathy?

3) Should we, as Saint Francis advised, act more and preach less in our dealings with others? Why do we often opt for words, not actions?

4) Is nature a means for seeing the creation of God? Where do you see the hand of God in nature?

5) Does Francis's sense of joy in suffering for Jesus make sense to you? Why or why not?

Resources

Doebler, Peter L. "Jest in Time: The Problems and Promises of the Holy Fool in Francesco, Giullare di Dio, Ordet, and Ikiru." *Journal of Religion and Film* 17 (2013). http://digitalcommons.unomaha.edu/jrf/vol17/iss1/35.
Gallaher, Tag. *The Adventures of Roberto Rossellini*. Boston: Da Capo, 1998, 340–366.
Ponder, Justin. "O Great God, Humility and Camera Movement in Roberto Rossellini's The Flowers of St. Francis." *Journal of Religion and Film* 17 (April, 2013). http://digitalcommons.unomaha.edu/jrf/vol17/iss1/36.

chapter 3

The Mission (1986) (PG)

Director: Roland Joffe

Screenplay: Robert Bolt

Awards: Cannes Film Festival—Palme D'or; Academy Award—Best Cinematography

Values: conversion, redemption, meaning in suffering, forgiveness, respect for human dignity, justice, fortitude, conscience

The light shines in the darkness, and the darkness has not overcome it.
—JOHN 1:5

Imagine you are in eighteenth-century South America. Facing the camera, the papal emissary, Cardinal Altamirano, is dictating a letter. We are starting at the end. Altamirano's decision to require the Jesuits to abandon their missions has insured the destruction of the Guarani people that they have nurtured and protected. Altamirano is staring at us; he is a serious, thoughtful man, but also a man fully immersed in the machinations of the world, like Cardinal Woolsey in *A Man for All Seasons*. Reflecting the difficulty of his decision, Altamirano is set in chiaroscuro; half of his face is in light, and half is in darkness. There is a bit of ominous flute music in the background and the pounding of an occasional bass drum.

The Mission (1986) (PG)

Your holiness, I write to you in this year of our Lord 1758 from the southern continent of the Americas from the town of Asuncion ... two weeks' march from the great mission of San Miguel. These missions have provided a refuge for the Indians against the worst depredations of the settlers and have earned much resentment because of it. The noble souls of these Indians incline towards music ... [the visual now switches to a mission where Indian children are playing violins with Father Gabriel, a Jesuit priest]. Indeed, many a violin played in the academies of Rome itself have been made by their nimble and gifted hands. It was from these missions that the Jesuit fathers carried the word of God to the high and undiscovered plateau to those Indians still existing in their natural state and received in return martyrdom.

With these last words, we suddenly switch to the jungle. There is a small cross on a string in the foreground. Then, the camera pans to the background where a Guarani tribal chief's head is poking out of the ground like some animal coming out of its lair. There is the movement of childrens' legs, and there is on the ground a person strapped to a large piece of wood. A Jesuit priest is bound to a cross. The cross is carried rapidly through the jungle. The delirious priest is thrown into a river. As we follow the helpless Jesuit, the momentum of the river gains speed, becoming white water before the cross plunges over the enormous Iguazu Falls.[1] It is a stunning visual sequence. We reel from the gentle image of children playing classical music to a horrendous martyrdom. Such is the history of humanity; we are part angel, part beast.

It is perhaps natural that we will initially have sympathy for the "civilized" world represented by the classical music and revulsion at the brutality of the Guarani, but this assumption will be tested. At the end of the film, the cycle of violence comes full circle as a Jesuit priest, Father Gabriel—played by Jeremy Irons—and many of the Guarani in his mission village are slaughtered as "civilized" troops shoot defenseless women and children and burn a village.

The film begins and ends with horrific deaths that were common in colonial clashes between Europeans and indigenous peoples. In the end, the indigenous people were inevitably subdued and often enslaved. Surprisingly, we learn that between these two extreme options there was another possibility. To explain this third option, it will be helpful to locate the

---

1. Historically, this would have been the Guaira Falls, but the movie uses the dramatic Iguazu Falls because the Guaira Falls were eliminated by a dam in 1982.

movie in its historical context. For more than a century and a half, from 1609–1767, over forty Jesuit missions—also called "reductions"—numbering in total as many as 150,000 people—existed in an area encompassing parts of modern Brazil, Paraguay, Uruguay, and Argentina. These missions were granted some degree of autonomy. The tribes were allowed to reap the benefits of their reasonably prosperous missions, raising cattle and harvesting plants like the yerba mate leaf that was drunk like tea. The missions also employed skilled tradesmen such as printers, tanners, carpenters, cloth makers, hat makers, boat builders, silver smiths, and violin craftsmen. The mission churches were often substantial Baroque buildings.[2]

The Enlightenment philosophers Jean Jacques Rousseau and Montesquieu praised the Jesuit approach. Montesquieu admired in his *Esprit de Lois* how the Jesuits molded the Guarani tribe into a civilized people. He saw them as akin to an ancient Greek civilization. Rousseau, in his *Discourse on the Origin and Foundation of the Inequality Amongst Men*, portrayed the Guarani as models because of their egalitarian self-sufficiency and harmony with nature.[3]

On a typical morning at a mission there were children's hymns, mass, breakfast, and then the workers would depart for the fields carrying aloft a saint on a pole. The workers stopped at small shrines to pray. They would gather at lunch for the Angelus and a meal followed by a *siesta*. They would return to work after the *siesta*. After dinner, they prayed the rosary. There were frequent festivals with fireworks, concerts, and dances.[4]

The movie employs some historical liberties in combining elements of different times and places. The mission of Father Gabriel above the Guairá Falls would have been founded around 1610. There was a river and land battle as in the movie, the Battle of Mbobore, against a slave raiding party, but this took place in 1641 and was won by the Guarani. The movie is closely connected to the Treaty of Lisbon in 1750 that prohibited the Jesuit missionaries from protecting the native peoples from Spanish or Portuguese slave traders.[5] The character of Cardinal Altamirano is loosely based on a real envoy, Father Luis de Altamirano, who was sent in 1752 from the Jesuit Superior General to transfer some missions from the Spanish to the

---

2. Ganson, *The Guarani Under Spanish Rule*, 52–84.

3. Ibid., 6.

4. The film is loosely based on McNaspy, *Lost Cities of Paraguay*. McNaspy was also a consultant to the film.

5. Miles, *Seeing and Believing*, 53.

The Mission (1986) (PG)

Portuguese. The Guarani received a pittance for their lands and property, getting roughly 28,000 *pesos* for seven missions that were valued at seven to sixteen million *pesos*. Not surprisingly, hostilities ensued in the Guarani War from 1754–1756. The Guarani initially won some battles but were eventually defeated. Then, the Jesuits were expelled from South America in 1767 and Pope Clement XIV suppressed the entire order in 1773. Slavers raided the remaining missions without Jesuit protection, and the missions either disappeared or were integrated into colonial culture.[6]

The freedoms taken with the collapsing of dates allows the movie to maintain an internal coherence and unity that would have been otherwise impossible. Perhaps less pardonable was the ignoring of the inconvenient historical fact that no Guarani had leadership positions and the use of corporal punishments by the Jesuits.[7]

While some elements of historical inaccuracy are troubling, the merits of the movie significantly outweigh its failings. So let us return to the movie. After the horrifying death of their priest, the Jesuits tried again to found a mission deep in the jungle. Father Gabriel, in his bare feet, climbs up the sheer face of a cliff to bring the good news of the faith above the falls. After this harrowing feat, he begins to play his oboe in the heart of the jungle and is soon surrounded by the bows of the Guarani. He risks a horrific death that seems imminent when the Guarani chief yells and breaks his oboe. Another Guarani collects the pieces of the oboe, gives it to Father Gabriel, and gently taking his hand, helps him walk into the jungle. Father Gabriel subsequently begins to connect with the Guarani through music. Indeed, music is a central aspect of the movie. For example, a young boy plays on the violin the "Ave Maria" before Father Gabriel makes his petition to the cardinal for the Guarani. When the village is reduced to embers, a single boy who survives the massacre sings the "Miserere."[8]

Eventually, Father Gabriel builds a mission where the Guarani are brought out of the jungle and into the faith. Unfortunately, there are slave traders, like Captain Rodrigo Mendoza—played by Robert DeNiro—who

---

6. Saeger, "The Mission and Historical Missions," 393–415.

7. Miles, *Seeing and Believing*, 48–61.

8. The film score for *The Mission* was selected by the American Film Institute as one of the twenty-five greatest film scores of all time. The "Ave Maria" (Hail Mary) is a very common Catholic prayer of petition to the virgin Mary, mother of Jesus that is also sung. The "Miserere" (Have mercy upon me, O God) is a polyphonic piece of music based on Psalm 51 and was composed by Gregorio Allegri during the 1630s for Pope Urban VIII for Holy Wednesday and Good Friday services.

illegally trap them in nets and sell them to the planters. The mercenary and the mercantile represented by Mendoza at this point eventually combines to seal the fate of the native peoples.

The larger geopolitical realities of empire provide an important background for the individual stories of a number of figures, including Captain Mendoza. In an early scene in the movie, Mendoza rides into a colonial town with his bounty of bound Guarani. In contrast to the greenery of the jungle canopy, Mendoza and his men on horseback ride in clouds of dust between large and imposing structures. Such men live for domination, glory, and profit.[9]

Soon, Captain Mendoza discovers that his beloved brother is sleeping with his mistress. Mendoza then kills his brother and is at the point of suicide when Father Gabriel decides to save him.[10] For Mendoza, despair is easy, but repentance requires spiritual courage. Hope and despair are pretty evenly matched between the priest and the soldier.

> **Gabriel:** God gave us the burden of freedom. You chose your crime. Do you have the courage to choose your penance?
>
> **Mendoza:** There is no penance hard enough for me.
>
> **Gabriel:** But do you dare try it?
>
> **Mendoza:** Do I dare? Do you dare to see it fail?

Father Gabriel offers repentance by trial. Mendoza will place all of the tools of his former life—his armor and weapons—in a net that is attached by a rope to his waist. In stifling heat, he drags this attachment over falls, up the sides of cliffs, and through jungles to a remote mission. There are poignant scenes of Mendoza struggling in his bare feet sliding down a mud bank and then trying again like Sisyphus to climb the embankment. One of the Jesuit brothers, Father Fielding—played by Liam Neeson in one of his first film roles—pleads that Mendoza has done enough and begs Father Gabriel to end this torture. Father Gabriel responds that what is important is that Mendoza must believe he has done enough. Here, we witness Father

---

9. Some of the tribe of Wuonaans, a jungle tribe used to represent the Guarani, who were for the first time exposed to white men during the filming of *The Mission*, later visited Europe. They were impressed by the buildings, but they wanted to return to their jungle, as they were oppressed by all the dead material surrounding them in the cities. "Interview with Roland Joffe" on *The Mission* DVD.

10. Cain too desired death in Gen 4:14, but receives a mark to protect him during his exile.

The Mission (1986) (PG)

Gabriel's wisdom, because the demands of the penance must match what is psychologically required to offset the enormous guilt.

Mendoza begins his penitential pilgrimage below the falls in the land of a fallen humanity. After struggling for three days, the penitent arrives near the village and the Guarani are furious at their foe, the mud-covered and dazed Mendoza. They think about slitting his throat. Seeing his helplessness, they cut the ropes, ending his penance as his armor and swords tumble into a river. The Guarani forgive him in a wonderful scene of tears and laughter.

Mendoza is invited into "a community of the reconciled and liberated, those who extend reconciliation and liberation to their enemy and their neighbor."[11] The subsequent healing of Mendoza takes place in a community where he contributes to the common good as they build the mission. He adopts a new rhythm of life. He watches the children being washed in a stream, and they play tip the canoe with him. A young girl paints his body. He is discovering the meaning of love and community. There are scenes of his planting trees and interacting with the Guarani, and he also reads these words from the First Letter to the Corinthians 13:2–13:

> Though I have all faith so that I could remove mountains, and have not love, I have nothing. And though I bestow all my goods to feed the poor and though I give my body to be burned, and have not love, it profiteth me nothing. Love suffereth long and is kind. Love envieth not, love vaunteth not itself, it is not puffed up. When I was a child, I spake as a child. I understood as a child, I thought as a child, but when I became a man I put away childish things. But now abideth faith, hope, love, these three, but the greatest of these is love.

Mendoza fully integrates into the life of the Guarani mission, and he soon takes the vow of a Jesuit.[12] Alas, this Eden cannot last. A papal emissary and a former Jesuit cardinal, Altamirano, arrives in the colonial city to determine the fate of the Guarani. He is an intriguing figure who is seeking to make the right choice. When asked by the Portuguese what he will do about the missions, he responds, "What else, what my conscience dictates." Altamirano is caught in a difficult ethical conflict. The Treaty of Madrid in 1750 has ceded the Jesuit missions in Spanish lands to the Portuguese. The

---

11. Stone, *Faith and Film*, 146.

12. One of the Jesuits at the mission is played by an actual Jesuit, the peace activist Daniel Berrigan.

Portuguese permit slavery and giving them sovereignty over the Guarani missions will insure their destruction. Altamirano is sympathetic to the Jesuits and the Guarani; he travels to a number of missions and observes their beautiful communal lives. Despite the Edenic life in these Jesuit "reductions," Altamirano knows that if he rules in favor of the autonomy of the missions, the Jesuits may be thrown out of Portugal or other European countries as in fact they were despite his efforts.

Altamirano seeks an alternative and attempts to serve—in the words of Thomas More—"God wittily in the tangle of his mind." He praises the Guarani before the Spanish and Portuguese colonials and the Guarani obviously have his sympathy. He even suggests to the Spanish leader, Cabeza,[13] that they wait until they can get assurance for protection of the missions from the Portuguese, and he further suggests that nothing less than their very souls are at stake in this decision. He is rudely rebuffed; the colonials will not cede any ground. God's will is that they should rule how they see fit. Altamirano is trapped. Fully aware of the human cost of his decision, he orders the Jesuits to leave on pain of excommunication. The Guarani will have no sanctuary; they will be hunted like animals and enslaved. At the end of the movie, continuing his letter to the Pope, Altamirano rues that "A surgeon to save the body must hack off a limb, but nothing prepared me for the beauty of the limb that I was about to sever." Perhaps, this is why the good Cardinal spends hours praying in a mission church reflecting on his agonizing decision. How can he seal the fate of the innocent? Altamirano is a tragic figure torn between his humanity and his loyalty as a former Jesuit to preserve the order. We see a foreshadowing of his decision in an exchange with Father Gabriel early in the movie.

> **Cardinal Altamirano**: "Father Gabriel, what do you think is at issue here?"
>
> **Father Gabriel**: "I think the work of God is at issue here."
>
> **Cardinal Altamirano**: "No, what is at issue here is the very existence of the Jesuit order both here and in Europe. And I assure you, Father Gabriel, that the courts of Europe are a jungle in comparison with which your jungle here is a well-kept garden."

With Altamirano's decision that they must leave, the Jesuits must choose loyalty to their missions or the institutional Church. The Jesuits at

---

13. The haughty Cabeza is played quite well by Chuck Low, who was not an actor but Robert DeNiro's landlord.

The Mission (1986) (PG)

the mission choose the former, but they do so in different ways. Father Mendoza reluctantly chooses the sword, while Father Gabriel follows the path of passive resistance. A military expedition insures that both options, despite the nobility of their efforts, end in death.

Here, as in *A Man for All Seasons*, we once again confront the issue of conscience. What are the obligations of the faith in this difficult situation? Digging a little deeper, Father Mendoza confronts his conscience, but he is torn on the use of violence that he has repudiated. He is sick of violence. Earlier in the movie, this is symbolized by Mendoza's refusal when offered the honor by the Guarani to kill a trapped wild boar at the end of a hunt. He abandons his pacifism, however, when a Portuguese colonial force threatens the mission. His sword is retrieved from the water by one of the children of the village, who cleans it and hands it to him. He has to choose, and his choice is to fight.

Should Father Mendoza, the other Jesuits, and the village pursue a just war or adopt a pacifist approach? The just war approach has dominated for more than a millenium the Catholic tradition.[14] The just war criteria require the following:

1) The exhausting of all possibilities for peace;

2) Be used only for self-defense;

3) Seek the reestablishment of a just peace;

4) Must be carried out by a justly instituted authority;

5) Requires a serious possibility of success.

In the movie, Mendoza's military resistance appears to have met the first three criteria, while the last two are more doubtful. Are the Jesuit "reductions" properly instituted authorities under a just war theory? Who has authority in these lands is what is at the heart of the dispute. Applying this last criterion, the prospects for success by the Guarani seem very limited. Is fighting the good fight enough when there is little hope of success? In retrospect, the answer seems clear, but how could they judge in advance the prospects for success?

---

14. Recently, the Church has initiated a process of discernment on whether to continue with the just war tradition. A recent conference sponsored by Pax Christi, a Catholic peace organization, and the Pontifical Council on Peace and Justice declared that the just war tradition must be superseded by pacifism. Magliano, "Vatican Conference Urges Church to Abandon Just War Theory."

The pacifism represented by Father Gabriel has certainly had its vigorous proponents in Catholic history, especially since the Second Vatican Council. Christian pacifism is grounded in the example of Jesus, who resisted the temptation to violence, spoke of turning the other cheek and loving your enemies, and told Peter to put away his sword in the Garden of Gethsemane because he who lives by the sword perishes by the sword. For the pacifist, the taking of life is a disordered act contrary to the New Testament, and no amount of justification will make it good or even licit. Father Gabriel does not want to live in a world where the taking of human life is an acceptable option for the Church. It would appear that the lines of just war versus pacifism have also divided the village. Half of the village will fight, and the other half will remain with Father Gabriel, saying mass and then processing with a monstrance in a show of peaceful resistance.[15]

The leaders in this movie must make extremely difficult decisions based on imperfect knowledge regarding the consequences of their actions. Altamirano listens attentively, weighs the facts carefully, and seeks alternatives. Despite this commendable process, in the end, however, Altamirano does not privilege the Catholic principle of human dignity that will not condone immoral means even to achieve a good end. He will seek to save the Jesuit order and to this end he sacrifices the missions and their people.

For his part, Father Gabriel is a commendable servant leader who leads from the front. He is always willing to sacrifice his personal interest to achieve a greater good as when he climbs the cliff and seeks out the Guarani. As a leader, he serves God by using a universal point of contact with the indigenous people—music—where words would have been useless. He makes a careful prudential judgment about how far to push Mendoza to accept an appropriate penance. He seeks a peaceful resolution with external forces, but remains consistent with his values and offers only God in a Eucharistic monstrance as his defense. He also knows how to apply religious discipline; he reminds Brother Fielding that the Jesuits are not a democracy. His word is final, but such discipline must be prudent and must not be applied without compassion. When Mendoza ignores him and decides to fight, Gabriel cannot bless his actions, but he does offer him a cross—the cross of a martyr. For this servant leader, love and mercy balance judgment and rigor. As for his personal duty to submit to authority, Father Gabriel

---

15. In the making of the film, the director, Roland Joffe, told the Waunaan Indians playing the Guarani that they could decide whether to join DeNiro and fight or remain with Father Gabriel and pray. They split almost exactly in half.

The Mission (1986) (PG)

obeys his orders except when it is a direct violation of his conscience and his duty to the Guarani. He will not choose to leave per Altamirano's order because he cannot abandon those in need. The good shepherd does not abandon his flock.

The film depicts how decisions by distant rulers can have catastrophic consequences for real people and their communities. I am reminded of the rebuke of Doctor Zhivago to the Communist general: "your point, their village." The Guarani are a native people who resist, but then accept and trust the Jesuits, and they are repaid for adopting their new faith with expulsion from their mission. There is a wonderful scene with the cardinal commanding the Guarani to abandon the mission. The cardinal explains that it is God's will. The Guarani chief counters that the cardinal speaks for the king of Portugal, not God—the cardinal must speak to the king. The cardinal responds that the king will not listen. The leader of the Guarani exclaims that he is a king, and he will not listen. The Guarani decide to resist and are slaughtered.

So, at the end of the eighteenth century, the Guarani are scattered and homeless. The Jesuits are disbanded. The defeat appears to be complete. Yet, at the end of the movie, a small group of Guarani children leave the mission and paddle down the river into the jungle. There appears on the screen John 1:5, "The light shines in the darkness, and the darkness has not overcome it." The Jesuits are eventually resurrected as an order in 1814. The movie notes that today they continue to help indigenous people in South America. Moreover, the movie has brought renewed awareness to the plight of indigenous people around the world. *The Mission* thus raises the important question of how we can live together even under the long shadow of a history of cultural confrontation. Christianity, at its best, offers an alternative. As Saint Paul declares in Galatians 3:28, for Christians, "There is neither Jew nor Greek, there is neither slave nor free person, there is not male and female, for you are all one in Christ Jesus."

In a globalized world, the challenges to living these words is as difficult as it was in eighteenth-century South America. This movie can help us to intelligently discuss these issues and hopefully to act with prudence and compassion. We can seek to build like Father Gabriel a just and humane world that is in harmony with nature. If we fail in creating a more just world then we are like Cardinal Altamirano who recognizes his guilt and laments at the end of the movie: "Thus have we made the world; thus have I made it."

Questions

1) What is the nature of our moral conscience? How is it formed? How do we know how to proceed when there is a conflict of values as was the case with Father Gabriel, Father Mendoza, and Cardinal Altamirano?

2) Discuss the nature of conversion, a turning in a new direction in your spiritual and personal life. What prompted your conversion? Consider Mendoza and his conversions; are you comfortable with all of them?

3) What is justice? What does justice require in the movie and why? Why do we sometimes not act justly to those who are different from us?

4) In the end, which would you favor, the pacifism of Father Gabriel or the just war position of Father Mendoza?

5) In the final scene, the children get in the canoes and head upriver into the jungle, and we see the words of John 1:5, "The light shines in the darkness, and the darkness has not overcome it." Why were these words selected? Is there hope in the darkness?

Resources

Resources on the Movie

Anker, Roy M. "The Laughter Beyond Tears: Love's Redemptive Call in *The Mission*." In *Catching Light: Looking for God in the Movies*, by Roy M. Anker, 162–90. Grand Rapids: Eerdmans, 2004.

Barkley, Elizabeth F. *The Mission: The Film and Its Music*. Center for History and New Media, 2004. http://chnm.gmu.edu/worldhistorysources/d/268/whm.html.

Stone, Bryan. *Faith and Film: Theological Themes at the Cinema*. Saint Louis: Chalice, 2000, 142–55.

Resources on the Guarani and the South American Missions

Ganson, Barbara. *The Guarani Under Spanish Rule in the Rio De La Plata*. Stanford: Stanford University Press, 2005.

McNaspy, C. J. *Lost Cities of Paraguay*. Chicago: Loyola University Press. 1986.

PART II

Religious in the Modern World

chapter 4

Diary of a Country Priest (1951)(NR)

Director: Robert Bresson[1]

Screenplay: Robert Bresson

Awards: Venice Film Festival—Best Cinematography, Venice Film Festival—International Award, Prix Louis Delluc

Values: fortitude, faith, hope, sacramentality, forgiveness, pilgrimage, grace, meaning in suffering

When Jesus heard this he said, "This illness is not to end in death, but is for the glory of God, that the Son of God may be glorified through it."

—JOHN 11:4

In the films selected so far, the challenges to faith come in many forms. As we have learned, it can be from a royal persecution for Thomas More, the pain of viewing a leper for Saint Francis, or in the helplessness of Father Gabriel in protecting his mission. These are dramatic and historically

---

1. Robert Bresson is our first Catholic director and screenwriter, although with a Jansenist tendency. Jansenists were Catholics suspected of Protestant tendencies in the seventeenth and eighteenth century who focused on original sin, human depravity, and God's unmerited grace.

significant challenges, but what about the challenge of everydayness of a priest in a village where God seems to be an absentee landlord? The cross that is carried in *Diary of a Country Priest* is living with ourselves and our neighbors.[2] It reminds me of Jean Paul Sartre's play, *No Exit*, where the three characters are locked together in a room, and one of them has this revelation: "So this is hell. I'd never have believed it. You remember all we were told about the torture-chambers, the fire and brimstone, the 'burning marl.' Old wives' tales! There's no need for red-hot pokers. Hell is—other people."[3] With our careless words and petty actions, we can mentally torture one another through a thousand small cuts.

Other people are also at the heart of misery for the nameless curé in *Diary of a Country Priest*. He lives in a tattered house in a bleak landscape of a small French village where he is in turn ignored, taunted, and rebuked. His plans fail miserably. He has no real friends or companions. He cannot pray. He is in a state of physical and emotional agony. The camera lingers and records the pain that is subtly expressed in the play of his expressions. Somewhat surprisingly, at the end of the movie, the priest concludes, "All is grace." How can the priest proclaim this? Robert Bresson, the brilliant director and screenwriter, always had, at the heart of his works, the question of God and his presence or absence. The path to God requires fortitude, a persistent faith in the reality of God, according to the Canadian theologian Gregory Baum, that guides a person through "growth in the many necessary and often painful choices by which he perseveres in the movement toward growth and reconciliation."[4] This is the path of the young priest.

The movie opens in the most mundane of places—the French village of Ambricourt. In this film based on the novel by the Catholic writer Georges Bernanos, the young priest arrives in a town full of cynicism, despair, anger, and indifference.[5] The movie opens with our observing the diary of the priest in which he records,[6] "I don't think I am doing anything wrong in

---

2. This appears to be a white martyrdom where one abandons everything for the faith and can include exile to an alien land. See Cunningham, *The Catholic Heritage*, 29.

3. Sartre, *No Exit and Three Other Plays*, 47.

4. Baum, *Man Becoming*, 40.

5. Georges Bernanos was a soldier in World War I and a Catholic with monarchist leanings. He was awarded the Grand Prize for Novels by the French Academy for *The Diary of a Country Priest* (1938). He was very conservative, desiring the spiritual renewal of France, but he bitterly opposed the collaborationist Vichy regime in France during the Second World War.

6. The handwriting and the hand doing the writing are that of the director, Robert

Diary of a Country Priest (1951)(NR)

writing down daily, with absolute frankness, the simplest and most insignificant secrets of a life actually lacking any trace of mystery." We fade into a view of a solid, concrete sign by the highway—Ambricourt. We then view the young priest on his bike dressed in his black cassock mopping his brow with a handkerchief. As the camera pulls back, we see him beside a bike, and there is a gate with bars between the audience and the priest. Then we see the count and the governess, Louise, apparently finishing an embrace next to the gate. Did the priest see the furtive embrace? Probably, but we are not certain.

These four quick scenes lay the foundation of many of the themes of the movie. In his diary, the priest records what he deems a simple life without any mystery. If that is true, why have a diary? Despite his protestations, he is onto something of significance. Through the course of his writing and narration, the priest develops a profound self-awareness. The entries in the diary probe, analyze, and ultimately clarify how his experiences relate to his journey of faith. The priest is onto the quest that the novelist Walker Percy, describes this way in the novel *The Moviegoer*: "The search is what anyone would undertake if he were not sunk in the everydayness of his own life. To become aware of the possibility of the search is to be onto something. Not to be onto something is to be in despair."[7]

This spiritual quest is not an easy one. Returning to the film, the priest wipes his brow, and we detect sickness etched on his pale and gaunt face. His sickness is both a medical condition (we eventually learn he has cancer) and a state of mind, for he is world-weary. Returning to the opening scene, he seems to be behind the bars of the gate and in a sense he begins from that moment serving a sentence of terrible isolation. How can he be freed from such a fate?

The town will turn its back on the priest many times. He is provided mildewed living quarters, without light or heat in his rectory, and this absence of lighting is reflective of the decayed state of the town. The lighting will come, but only in three to four months. For the moment, darkness reigns.

A different kind of illumination—the gift of grace—will come, but it too is also delayed. It is revealed only after many trials and tribulations. The young priest wants to act, to correct things, but he initially feels impotent. When the deputy mayor informs him that his request for lighting has been

---

Bresson.

7. Percy, *The Moviegoer*, 13.

approved but will not come for many months, the priest wants to chastise him for sponsoring Sunday drinking parties with young men and women. He confesses that he doesn't dare say anything. Why? "The simplest tasks are by no means the easiest." Confronted by everyday error, falsity, bias, hatred, or indifference, do we not also ignore what we should do? These simple tasks are not easy because it is human nature to avoid confrontation; there may be repercussions. The priest may endanger his chances for lighting. Other interactions with the village do not end much better. Old Fabragars chastises the priest for being greedy and exploiting the poor with a charge for his wife's funeral, despite the fact that Fabragars has plenty of money. Once again, the priest is largely passive. He turns the other cheek.

The priest also discerns improper motives in Seraphita, his star pupil in the catechism class. Seraphita confesses that she is not learning because of religious conviction, but because the priest has beautiful eyes. For his part, the count does not commit to the priest's request to create a youth sports team and brusquely escorts him from his chateau. The priest is often in transit, a liminal figure in the village who rarely engages with others for long. He is often walking in muck as if the land itself is working against him. He is shut out of houses; he is advised by an anonymous letter to leave the village. The priest despondently observes, "I know nothing of people and never will." He yearns for connection. At one point in the film, he goes to sleep as sadness overwhelms him. When he awakens, he opens a window and silently records, "I'd have done anything this morning for a word of compassion or kindness."

Perhaps, there are mentors who can guide the priest on his lonely pilgrimage. Surprisingly, it is the atheist doctor who might be of assistance in the village because he too seeks to aid others and is abused for his efforts. His patients, thanks to rumors of his being brutal and ineffective, have abandoned him. The doctor invites the priest to visit him. Shortly after this request, the doctor dies in a hunting accident. He is rumored to have committed suicide. The priest records this loss as one more test of his faith.

> No, I have not lost my faith. The cruelty of this test, its devastation, like a thunderbolt, and so inexplicable, may have shattered my reason and my nerves, may have withered suddenly within me the joy of prayer—perhaps forever, who can tell? May have filled me to the very brim with a dark, more terrible resignation than the worst convulsions of despair in its cataclysmic fall. But my faith remained. I can feel it.

Diary of a Country Priest (1951)(NR)

The priest from nearby Torcy is a potential mentor, but he is a career churchman. One time when the young priest needs him, he is not around. When the older priest is available, his words are not encouraging. He wonders how desperate the bishop must be to send a young priest who lacks common sense and pursues grand, impractical schemes. Like the count, he advises caution and then urges the priest to soldier on. The walls of despair close in around the young priest. He records in his diary one stormy night that there is nothing behind him and a dark wall in front of him. In the dark night of the soul, the priest lays face down on the floor and accepts his fate and abandons himself to God despite the nothingness he faces. Once again, he perseveres.

The count's house is dysfunctional like the village. The count is an adulterer, and the countess is embittered by the death of her only son. The governess, Miss Louise, is in despair and is despised by the count's daughter, Chantal. Chantal, in her turn, is enraged by her father's adultery and her mother's indifference. She attempts to manipulate the fate of everyone around her and tries to poison the life of the priest by seeking to turn him against the governess and then by circulating a false rumor of his emotionally blackmailing the countess shortly before her death. This time, the priest decides to act within this swirling maze of dysfunction. He tells the count that he is worried about Chantal's sadness. The count dismisses the priest and calls him a fool.

Subsequently, the priest meets with the countess about the daughter being sent away. He confides that Chantal may not return; she may run away or kill herself. The issue soon turns to the spiritual state of the countess. In a battle of wills, the countess is filled with anguish from the death of her son and her husband's infidelity and is therefore indifferent to the plight of her daughter who must resign herself to pain and despair like her mother. This would appear to be an uneven match between the proud and angry countess and a priest teetering on the brink of despair.

After initially feeling faint and weak, the priest regains his equilibrium. He rebukes her for letting the death of her son harden her heart towards God, which threatens her soul and may separate her from God as well as her son. The priest declares that God is love so she should not place herself beyond his reach. Her prideful pain resists; it has deep roots and it threatens the life of others. Then the priest warns, "Our hidden faults poison the air others breathe." The priest connects to her through his suffering and weakness. The countess begins to display a maternal concern for the priest.

The priest counsels that the countess must come face to face with God. She must offer all to him and accept the kingdom of God. The priest asks her to repeat, "Thy will be done" and "Thy kingdom come." She does this.

Can the countess truly convert and be redeemed? The answer is yes because, as the priest observes, "God is no torturer; He wants us to be merciful with ourselves." Then the countess sinks to her knees and offers everything to God. The priest blesses her with the sign of the cross on her head and softly and slowly intones, "Peace be with you." The countess writes the priest a letter immediately after his departure. She admits that her son's death locked her into a "terrifying solitude." It was another child (the priest) who led her out of her despair. The countess receives a new peace and offers the priest friendship and love.

While his childlike innocence and candor transform the countess, the victory is short-lived. That night after the conversion, the countess dies. The priest is overwhelmed and feels faint again. He recalls granting her peace—a peace that he paradoxically does not possess. We are reminded at this juncture of a central point of Catholic doctrine. A priest's ability to act as a conduit for God's grace does not depend on the sanctity or psychological state of the person performing the acts. Sacramental rituals, properly performed, invoke and transmit grace. We can give others more than we possess; the curé notes that this is the "gift of the empty hands."

The priest's peace is short-lived. He is an irritant in the community. The priest is banished from the count's family for meddling in their affairs. The count accuses him of certain unspecified indiscretions. Moreover, the parish labels his character and habits as dangerous. Later from the curé of Torcy, the priest learns that Chantal has spread the rumor that he forced the countess to burn the only picture of her son. He is alleged to have tried to blackmail her into faith. When asked by the older priest if this is true, the priest says he could tell another story, but the facts are essentially true. Like Jesus before Pontius Pilate, he opts to remain largely mute—"It is as you say."[8] Chantal mocks the priest as he is leaving Ambricourt; she declares that everyone in the town now believes that he is a drunkard.

Despite the wounds from such hatred, grace in the second half of the movie is revealed not only in the countess's rebirth of faith, but also in a scene where the priest recovers from a fainting spell that leaves him passed out on a muddy road. Arising, he is dazed and follows an image of the Virgin Mary down a road. He then places his hand in hers, but it is the hand of

---

8. Mark 13:1–5.

Diary of a Country Priest (1951)(NR)

a child, a working farm girl's hand. He awakens next to a lantern. Seraphita[9] kneels beside him with water and a cloth to wash his face on which he has vomited. She confesses to saying terrible things about him. Carrying her lamp, she walks with him to the main road. The lamp reminds me of the ancient Greek, Diogenes,[10] who with his lamp looked for the one honest man. Perhaps, Seraphita has found the one honest man.

There is a sacramental source of strength for the suffering priest. There is his wine and bread. He is living on a diet similar to the elements that are transformed in the Eucharist in the celebration of the Mass. He even lets the bread harden so it is like the wafer used in the Mass. He believes that the wine and bread strengthen his body and renew his spirit.

The final thirty minutes of the movie parallels in many ways the Passion of Christ. Like Jesus coming to Jerusalem, it begins with a journey and great joy. Olivier, a cousin of Chantal and a member of the Foreign Legion, offers the priest a lift to the train station on his motorcycle. The priest smiles and remembers the blessings of youth. This moment of joy allows the priest to comprehend what he will be sacrificing when he dies. Olivier mentions a military expression "all or nothing," and recognizes that there are great sacrifices demanded of both young soldiers and priests.

In Lille, the momentary path of joy and youth ends with a diagnosis of stomach cancer. His time is now short and his path will be thorny. He cannot pray; he is restless and forlorn. He resists a return to Ambricourt and instead he visits an old friend, Louis Dufrety, who left the seminary. He passes out again and when he awakens he doesn't want to die in such a disgusting room. The priest is gently helped by Dufrety's girlfriend, a tender cleaning lady who is willing to sacrifice her desires for the future of Dufrety.

Now, we are at the end. The priest becomes too tired to write. The camera closes in on his face that looks slightly upwards; his expression is yearning, resigned, and expectant. You can almost hear the words of Luke 23:46, "Father, into your hands I commend my spirit." The final scene is the priest of Torcy reading the letter from Dufrety about the final moments. Dufrety found the priest unconscious at 4:00 AM on the floor. He carried his friend back to a bed where he vomited on the floor. The letter on the screen fades into an out-of-focus, simple black cross against a white

---

9. Here Serpahita acts more like a seraphim, one of the highest levels of angels. These angels are known for the special quality of their light. Aquinas, *Summa Theologiae*, I q.108.

10. Diogenes (412–323 BCE) was an ancient Greek philosopher of the Cynic school.

background. The priest regained consciousness. With sweat covering his brow, his face expressed great anguish. He motioned for his rosary that he pressed against his chest, then asked for absolution. He grew calm and smiled. He held his friend's hands and drew him close. The friend expressed reluctance in granting him absolution. The young priest died saying, "What does it matter, all is grace."

The priest has the fortitude—a courageous persistence—to carry his faith to the end. He is faithful despite indifference, hostility, doubt, and despair. The death of the doctor does not shake him. The doctor told the priest that they belong to the same race, the race that "holds on." Where does he find such fortitude? One time, when he is alone in his room, he feels the temptation to despair, and he believes that he lacks courage. Yet, the next day with the priest of Torcy, he is reminded of the passion of Jesus and he cries. He is shown God's grace and realizes that nothing would remove him from his place in eternity. He is a willing "prisoner of the Holy Agony."

With his faith restored, the young curé tells the priest of Torcy that he cannot shut his doors to even those like Chantal who seek to harm him. "I'll close my doors to no one while I am the priest here." He tells Olivier that he will not reject the world even if "it lacks love." So the young priest holds onto faith, hope, and love until the hour of his death. In the end, he sees that life is suffused with grace—a special gift of God.

A warning is in order about *Diary of a Country Priest*. This film is about the movement of a soul, the life of the spirit. External actions are minimal. This is perhaps a bit disconcerting to those raised with action-packed movies. There is good news, however, if you persevere. The film critic Roger Ebert has noted that the rewards of this film "unfold slowly, but they pierce deeply." For example, you are haunted, long after viewing the film, by the memory of the priest's face in this movie.[11] It leaves an indelible impression. Bresson captures each twist and turn of the priest's many struggles and illuminations. As the film critic André Bazin concluded (I think quite correctly) about a Bresson protagonist, "What we are asked to look for on their faces is . . . an uninterrupted condition of soul, the outward revelation of an internal destiny."[12] In the journey of the young priest to his eternal destiny, he learns, often the hard way, to not focus so much

---

11. The actor playing the priest, Claude Laydu (1927–2011), had some major roles in the 1950s and early 1960s. He then created and produced a famous children's television show in Paris, *Good Night Little Ones*, and unlike the young priest lived a long and apparently happy life.

12. Bazin, *What is Cinema?*, 133.

Diary of a Country Priest (1951)(NR)

on his plans, expectations, and hopes. Rather, he learns that faith, hope, and love can expand his vision of the world and prepare him for the gift of grace that makes sense of all the pain and prepares the transition to another life. He has prepared himself well for his arrival in the communion of saints. Like Saint Paul he can declare, "I have competed well; I have finished the race; I have kept the faith."[13]

Questions

1) The young priest says, "The simplest tasks are not the easiest." Why do we not do the right things that we know we should do?
2) The priest feels very lonely, is in need of compassion, and seeks a kind word. Why is that often so difficult to give? Why are we too often disconnected, lacking in compassion?
3) Why is the Church not a source of sustenance for the people of Ambricourt?
4) The priest's last words are "all is grace." How can he say this?
5) How do we deal with loss, depression, pain, and death? Does the scene between the countess and the priest offer any insights on this issue?
6) Like the priest, do we keep our doors open to all, even to those with whom we disagree?

Resources

Avila, Wanda. "*Diary of a Country Priest*: The Transcendent on Film." *Journal of Religion and Film* 10 (October 2006). http://www.unomaha.edu/jrf/Vol10No2/Avila_CountryPriest.htm.
Ebert, Roger. "Diary of a Country Priest" (2011). http://www.rogerebert.com/reviews/great-movie-diary-of-a-country-priest-1951.
Keegan, John E. "Robert Bresson's 'The Diary of a Country Priest': The Experience of God as Grace." *Sewanee Theological Review* 54 (Christmas 2010) 47–59.
Pipolo, Tony. *Robert Bresson, A Passion for Film*. New York: Oxford University Press, 2009.

---

13. 2 Tim 4:7.

chapter 5

Of Gods and Men (2010) (PG-13)

Director: Xavier Beauvois

Screenplay: Xavier Beauvois and Etienne Comar

Awards: Cannes Film Festival—Grand Prize; National Board of Review—Best Foreign Film

Values: common good, solidarity, conscience, integrity, faith, hope, compassion, fortitude, wisdom

God is love, and whoever remains in love remains in God and God in him.

—1 JOHN 4:16

Of Gods and Men recounts the story of Trappist monks in Tibhirine, Algeria in 1996 who suffered martyrdom in a vicious war waged between a corrupt military government and radical Muslim guerillas. When this film was released in 2010, it was a sensation. In a largely secular France, it was the top-rated movie for four consecutive weeks. It won the Grand Prize at the Cannes Film Festival. The noted American cultural critic, Father James Martin, SJ, declared, "*Of Gods and Men* is the greatest film on faith I've ever seen." For Father Martin the film is a realistic, not idealistic, portrayal of the

Of Gods and Men (2010) (PG-13)

life of faith, intelligently reveals the life of religious, is artistically deft and understated, and effectively uses talented actors.[1]

The film is both a glimpse into how a combination of historical forces resulted in the terrible deaths (they were beheaded) of the monks and a deeply moving personal and communal story of religious trying to be true to their vocation under extreme circumstances. Some historical background will help to orient the viewer to the religious, cultural, and political forces that collide in the film. For example, why are there French monks in Algeria? It began with a flyswatter. In 1827, the *dey*[2] or governor of Algiers smacked a French consul with a flyswatter over the issue of debts owed to the French government. This initiated a series of events that led to the French invasion of Algeria. The seeds of resentment between the French and the Algerians were sown in these nineteenth-century conflicts and would boil over again after the Second World War. Algerian nationalism ignited a guerilla war against the French in 1954, lasting until national independence in 1962.

One of the young officers in the Algerian War, Christian de Chergé, was attached to a Special Administrative Service unit that sought to pacify the Algerian population through building houses, hospitals, schools, and mosques. Christian was drawn to this new land and the hospitality and piety of its people. One evening, Christian was walking with his friend, an Algerian policeman, Mohammed, when they were suddenly surrounded by rebels who pointed their guns at his chest. Mohammed stepped between the guns and his friend and told the rebels that the Frenchman was a godly man and a friend of Muslims. The rebels withdrew. That night, Mohammed had his throat slit by the rebels, leaving behind a wife and ten children. Christian declared that Mohammed "changed my life by liberating my faith in spite of the complexity of daily life, and showed me how to live it simply as a response to what is authentic and natural in others."[3]

Mohammed had given him a gift of love, a gift that Christian was now willing to offer others as a *mendiant de l'amour*, a mendicant of love. In exploring his new vocation, the historical themes in Western monasticism of humility, good works, discipline, and purity of heart appealed to the ex-soldier. When he was assigned to the small Trappist monastery in Tibhirine, a two-hour drive south of Algiers, Christian startled some of

---

1. Martin, SJ, "A Profound Work of Art."
2. A *dey* is a governor in the Ottoman empire.
3. Kiser, *The Monks of Tibhirine*, 9–10.

the older brothers with his interest in Arabic and the Koran. He spent two years studying at the Papal Institute of Islamic and Arabic Studies in Rome. Combining the themes at the Second Vatican Council of dialogue with the older vow of monastic hospitality, Christian regularly organized *ribats* or dialogues of Muslims and Christians in the monastery guesthouse. He sensed common values in Islam and Christianity, since the religions shared a common heritage as Abrahamic faiths. This heritage included a shared "devotion to the Absolute, regular communal prayer, fasting, submission to the will of God, giving alms to the poor, offering hospitality, self-transformation, trust in Divine providence, and spiritual pilgrimage."[4]

The Algerian Civil War (1991–2002) placed these efforts in jeopardy as the monks were caught between the goals of the national government and Islamic rebels. This guerilla war resulted from elections cancelled by the military because of fears that the Islamic Salvation Front might win. A military coup then plummeted the country into a civil war. The rebels initially focused on the military and police but eventually began targeting civilians—sometimes in horrifying attacks that killed women and children. The government retaliated with its own harsh measures. It is estimated that as many as 150,000 people died in the civil war.[5]

At the beginning of the movie, the monastery seems a peaceful refuge, far from the civil war. We witness the measured patterns of *ora et labora*, the ancient monastic disciplines of prayer and work. In the first scene, the monks shuffle out of their cells to the daily office[6] with its chanting of the psalms. The actors playing the brothers noted the impact of praying the psalms. Lambert Wilson, who plays the abbot, Christian, observed that through chanting the psalms, the actors "became brothers." Olivier Rabourdin, who plays Brother Christophe, discovered that "To chant Psalms is to breathe together, to share the Breath of Life."[7] After the chanting of the psalms, the film documents the measured, daily work of the monastery—sweeping, fetching firewood, tending the bees, and watering the gardens.

---

4. Ibid., 48.

5. This is the official number of deaths although the actual number is debated. Hagelstein, *Explaining the Violence Pattern of the Algerian Civil War*, 9.

6. "The Divine Office . . . is the daily prayer of the Church, marking the hours of each day and sanctifying the day with prayer. The Hours are a meditative dialogue on the mystery of Christ, using scripture and prayer." USSCB, "Liturgy of the Hours." Online: http://www.usccb.org/prayer-and-worship/liturgy-of-the-hours/.

7. Beaty, "Of Gods and Men."

Of Gods and Men (2010) (PG-13)

There are always interludes for silence in a space created for the heart and soul to encounter the transcendent.

There are also simple yet telling scenes of interaction between the monks and the people of Tibhirine. The villagers come to the dispensary to get medications from the avuncular Brother Luc, who gently examines the children and prescribes medications. He is a healer of more than illness. When he sees a young girl without proper shoes, he offers her a better pair. Health care at the monastery considers the needs of the whole person. Luc is also the confidant of a young woman who is worried about a marriage that her father wants to arrange for her. Here, he provides some balm for the pain of love. She asks him, "How do you know when you are in love?" He reveals that he had known love, the thrill of being in the presence of the other. Luc provides insight, but he does not propose a final solution. He is sensitive to the role of the parents. A review in *The New Yorker* admitted that Brother Luc—played beautifully by Michael Lonsdale—"looks like someone who knows all the mysteries of the universe but has decided, in the interest of public order and private amusement, to keep them to himself. In short, he makes one heck of a monk."[8]

Unfortunately, the ebb and flow of the monastery's common life and the mutually supportive interactions with the village, however, are eventually interrupted by political turmoil. Muslim fundamentalist rebels are waging a brutal guerilla war. Rebels slit the throats of nearby Croatian workers. A villager tells Christian that his niece was murdered for not wearing a head scarf. The Algerian government orders the monks to leave or accept armed guards. Speaking as the abbot for the whole community, Christian abruptly refuses.

In a tense meeting, the apprehensive monks gather around a table to discuss their options. A large map of the world is behind them. The problems of the larger world are indeed coming to their monastery. What is the correct path of discernment? One of the other monks complained that Christian had acted without their input. "All our lives are at stake," he complains. "The very principle of community is compromised by your attitude." Christian is a strong personality with a quick temper. His deep commitment to Muslim and Christian dialogue and fraternity would be compromised by the government's offer. The monks should not take sides. He initially rejects further discussion, but he relents, for even an abbot must listen.

---

8. Lane, "Brothers: 'Cedar Rapids' and 'Of Gods and Men,'" 81.

The discussion then turns to an even thornier issue. What are they called to do? Are they not headed for collective suicide? For Christian, the issue relates to his vocation; he is called to live in this country with the village that is also afraid. There is uncertainty, but Christian observes, "We will live with this unknown." Other monks are less sanguine about the unknown. Brother Luc asks what each monk could do if the rebels come? Ending this scene with levity, Luc suggests they play hide and seek.

The tension at the monastery mounts. Everyone is becoming pensive. Daily activities are no longer normal. A brother visiting the village to make photocopies is asked by the shop owner if he still has his head. He responds dismissively, "They can have my head." The brother's confidence dissipates when he watches a scene of a bombing on television. He sees women and children being hurt. There is fear and anguish on his face. In another scene, a door closing in the kitchen startles a brother. The monks are short with one another. The rectory reading at a meal counsels them to accept powerlessness and poverty and to create relationships based not on power but on love. Another reading reminds them of the bitterness of the life of an apostle and the anguish at times of God's apparent silence.

It is not long before their fears are realized. On Christmas Eve one of the monks sings as he lights candles celebrating the coming of Christ and the creating of the earth as a cradle for the Savior. A monk is walking with keys through the cloister. A door bursts open and rebels pour into the monastery. Christian bravely tells the invaders that this is a place of peace; no guns are allowed. The guns and the discussion must move outside the walls. The rebel leader, Ali Fayattia, wants to take Brother Luc to provide for their medical needs. Christian responds that Luc is too old. Fayattia also wants their limited medical supplies. He stares at Christian, "You have no choice." Christian counters, "I have a choice. We can't give what we don't have." Christian then cites the Koran noting that Christians are nearest in faith to the believers and among Christians, priests and monks "wax not proud." Christian explains that this is why the monks are friends with their Muslim neighbors. Christian reminds him that it is Christmas Eve, and the monks are celebrating the birth of the Prince of Peace. Fayattia then apologizes and shakes Christian's hand.[9]

The monks are rattled by the rebel intrusion and by the subsequent incursions of the Algerian military. They are adrift with their fears and

---

9. This exchange is almost exactly as it happened according to diaries and letters of the monks. This is true for much of the dialogue in the film.

Of Gods and Men (2010) (PG-13)

choices. They meet again to discuss their fate. Should they give the rebels medicine? Should they accept military protection? The middle way between the rebels and government is not placating either side. They wander amidst an array of questions, both practical and sublime. What are the demands of the faith? What do the rebels really want? How great is the threat? What do we do now? The monks could leave at once, leave gradually, or commit to staying. This time, instead of deciding for the monks, Christian, having perhaps learned his lesson, allows for a process of dialogue that permits each monk to express his opinion since it is a matter of conscience. The monks are fairly evenly split. There are those who fear for their life and health. Perhaps, they could fulfill their mission in another location. Others wish to stay, either in solidarity with the village or because they have no other option. Amédée and Christian suggest that it is too early to decide. They must pray and reflect some more.[10]

The agony of the pending decision weighs heavily on the monastery. Christian goes for a walk in the beautiful countryside. He is seen walking among sheep; the good shepherd is pondering how to guide his flock. As Christian walks by a lake surrounded by hills, we hear a psalm about the troubled nature of man and the infinite mystery of a God who weeps for us. Geese fly over a lake. They can fly away. Christian closes his eyes.

While the rebels and government make demands and threaten, some villagers beg the monks to stay. Two men and a woman meet with the monks and tell them, "We are like birds on a branch. . . . If you go we lose our footing." The monks are also disoriented. Paul felt on his last visit home that he was completely removed from his former life. Christophe gets angry with Luc over a mild comment and tells him to "Fuck off." Luc suffers a severe asthma attack. He is overwhelmed by his medical work. A trip by some of the monks in a car results in a stop by the military at a heavily armed checkpoint. They view a dead rebel by the side of the road. Later, Christian is asked to identify the body of Fayattia. In perhaps the most evocative scene in words that resonate with some of the last words of Christ, Christophe screams in his cell one night, "Help me! Help me! Don't abandon me!"

In the midst of the turmoil, there is compassion and tenderness. A guerilla comes to the monastery, and Luc gently cleans his wounds. Later,

---

10. Interestingly, the film critic Roger Ebert, who liked the film and the monks in general, found their choice to stay selfish because of their ability to do good elsewhere. Ebert, "Of Gods and Men."

seeing his friend asleep, Christian gently removes Luc's glasses, lifts a novel from his chest, and turns off the light. Christophe is troubled by the monks' plight. He walks with Christian and asks, "Dying here, does it make a difference?" Christophe confesses to praying and hearing nothing in return. He is losing his faith and probing his heart: are they seeking martyrdom to be heroes, to be the most spiritual? Christian reminds Christophe of all the sacrifices they made to become monks and the meaning of their vocation, including martyrdom. "We are martyrs out of love, out of fidelity. Love endures everything," Christian says, embracing Christophe. "It is through poverty and death that we advance towards him." Echoing Thomas More, Christian also counsels that they must not seek death. They must seek rather to be brothers to all in a love that is based in a faith and hope that endures everything. They embrace and walk back to the monastery.

There is a final meeting of the monks. It is the moment of decision. Luc and Amédée are for solidarity with the villagers and for staying. Celeste notes that leaving would not lead anywhere. Paul has thought about leaving, but it would not bring him peace. Their mission is not about their personal interests. Jean Pierre does not think their mission is finished. For Michel, the disciple is not above the master. Christophe, who has struggled, is finally at peace. He is prepared for God's will. "Let God set the table here." They all vote to stay. They will do their duty to God, one another, their neighbors, and even to those who threaten them.

The vote does not end all questions. Christian strains in the rain to pray. Luc recognizes that the rebels and the government are in a death struggle. The monks are caught in between where they are not trusted by either side as they refuse to become a part of an ideology. Luc realizes ideologies too easily blind people to their common humanity. This can be true, most regrettably, even of religions. Luc writes a letter in which he cites Pascal, "Men never do evil so completely and cheerfully as when they do it from religious conviction." In a "high-risk situation," what the monks can do is "persist in our faith and in our confidence in God." Fortitude, the persistence of faith despite doubt and despair, has become a key virtue. They must do their duty until they receive the final peace and joy of Jesus. Luc goes to a painting and tenderly kisses the chest of the Savior and puts his hand on Jesus' wound.

Military helicopters buzz the monastery. Amidst the clatter of the helicopters, the monks put their arms around one another and chant the psalms. Their faith and fortitude is grounded in the spiritually sustaining

Of Gods and Men (2010) (PG-13)

grace of their liturgy. Their growing solidarity is also reflected in their last supper. They gather around a table. Brother Luc has brought out some wine and puts on Tchaikovsky's *Swan Lake*. With the dramatic music playing, the camera pans across their faces full of joy and love. They cherish, as good Frenchmen, a fine meal with some good wine, but their faith binds them to something larger, something infinite, ineffable, and yet so very tangible at this moment. God's grace is present. There are also tears and longing looks. They do not want to forfeit this fellowship or their lives, but they have made their choice and they will accept the future.

The next scene shows the monastery invaded by the rebels late at night. The monks are quickly herded outside and taken away. Two monks hide and are saved. The rest become prisoners and are killed. The movie ends with a reading of Christian's final testament. He begs that people reading his letter refrain from imputing collective guilt on Muslims. Christian writes in words that appear against a winter landscape. The landscape includes the crosses of the monks' final resting places.

> I would like my community, my church, my family to remember that my life was given to God and to this country, that the unique master of all life was no stranger to a brutal departure. And that my death is the same as so many other violent ones consigned to the apathy of oblivion. I have lived enough to know I am complicit in the evil, the evil that, alas, prevails over the world and the evil that will smite me blindly. . . . And to you, too, friend of the last moment, who knew not what you were doing. Yes, to you as well, I address this thank you and this farewell, this "A-Dieu," which you envisaged. May we meet again, happy thieves in paradise, if it pleases God, the Father of us both. Amen! Inshah Allah.[11]

This message is in part the plea of Jesus on the cross, "Father, forgive them; for they know not what they do."[12] It is a plea for forgiveness to even those who harm us. The movie ends with the monks and their captors marching through the snow into the mists. The monks support one another when they fall. Then they are gone. Such is life. We disappear into the mystery from which we come. Christian was wrong about one thing: the lives of these monks are no longer anonymous. *Of Gods and Men* is a powerful testament to their struggles, solidarity, and love of one another and all people. We have much to learn from them.

---

11. *Inshah Allah* (God willing).
12. Luke 23:24.

Questions

1) Like the monks, what are the routines of your life that sanctify your existence, providing a rhythm attuned to God's creation? Or do you struggle to find such rhythms? Why?

2) How do we live with others different from ourselves amidst the diversity of the United States? Are there lessons you can learn from the monks on this point?

3) What would you have done in the situation of the monks? Why?

4) How do you pursue spiritual discernment in times of crisis? Why is silence important for the spiritual life?

5) Can we, like Christian, forgive our enemies—those who harm us, threaten us?

Resources

Greydanus, Steven. "SDG Review 'Of Gods and Men', A Transcendent Spiritual Portrait of Faith, Love, and Martyrdom." *National Catholic Register* (March 9, 2011). http://www.ncregister.com/daily-news/sdg-reviews-of-gods-and-men/.

Kiser, John W. *The Monks of Tibhirine, Faith, Love, and Terror in Algeria*. New York: St. Martins, 2000.

Martin, James. "A Profound Work of Art." *America* (February 27, 2011). http://americamagazine.org/content/all-things/profound-work-art.

Wright, Wendy. "Of Gods and Men." *Journal of Religion and Film* 15 (2011). http://digitalcommons.unomaha.edu/cgi/viewcontent.cgi?article=1055&context=jrf.

Wyndholm, Anne M. "The Terrible and Sublime Liturgy: Sustaining Mission to the Suffering in Beauvois' *Of Gods and Men*." *New Theology Review* 26 (September, 2013) 63–74.

PART III

The Common Good

chapter 6

Babette's Feast (1987) (G)

Director: Gabriel Axel

Screenplay: Gabriel Axel

Award: Academy Award—Best Foreign Film

Values: solidarity, sacramentality, conversion, redemption, common good, servant leadership, gratitude, grace, hospitality

This is how all will know that you are my disciples, if you have love for one another.

—JOHN 13:35

In April of 2013, the recently elected Pope Francis is asked about his favorite movies. He likes the Italian neorealists[1] and *Babette's Feast*. According to his holiness, *Babette's Feast* demonstrates "the transformation of a group of people who took denial too far, and didn't know what happiness was. The sumptuous meal helps free them from their fear of love."[2] As Pope Francis indicates, the film centers on a single meal and its transformative consequences such as freeing people to connect in a spirit of love. The film relies on subtle colors, music, and a nuanced story to unpack its layers and

---

1. See earlier review of a neorealist film, "chapter 2, *The Flowers of St. Francis*."
2. Glatz, "Homebody, soccer fan, tango-lover."

depths. As a result, the film has been aptly described as "delicate, lyrical, haunting, and complex."[3]

The development of the short story and its adaptation into a movie does not follow a path of traditional piety. The movie is based on a short story by the Danish writer Karen Blixen, whose pen name was Isak Dineson.[4] Blixen was a baroness, an eccentric diva, and suffered from an illness that left her physically incapable of even tasting food as she wrote the story. The baroness composed the story because of a bet that she could not get a story published by a mainstream American journal. After several rejections, it was finally published in *Ladies' Home Journal*. The Danish director and screenwriter for the movie, Gabriel Axel, was noted for his sexually explicit movies and Viking films. The film owes its development and creation to a literary diva suffering from an eating ailment writing on a bet and a director noted for films of sex and violence. Although both Blixen and Axel were open to a religious reality, they remained agnostic. What an odd pair to produce such a luminous film.

In the movie version, *Babette's Feast* is located in a hamlet in Jutland, Denmark[5] in the nineteenth century and focuses on the lives of two elderly maiden sisters, Martine and Phillipa, and their French housekeeper, Babette. The sisters are the daughters of a long-deceased preacher who was the minister of a pious Protestant sect. They devote their lives to assisting the remaining members of their father's congregation.

Everything seems to be in its place, but there is more to the background story. In a couple of early flashback scenes, we learn that the sisters were beautiful as young women. Not surprisingly, they attracted attention from suitors. One of those was Lorens Lowenhielm, a dissolute cadet infamous for his gambling debts who had been sent by his aunt to an isolated community to remove him from the temptations of other locations. Lorenz, while riding on his horse, spots Martine and is captivated by her beauty. Introduced to this special young woman, he is attracted to the possibilities of a simple, holy life, but he cannot commit to it, and he leaves the town vowing to achieve worldly success.

A second suitor, Achille Papin, is a famous opera singer seeking rest in the coastal town. Depressed in these surroundings, he hears the young

---

3. Anker, *Catching Light*, 91.

4. Blixen would also write *Out of Africa* about her many years on the continent.

5. The short story was set in Norway, but the movie was filmed for visual and financial reasons in Denmark.

Babette's Feast (1987) (G)

Phillipa in church and believes she has a future as a famous singer. He offers his services as a tutor, but Phillipa is made uncomfortable by the sensuality of the lyrics and the romantic intentions of her tutor and rebuffs his plans.

The father and the patriarch of the family and community is a devout minister who refuses to permit his daughters to marry since they are critical to his work for the Lord. At the time of the movie, the father is deceased and the sisters are elderly and they are fulfilling their pious mission with the assistance of Babette Hersant, a political refugee from France who joined them fourteen years earlier after losing her husband and son in the revolutionary Communard uprising in Paris in 1871. Achille Papin recommended Babette to the sisters, and she becomes their cook and servant.

The pious religious community that was once well disciplined and united is now elderly and has fallen into bickering and petty feuds. In an effort to reconcile the community, the sisters plan to host a dinner to celebrate what would have been their father's one-hundredth birthday. Before the birthday celebration, Babette wins a lottery in Paris worth ten thousand francs. While at the beach, she ponders her situation. Gulls skim over the ocean. She can now be free like the birds; she can leave. Babette decides to spend the money, however, on a gourmet Parisian meal for the birthday celebration including quail, rare wines, turtle soup, and many other delicacies. In a bit of an odd twist, the sisters, who have been faithfully served by Babette, are fearful that something terrible is afoot—perhaps some kind of pagan ritual or witchcraft—and agree with the other members of their community[6] to attend but to not be trapped by sensual indulgence. The nephew of the aunt, who is now General Lowenhielm, joins the somber guests.

The meal is a catalyst—a point of connection as it has been in many civilizations. This was true in Homer's *Odyssey* in the guest-host relationship of xenia. In the custom of xenia, failure to provide hospitality in Ancient Greece often invoked the wrath of the gods. In the Bible, hospitality in the form of a meal was a holy obligation. Lot insists on feeding the angels visiting him.[7] Abraham's servant is welcomed in Rebekah's home.[8] In the New

---

6. The sisters and several members of the community are played by well-known Danish actors who often acted in the films of the famous director Theodore Dreyer.

7. Gen 19:1–3.

8. Gen 24:22–25.

Testament, Jesus received hospitality from people of many backgrounds. Levi held a banquet for Jesus that included tax collectors and sinners.[9]

From a Catholic perspective or the Lutheran perspective of the attendees, for that matter, the meal is reminiscent of the Last Supper—a place of ultimate transformation. The Eucharist brings God to dwell with and in us. The breaking of bread in the meal of the Eucharist is where we renew our commitment to God, life, and one another. As it proclaims in John 6:51, "I am the living bread that came down from heaven. Whoever eats this bread will live forever; and the bread that I will give is my flesh for the life of the world." With twelve people gathered at the dinner, Babette's feast "is genuinely Eucharistic, a love feast that transfigures ordinary elements, bread and wine, into agents and portents of divine love for the world."[10]

The dinner thus reveals the sacramental nature of the world. God's grace operates through a meal revealing points of solidarity in our common need for nourishment, both physical and spiritual. There is also the role of selfless sacrifice. In a form of *imitatio Christi*, Babette relinquishes her personal hopes for returning to France and independence to offer her time and treasure on behalf of a splendid meal that will alter the lives of the community. Among the diners, the outlines of a renewed covenant are present in their adoption of hope, forgiveness, and reconciliation.

Babette's actions are central to unlocking these new possibilities. She labors over the meal with a small gold crucifix on her chest and does not sit down to eat the fruits of her efforts. She is open and inviting to all. Even the coachman and the boy who helps in the kitchen gratefully join in the banquet. The generosity of Babette, the unconditional giving of her resources and energies for others, allows for grace to operate in the lives of everyone in the house. As Lloyd Baugh, SJ, a professor of film studies and theology, summarizes the impact: "Babette's is an open, sensual, culture affirming, inclusive world where spirit-incarnated-in-matter leads to salvation, a world which does not repudiate or deny the other world. In a very Christological way, it enters into that world, liberates and redeems it, bringing it to fulfillment."[11]

Babette's Feast has layers of meaning that are not always self-evident. Take for example the *calles en sarcophage*, which are quails in bread. This is

---

9. Luke 5:29.

10. Anker, *Catching Light*, 214.

11. If you want to further unpack the theme of Babette as a Christ figure, see Baugh, SJ, *Imaging the Divine*, 137–45.

a specialty of Babette's when she was a famous chef in Paris. The quail and bread mirror the manna and quail given to Moses by God for the starving Israelites in the book of Exodus. The Israelites, like the pious villagers, doubt what is given to them. Also, *sarcophage* in its Greek etymology literally means "flesh eater," which is shorthand for Catholics.

In *Babette's Feast*, the initial reluctance to enjoy the meal wanes as the conversation gradually lightens, and the mood shifts from somber to celebratory as each course reveals sumptuous new possibilities for the senses with Babette as the conductor of a feast. The timing of the meals with their mixtures of visual artistry and culinary complexity parallels how the diners move from the simple and the formal to a richer dynamic of human interaction.

For the pious community, the meal and its joy remind them of how they once were. From a band of believers ablaze with God's word and compassion for others, they have devolved into captives of a web of petty quarrels. Quarrels and settling scores have replaced the possibilities of the kingdom of God on earth. Their usual fare of cod and ale bread reflects the dreariness of their lives.

There is a temptation to interpret the movie as a celebration of secular values against the dangers of religious narrowness, but this is far too simple an analysis. For one thing, Lorens and Achille, the denizens of the secular world, are hardly ethical exemplars. They have fecklessly pursued the vanities of the world. At one point, General Lowenhielm stares in a mirror and quotes Ecclesiastes 1:2, "Vanity, all life is vanity." By comparison, the religious sect with all its narrowness and rigidity has at least not surrendered to the idols of aesthetic indulgence, romanticism, high office, fame, power, wealth, or control. This is no small accomplishment.

The meal is also a charitable act of extreme beauty and artistry for the good of others. After the meal, Babette admits that she is like every artist who wants to produce something spectacular. For me, this effort echoes a theme of J. R. R. Tolkien that the artist through his or her work mirrors and reflects the possibilities of the initial creation.[12] The artistry of the film also offers us a lens from which to view the special qualities of the created world. We can luxuriate on life through the film's soft and subtle coloring,[13] the poignant music, and the landscapes. The china, the dress, and the meal are

---

12. Tolkien, "Leaf by Niggle," 46–61.

13. The director, Gabriel Axel, wanted the film to reflect the colors of the Dutch painter Johannes Vermeer (1632–1675).

all authentic and researched with scrupulous detail to heighten the veracity of the film.

More importantly, the sights and sounds of the meal combine to point to something beyond the reality of the world, to the sublime possibilities of the transcendent. To this end the world unveiled in *Babette's Feast* is presented in alternating aspects of simplicity and elegance, with sometimes a mixture of the two. This contrast helps us to appreciate the need for both, the simple and nuanced, the ordinary and the extraordinary. These points of contrast remind us of the depths of creation and its mysterious fecundity. There is elegant food in simple bowls. Note how the general's ostentatious uniform contrasts with the simple, dark clothes of the villagers. The elegant music of Brahms is contrasted with popular hymns. Babette's ornate meal reflects a kind of Catholic sacramental sensibility assuming the goodness of the word compared to the restraint of the pious villagers,[14] who shun the false material realities of the world.

In the film, we are invited to take a slow and loving look at the world in order to glimpse a sacred dimension. For example, there is a spiritual awakening during the meal where old wounds are confronted and resolved in charity. A long feud of a husband and wife ends in a tender kiss. Other grudges are forgiven. The grand meal of Babette echoes the biblical calls to a heavenly banquet at the end of time, where, in the words of Matthew 11:15, the blind will see, the lame will walk, and every sorrow will be healed. All will be reconciled. Early in the movie, the congregation sings of a new Jerusalem, a transfigured world. During the meal, this hope, to a degree, is realized.

The movie also explores the unrequited love between Lorenz and Martine. As a young man, Lorenz had left and proclaimed to Martine that he had learned one thing: that "life is hard and cruel," and that there are things in life "that are impossible." However, Lorenz gives a toast that recalls the words of their father, citing Psalm 85, that "righteousness and mercy shall meet" and "righteousness and bliss shall kiss." He confides his feelings for his lost love but also his reconciliation to the path of his life. "I have been with you every day of my life. Tell me you know that! . . . You must also know that I shall be with you every day that is granted to me from now on. Every evening I shall sit down to dine with you—not with my body, which is of no importance—but with my soul. Because this evening

---

14. The inspiration for his image of the villagers for director Gabriel Axel was the painting of Neils Bjerre, "The Prayer Meeting" (1897) of the Home Mission Evangelical Movement. See http://www.the-athenaeum.org/art/full.php?ID=57185.

Babette's Feast (1987) (G)

I have learned, my dear, that in this beautiful world of ours, all things are possible." He knows that there is beauty and love, and that he has touched it even if only in a fleeting way. There is an ultimate beauty that is momentarily mirrored in this world that transcends the troubles of this life.

The movie reveals the journey of a fractured collection of individuals who are reunified and anchored in a renewed community of faith. At the beginning, the camera is focused on the ocean and as it pulls back, we view a small village by the sea. The sea, the land, and the village are in a kind of dull mist. We then see cod that are scarred, gutted, cleaned, and very dead. Is this not a metaphor for the village—scarred lives lost in a mist of disillusionment? The members of the pious sect sing in the church in the first few minutes of the film and several other times the hymn, "Jerusalem, Jerusalem" with the opening lines of "Jerusalem, my heart's true home." There is a yearning of these restless hearts for a true spiritual home, a loving community of believers. Babette's feast lifts the haze over them and reignites the possibility of a real community.

After the meal in the village, we view the diners who grasp hands and begin to dance and sing around a well. A well is a very biblical symbol. It is where connections often lead to marriages in the Old Testament. In the New Testament, Jesus tells the Samaritan woman at the well that he is the living water that leads to eternity.[15] Perhaps the village has found this living water again, for we hear them sing, "Let us use this time to try to serve the Lord with heart and mind so that our true home we shall find."

The writer, D. H. Lawrence, once said that wonder was a religious sense, our sixth sense.[16] In this movie, our first five senses evoke and cherish this final sense of wonder. In *Babette's Feast*, it is a wonder that is grounded in the kenosis or emptying of God into his good creation. The celebration of this good creation unlocks spiritual possibilities. In the end, the joy and wonder of the meal restores old bonds and unlocks new possibilities. As for Babette, she is reconciled to being in the village. Phillipa exclaims that there is more ahead for her. "In Paradise, you will be the great artist that God meant you to be. Ah, how you will delight the angels!" Here on earth, we have a movie that should delight any audience by both its artistry and its offer of faith, hope, and love as sure spiritual guides to explore the wonders of a good creation on our pilgrimage to paradise.

---

15. John 4:1–13.
16. Lawrence, *Late Essays and Articles*, 132.

Questions

1) Do you remember a special meal? Was it with your family? Why was it special—the company, the excellence of the food?
2) Why do meals or eating have a religious meaning? Why do we say grace before a meal?
3) In Babette's feast, are the reconciliations plausible for you? Why or why not? What was it about the meal that prompted these reconciliations?
4) In one scene, Babette watches a seagull skim across the ocean. The bird is free to go where it will, but Babette chooses to stay and prepare a special meal. Does Babette discover freedom, or does she just accept her fate?
5) In what way does Babette's feast mirror the Last Supper in its form and meaning?

Resources

Anker, Roy M. *Catching Light: Looking for God in the Movies.* Grand Rapids: Eerdmans, 2004, 191–214.

Baugh, Lloyd. *Imaging the Divine: Jesus and Christ Figures in Film.* Franklin, WI: Sheed and Ward, 2000, 137–45.

Wright, Wendy M. "Babette's Feast, A Religious Film." *Journal of Religion and Film* (October 1997). http://www.unomaha.edu/jrf/BabetteWW.htm.

chapter 7

The Spitfire Grill (1996) (PG-13)

Director: David Lee Zlotoff

Screenplay: David Lee Zlotoff

Award: Sundance Film Festival—Audience Award

Values: forgiveness, conversion, redemption, common good, pilgrimage, solidarity, family, the value of life, hospitality

Is there no balm in Gilead, no healer there?
—JER 8:22

In a clearing overlooking a valley with mountains in the distance, a young woman with her back to us is sitting on the ground singing. She is apprehensive about the ragged man approaching her slowly from behind. We hear her heartfelt words when she sings, "There is a balm in Gilead to make the wounded whole, there is a balm in Gilead, to heal the worried soul." The man stops beside her; she continues to sing as he gently puts his hand on the back of her head. In this scene from *The Spitfire Grill*, we witness a moment of contact and redemption made possible by an overcoming of doubts and fears.

This moment between the two characters—Percy Talbot and Johnny B—reflects the thrust of the movie, where wounded souls seek and at times find connection and discover a sense of community. The opening scene in the film has a young woman, Percy Talbot, in a woman's prison. She is answering phones for the Maine Tourism Division. This is an apt occupation for Percy, because the movie is about a variety of journeys, both geographic and spiritual. We also observe in the opening scenes Percy reading *The Odyssey*. She is on a journey like the ancient Greek hero, Odysseus, who seeks a way home from the Trojan War to restore his community. There are differences too. Unlike Odysseus, Percy has no family awaiting her release from prison. She must select a place of community and refuge. Upon leaving the prison, she chooses the small town of Gilead, Maine.

The name of the town is highly symbolic—Gilead was a place of refuge in the Bible. Jacob went to Gilead to escape Laban (Gen 31:21–55), and David went there during Absalom's revolt (2 Sam 17: 22–29). Jeremiah laments the need for a balm or a physician from Gilead to help cure his people (Jer 8:21–22). There are other biblical resonances in the names Hannah, Eli, and Nahum in the movie, although they are often used ironically. Hannah has many Hebrew meanings, including grace or God has favored me, or passion. In the movie, Hannah Ferguson certainly has a passionate desire to assist her long-lost son and eventually extends her compassion to Percy. She is the conduit through which much good flows as she sacrifices herself like the biblical Hannah by giving food to her son, Eli, a Vietnam veteran who lives secretly in the woods. She also sells the Spitfire Grill to secure funds for some mental health treatment of Eli. Hannah in the Bible is barren, but God grants her a child whom she promises to make a priest. In the movie, Hannah has a son, but he has been taken away in a sense because he cannot live with her because of the traumas of the war. The biblical Eli, a high priest, hears Hannah's lamentation about no children and blesses her and she has children.[1] In the movie, Eli is Hannah's child and he eventually gives himself back to his mother.

Nahum is a minor prophet in the Old Testament. The term Nahum means comforter, compassionate, or regretful. The prophet Nahum condemns Ninevah.[2] In the movie, Nahum accuses Percy of theft. In the end he is regretful and becomes a comforter when, at Percy's funeral, he confesses that his actions led to her death as the result of his judgmental attitude and actions.

---

1. 1 Sam 1.
2. Nah 1.

The Spitfire Grill (1996) (PG-13)

Percy's efforts at seeking refuge and healing have a rocky genesis. When she arrives in Gilead, the sheriff takes her to Hannah, the cranky elderly owner of the Spitfire Grill who reluctantly agrees that she could use some help. Soon, there are incessant whispers at the Spitfire and Percy feels the stares. Having had enough one day, Percy yells to Hannah in the kitchen, "Say, Hannah, did I forget to mention that I was imprisoned down in Wyndham for the past three years and I only got sent to solitary three times?" When she goes out for a beer with Joe, a young man in Gilead, the loud music and a woman being harassed by a man unnerves her. She cannot talk to Joe; she does not want to answer any more questions. She senses the town is always judging her, but her harshest judge is Percy Talbot.

Despite this rough beginning, Percy has been compared to a Jesus figure that takes on the sins of the town. The screenwriter and producer, David Lee Zlotoff, is an Orthodox Jew, and hence I believe a more compelling interpretation is that her character is a healer who unites the community through her life and death. And what are the wounds? The crusty owner of the Spitfire Grill, Hannah, has some physical issues, especially after she falls. This wound is easily treated. Percy gets Hannah to a hospital and later she rubs a balm in the form of some ointment into her legs. Hence, we learn there is some balm in Gilead.

There are other wounds that will not heal so easily. Percy discovers that Hannah's son, Eli, a veteran of Vietnam, is secretly living in the forest nearby. Hannah leaves food in a bag for him each evening by the woodpile. Percy has to do this task when Hannah is hurt and cannot get out of bed. Percy sees Eli and follows him into the woods. On subsequent visits, she talks to him, and he leaves her little mementos like a feather at the woodpile.[3] Eventually, Eli becomes more trusting and leads Percy to his shack; this scene ends with Percy sitting and singing while overlooking the valley. The elusive Eli joins her there.

Sometimes, a wound can inhibit the full development of a person. Shelby, the wife of Hannah's nephew, Nahum, is mousy, and lets her husband mock her. The name Shelby has a derivation in English, meaning "sheltered town." Shelby has been sheltered and controlled by her town. Nahum tells Shelby that she is not smart enough to come up with the idea of selling the Grill through a newspaper lottery. Despite these slights, Shelby will grow during the course of the film. Percy needs assistance with the Spitfire Grill

---

3. The momentos were reminiscent to me of those left by Boo Radley for Scout in *To Kill a Mockingbird*.

when Hannah twists her ankle because she cannot cook. Percy is able to begin to draw out dormant strengths in Shelby after Percy asks her help with the cooking. Shelby becomes an adviser, comforter, and leader in Gilead.

Nahum is full of anxiety over his aunt's declining health and wants to protect her from Percy and her problematic background. He is constantly warning others about Percy, and yet it is his paranoia that has tragic consequences. Late one night, Nahum sneaks into the Spitfire, and to protect his aunt, he removes the money from her safe. Interrupted by Percy in this act, he drops the bag of money. Percy picks up the bag, and without noticing the money, places food in it and leaves it by the woodpile for Eli. The next day, Percy will be blamed for stealing the money. This leads to the arrest of Percy and the search for her accomplice in the woods. Hannah learns the truth from Shelby and springs Percy from the jail to find and protect Eli. Percy desperately searches for Eli, and seeing him, she tries to cross a swift stream and drowns. Nahum, at her funeral, confesses his fault in this episode and that he "never knew Percy Talbot." Although Nahum is apparently now separated from Shelby, we sense in the final scene that he is able to begin a journey of reconciliation as he walks over to his wife and daughter at a town picnic.

There are others who are adrift. An earnest young man, Joe, takes an interest in Percy. She loves the trees on his land that he thinks are useless. While Percy refuses to be his wife because she cannot have children, Joe's "useless" trees turn out to have medicinal properties. Ah, the balm of Gilead theme again.

Percy's many healing impacts derive from her empathy stemming from her wounds. She confesses the source of her pain to Shelby as they sit in an abandoned church. Percy's stepfather forced himself on her, resulting in a pregnancy. On the run, he beats her, killing the unborn child. Percy cannot forgive herself for not fulfilling her promise to protect her child that she named Johnny B. When the stepfather says the death of the child was a good thing, Percy kills him.

Despite her loss, Percy will choose hope over despair. Percy becomes, in the words of the spiritual writer, Henri Nouwen, a "wounded healer." Percy learns to live Nouwen's lesson that "Many people who have suffered the most horrendous rejections and been subject to the most cruel torture have been able to choose love. By choosing love they became witnesses not only to human resiliency but also to the divine love that transcends all

The Spitfire Grill (1996) (PG-13)

human loves. Those who choose, even on a small scale, to love in the midst of hatred and fear are the people who offer true hope to our world."[4]

Percy remains wounded and scarred from her experiences. When Percy is rubbing lotion into the leg of Hannah, she asks whether some wounds are so deep that the healing can be as bad as what caused it. She is leery of strangers, assistance, and intimacy. Percy's terrible pain has also brought extraordinary powers of empathy. Walking in the woods one day, Percy is talking to the non-responsive and elusive Eli, and she decides to call him Johnny B after her baby who was beaten to death by her stepfather. In the woods following Eli, Percy muses that it would not surprise her if something like that had happened to Eli as well. A connection continues to grow between them.

There is a broader connection being made by the townspeople. The contest to sell the Grill to the person with the best reason for receiving it ignites a mass of letters with one-hundred dollars in them as the fee for a chance to win the cafe. One evening, Hannah, Shelby, and Percy drink Apple Jack, and laugh and cry reading the letters. Since there are so many letters and the town is nosy about the contest, Hannah gets everyone involved in reading the letters. Even Joe's catatonic father is raised from his seat watching television after reading some letters. Bringing the story of journey full circle, the town awards the grill to a young, single woman, Claire, with a small child, Charlie. Claire means "clear" or "bright" in French, and with the coming of this young woman things become much clearer with a new moment of possibility. The young woman, like Percy, has dreams for her child. She wants the child to be part of a loving community. As she enters the town on a sunny day during a town picnic and is warmly greeted by the town of Gilead, we hear a narration of part of Claire's letter for the contest.

> It's really more for Charlie than for me anyway. . . . I don't pretend I'm ever going to amount to much myself. But even before I held him in my arms, I swore that no matter what it took I was going to do right by this child. I just gotta find someplace to give my boy a chance, Mrs. Ferguson. That's all he really needs, just a chance. And from reading from what you all wrote, well I got to wishing maybe your town could be that place.

Proverbs 29:18 proclaims, "Where there is no vision the people perish." Percy Talbot provides a new vision for Gilead, where nature, the people, and the community can reflect the goodness of creation. In her initial meeting

4. Nouwen, *Bread for the Journey*, 173.

in Gilead, the sheriff asks Percy why she picked Gilead. Percy meekly observes, "I mean if you give any account to the Indian legends it was just around here, well story goes that when the gods heard how beautiful the land was they had to see it for themselves." With her persistent hope in new possibilities, Percy never lets despair have the final word. When Shelby is searching for the right words for the essay contest for the Spitfire Grill, she remarks that there was nothing special about Gilead. Percy counters that she would write about the town, "There's enough country around it to lose yourself in and not so many people that you'd ever feel lost.... It's a place with roots so deep that no one could tear them out from underneath you."

In Percy and Gilead, we deal with a fundamental problem of humanity. We are made in the image and likeness of God, but we are also fallen, fractured, and broken. Whether we can restore nature and our communities is a big question. It will require an act of moral imagination and vision, but this movie suggests some paths if we are open to them. We can confess our sins, receive grace, seek reconciliation, live in solidarity with one another, and slowly build thick communities of hope. Percy is in many ways a Christ figure whose sacrificial life and death dissolves much of the cruelty, pettiness, indifference, and greed of the town's inhabitants.[5]

In a somewhat curious turn of events, the movie was criticized for being too sentimental, and even worse, for engaging in "sermonizing." For example, in Gustav Niebuhr's article for *The New York Times*, "Spiritual Values Are In, But, Please, No Sermonizing," he observed that the positive "buzz" around the film turned to "dismay in some quarters when it turned out the film was made by a religious organization."[6] Who was this shadowy presence backing the film? It was Gregory Productions, the film arm of the Sacred Heart League, a Roman Catholic charitable organization in Mississippi. The goal of Gregory Productions is to promote "reverence for God." This would seem to be rather tame stuff, hardly fodder for a Dan Brown novel. Wait, it gets better. The Sacred Heart League used the profits of the movie to finance a school. Gregory Productions never disguised its association with the film, but still there were rumors of a hidden agenda to proselytize, even though the movie has no overt trappings of the Catholic Church. The head of Gregory Productions commented that, "Catholics are not encouraged to proselytize." The director and screenwriter, David Lee Zlotoff, who is Jewish, told Gregory Productions he would not make a reli-

---

5. Blake, "Converts," 32–33.
6. Niebuhr, "Spiritual Values are In, But, Please, No Sermonizing."

The Spitfire Grill (1996) (PG-13)

gious film and he was instead interested in making a film with "lots of levels of possibilities and meanings." Commenting on the claims of proselytism, Zlotoff remarked that "It just seems to point to a very high level of cynicism these days."[7]

Given the aforementioned genesis, it is odd that the movie ignited exaggerated concerns of "sermonizing." I would readily concede that it is perfectly appropriate to have a concern about creating a simplistic movie because of certain religious commitments. A rigid and overtly didactic art that seeks to inculcate very precise doctrines and formulations of any kind of theology is problematic. Human life is messy, complex, full of layers and meanings, and our art forms should imitate this reality. This approach should not, however, exclude religious perspectives.

Such nuance and reflection is found in *The Spitfire Grill*. Perchance, the main character's actual name that is shortened to Percy, means by chance. The movie like the character seems to have a lot of chance encounters, small but important moments in a bigger picture. These chance events lead us to larger concerns, however, and by the end we have dealt with environmental degradation, the Vietnam War, murder, the loss of a child, a drowning, and many other difficult issues. There are losses and some of them are severe, but in the end, Percy Talbot, like Babette Hersant, transforms a mass of often isolated individuals into what is becoming a community. In our frenetic world, it is easy to miss possibilities for such transformations. Percy is attuned to these possibilities and we too can renew our paths and be transformed. We can build a true community if we want to, but it will not be easy. As the director and the writer of the screenplay, David Lee Zlotoff concluded,

> One of the things the Spitfire is about is the importance of community and the extent to which we have allowed community to whither. The Internet is hip, but I think it's important to walk next door and have a cup of coffee with your neighbor. Spirituality of all sorts is not only important; I think it is essential to living a meaningful life. Our lives are brimming with spiritual potential. All we have to do is stay open, sit quietly every once in a while, and just listen.[8]

Wise advice. So, watch this movie and listen.

---

7. Niebuhr, "Spiritual Values Are in But Please no Sermonizing," 7,14.
8. Baker, "Rediscovering Community Care of the Spitfire Grill."

Questions

1) What are the wounds in Gilead? How does Percy help to heal these wounds? Do we heal or open wounds in our lives? Why are some wounds so hard to heal?

2) What do you make of Percy seeing Gilead, Maine as a wondrous place? For example, she sees "useless" trees as magical. What is the power in our imaginations to recapture the divine creation of the world?

3) Why does Percy flee to the abandoned church? What was she looking for? It is in the church that we hear her confession. What did you make of her confession and why?

4) Nahum, at Percy Talbot's funeral, confesses that he judged Percy even though he never really knew her. How many people do you judge without really knowing them? Why do you judge in this way?

5) Percy lays down her life trying to save Eli. In her actions, we hear the echo of 1 John 3:16, "The way we came to know love was that he laid down his life for us; so we ought to lay down our lives for our brothers." How do we sacrifice for others? What compels or hinders these sacrifices?

Resources

Baker, Elizabeth Gaylynn. "Rediscovering Community Care of the Spitfire Grill." *Body Mind Spirit Magazine* 15 (September, 1996) 54–55.

Barsotti, Catherine M., and Robert K. Johnston. "The Spitfire Grill." In *Finding God in the Movies: 33 Films of Reel Faith*, 276–83. Grand Rapids: Baker, 2005.

McNulty, Edward N. "Spitfire Grill." In *Faith and Film: A Guidebook for Leaders*. Louisville: Westminster John Knox, 2007, 217–23.

PART IV

Justice and Human Dignity

chapter 8

Au Revoir les Enfants (1987) (PG)

Director: Louis Malle

Screenplay: Louis Malle

Awards: Academy Award—Best Foreign Film, Best Original Screenplay; Cesar Awards—Best Film; Venice Film Festival—Golden Lion Award

Values: solidarity, justice, human dignity, empathy, trust, mercy

> *What strength have I that I should endure, and what is my limit that I should be patient?*
>
> —JOB 6:11

The director and screenwriter Louis Malle, as a young student in Vichy, France during the Second World War, watched helplessly as three Jewish classmates and his Carthusian headmaster, Père Jean, were escorted from his school by the Gestapo. Père Jean looked at the assembled students and calmly bids farewell—"*au revoir les enfants.*"[1] It is a quiet scene. There is no dramatic music; everything is orderly, and this juxtaposition of the ordinary and the cataclysmic amplifies the horror. In *Of Gods and Men*, silence is a place for contemplation and communion with God. Here, silence is an

---

1. The translation is "goodbye children."

abyss; it is the absence of good. In the silence the schoolboys say goodbye to the innocence of childhood and confront the pain of a fallen world.

In *Au Revoir les Enfants*, Malle presents a very personal movie, and he narrates the final scene. He had been haunted by the inaction of everyone regarding these final events. How could this ever happen? Compounding the errors of this moment in history, Malle believed that the nation of France suffered from a collective amnesia about its past. He drifted away from his Catholic faith. It was twenty-five years before he decided on making the movie and thirteen additional years before it came to fruition.

The film centers on two children, age eleven, who undergo a series of separations. Some separations are familiar and relatively innocent—such as the departure of children from parents as they return to school by a train. One of the young boys, Julien Quentin, is preparing to board a train as he returns to his school after Christmas. He pouts at having to leave his mother. In his frustration, he lashes out; he claims to detest her. The machinery of the trains carries the boys away from their loved ones. It foreshadows another kind of departure of a darker and more traumatic kind—a train inexorably conveying Jewish students who had been hiding at the school to a concentration camp.

The film operates on several intertwined levels. On one level, the children are experiencing the usual difficulties of separation from family, creating their own identity at school, and confronting their attraction to the opposite sex as they look at some "dirty" cards. On this level, the film accurately portrays the erotic and neurotic elements of a boarding school run by the Carthusian order. In one of many bifurcations between surface and reality, Julien presents a tough image to his fellow students, but in reality he is deeply hurt by the separation from his mother. The constant taunting and petty cruelty around him exacerbate his bitterness. In the school, the monks are good-natured but largely blind to how the boys push, punch, and jab at one another both mentally and physically. Mirroring the cruelty of occupied France, the boys at recess walk on stilts and attack one another yelling, "Pig!" "Jew!" "Infidel!" There is scapegoating and gratuitous cruelty. The boys short-sheet beds and hurl derisive nicknames at each other. This kind of rough sport imitates in some ways the harsh realities of the external world as the necessities of life dwindle and the noose of German repression relentlessly tightens around them.

Painful separations and hazing exist concurrently. As a result, there is a desperate longing for connection. The same Julien who expresses disdain

Au Revoir les Enfants (1987) (PG)

for his mother relishes her perfume on a letter. One night, an unknown child cries for his mother. The separation from family is most keen for a new student, Jean Bonnet. Julien is hostile to the new student, advising him not to mess with him because he is tough. Bonnet's academic prowess does little to ingratiate him with his fellow students. The students mock him, calling him "Easter Bonnet."

Such educational hazing rituals at a boarding school are not unusual. Occupied France in 1944, however, was no ordinary place to be a child. The French nation has been disgraced by a military defeat and the subsequent collaboration by many French leaders and institutional forces like the police. In the middle of this chaos, Jean is also experiencing the normal distress of being at a new school and making friends, but the war makes his situation even more complicated. He is haunted and hunted by pitiless enemies beyond the school.

Julien becomes vaguely aware of this threat and slowly fills in the details. This is due in part to the fact that in wartime France little is as it appears. Jean Bonnet is presented as a Catholic child, but he is not. Julien covertly sees Jean praying with a kippa[2] on late at night. Searching through Jean's belongings, he uncovers a diary. He puts it up to a mirror, and he can see Jean's real last name that is perhaps a play on kippa—Kippelstein. Julien operates by deduction like Bonnet's favorite, Sherlock Holmes, to uncover facts and arrive at a deduction. In a world awash in hidden motivations and meanings, Malle offers a multifaceted reality where the truth can only be sifted by indirect means. The revelation of the truth finally allows the boys to accept one another. The passage to friendship is not immediate or easy; it has to be warily constructed through a series of challenges. For example, Julien offers Jean pâté, knowing that he will refuse it because it is not kosher, and then hisses, "Kippelstein." Jean responds with his fists to this cruel mockery. Enough is enough. Subsequent events lead to less cruelty and more connection. Both boys share a deep affection for their mothers, but Jean's situation is not the normal one of a lonely kid at a boarding school. His father is a prisoner of war, and his mother's whereabouts are unknown. Jean is on the run and is hiding for his life. The boys build their trust through joint acts of disobedience. Jean plays jazz piano for Julien during an air raid. They pilfer chestnuts from the kitchen.

---

2. A *kippa* in Hebrew or *yarmulke* in Yiddish is a brimless cap, usually made of cloth, often worn by Jews on the top of their heads during prayer and religious services and rituals.

Sometimes, the innocent world of youthful exuberance and hijinks is invaded by the stark reality of the occupation and its implications. The boys are playing a game in the woods with their fellow school children where there are teams seeking clues and a "treasure." Jean and Julien are pursued and they split up and run deep into the woods and boulders to avoid capture. The film captures Julien's efforts to escape. We hear the rasp of his heavy breathing and sense the closeness of his pursuers. The pursuers relinquish the chase as Julien finds the "treasure." Jean and Julien are reunited at this moment of victory. Now they have won the game, but are lost in the woods. Their companions are no longer around. They hear animal noises. Jean wonders, "Are there wolves in these woods?" It is getting dark, and the boys find a road but are suddenly caught in the headlights of a German military vehicle. Jean darts like a rabbit into the woods. The Germans point their guns at him, but only for sport—they do not intend to shoot. They then scoop up the boys and drive them back to the school. One soldier chats about how he is also a Catholic from Bavaria. He places a blanket over them. They hand the children over to the school, quipping, "Lost any children?"

The wolves, in the form of soldiers, are also at the public baths where the boys, as adolescents, already feel vulnerable. The tension is also palpable when Julien invites Jean to join his family for dinner. Soldiers of the collaborationist militia, the Milice, hassle an elderly Jewish man with the yellow Star of David on his coat in the restaurant. A German officer, perhaps interested in Julien's mother, intervenes and tells the French militiamen to leave. The humiliated Milice meekly submit. During the dinner, the mother comments that the elderly gentlemen appeared very noble and then notes, "Mind you, I have nothing against the Jews. On the contrary, except for that Socialist Blum, of course. He deserves hanging." Leon Blum was the former socialist prime minister who governed France in a time of economic chaos in the 1930s. The mother is also not a fan of Field Marshal Petain, who signed an accord with the Germans creating a puppet French state in southern France controlled by the Germans, and she observes that nobody likes him now. The mother's commentary on Blum and Petain begs the question: where are the loyalties of the French people? There was plenty of collaboration by the Vichy French regime with the Germans in passing anti-Semitic laws and by individuals betraying Jews. There was also in France a contrapuntal tendency to fight the invaders through the Resistance and the Free French forces. Most French were caught between these

AU REVOIR LES ENFANTS (1987) (PG)

views and were just trying to survive. So, if you were Jewish, the navigating of this swirling world of loyalties was quite complicated.

The film suggests how slowly, but inexorably, the full reality of the Nazi occupation is revealed to the boys. Certain ugly realities of submission and the betrayal of humane impulses are thrown into sharp relief. For his part, Malle rejects a post-war amnesia that neither he nor the French people were aware of the fate of the Jews in their country and declared, "When I heard or read that most people in France didn't know anything about the fate of Jews—That's an incredible lie. If they didn't know it was because they didn't want to know. As I said, my parents knew and told us about it. I remember how shocking it was when the yellow stars first appeared."[3]

So, is there no possibility for hope to survive in such a sick world? Malle offers a few glimmers of the victory of hope over despair. Curiously, the watching of a Charlie Chaplin film is one of the few uplifting moments. Elisa New—in her article on Malle, the Church, and the Holocaust—describes the redemption of this scene:

> In this, arguably the most religious scene in the film, what we see break over each boy's face is nothing less than his soul, nothing less than what God sees. Thus the lame and embittered kitchen boy, the Arab, Joseph, laughs uproariously and hysterically, showing us the desperation soon to be put at the Gestapo's disposal, while the school fat boy, usually wary and constrained, snorts with lusty, unself-conscious pleasure. Julien cracks a smile, Jean allows the corners of his mouth to curve, and Father Jean's face grows serene, as though in this piece of entertainment he recognizes some goodness cognate with that goodness to which he ministers.[4]

In this time of French equivocation, where was that powerful social and cultural force—the Catholic Church? The Church's response to the Holocaust was, like its leader Pope Pius XII, often enigmatic. The Church offered equivocal public statements and actions to preserve itself and its followers while it was also engaged in a form of indirect opposition through general statements condemning violations of human rights and a veiled and sporadic protection of some Jews. The response of the Catholic Church during the Holocaust has elicited an enormous firestorm of interpretation from high praise to total condemnation.[5]

---

3. Hayward, *French National Cinema*, 155.
4. New, "Good Bye Children; Good Bye, Mary, Mother of Sorrows," 133.
5. The response of the Catholic Church, especially Pope Pius XII, towards the

The response of Catholics in the movie are also diverse. A nun in the infirmary betrays one of the Jewish boys to the Gestapo. She, who healed their wounds, betrayed one of her patients to certain death. The leader of the Church in the world of the Catholic school was Père Jean, the Carthusian monk and head of the school. In real life as in the movie, he was a stoic character who on the surface was formal and removed. He accepted pain as part of living in a fallen world. When Julien complains of frostbite, he reminds him that others are worse off. He is committed to deep and unchanging principles. He chides visiting parents on the pride of wealth. One parent storms out of the church, but he continues and prays for the unfortunate and the persecuted.

Père Jean embodies the motto of the Carthusian order: *Stat Crux Dom Volvitur Orbi*—that is Latin for "The cross is steady while the world is turning." He does not alter his ideal of charity or acceptance of the innate dignity of all human beings because such ideas are dangerous. So, he protects Jewish students even at the cost of his own life. When he was arrested with the Jewish boys, he was sent to a concentration camp and upon its liberation refused to leave until all of the inmates were repatriated. He died in the camp. He is honored by the State of Israel as one of the righteous among nations.

Père Jean is no plastic saint. Julien comes to him when he feels a calling to become a priest. Père Jean quickly rebuffs this idea; the priesthood is a terrible life. Moreover, it is his rigidity that inadvertently causes the betrayal of the boys to the Nazis. The kitchen helper, Joseph, is part of the black market and many of the boys are his clients. When his machinations are discovered, Père Jean dismisses him even though he has no home. Rejected and without prospects, Joseph betrays the Jewish boys to the Gestapo.

In this instance Père Jean's decision is at least questionable. Yes, the black market in a perfect world may be wrong, but occupied France is not a perfect world. The pressures for survival test even the virtuous. Also, why are none of the boys at the school punished? Is not Joseph one more scapegoat in a world of scapegoats? There would be no under-the-counter dealings if the schoolboys did not participate in it. Why is there no response to the merciless taunting of Joseph? Is his suffering at the school not

---

Holocaust is a source of much debate. This subject has created busy hives of defenders and critics. For two examples, compare Cornwell, *Hitler's Pope*, and Rychlak, *Hitler, the War and the Pope*.

Au Revoir les Enfants (1987) (PG)

a problem for Père Jean and the other religious? Are they truly ignorant, or, like much of French society in regard to the Jews, are they willfully blind?

While these questions may and probably should trouble us, we can conclude that Père Jean is on balance a good man, and Joseph is both a victim and an exploiter who is driven by his immediate needs and lower impulses. His chances for survival are limited. He is at once crippled, not very smart, and an Arab in a French country. He angrily betrays the school, the Jews, and the religious. His terrible actions make him a character to be scorned, but Joseph has imbibed a common prejudice against the Jews in France that was fanned into extremism by the Germans. Joseph consoles Julien about the fate of the Jewish students, "Don't worry about it, they are just Jews." Here we witness, in unvarnished terms, that perverse human capacity to turn a group of people into something nonhuman. Lest we think this capacity is only in Nazis, remember in *Huckleberry Finn* how even an innocent like Tom Sawyer has accepted the almost universal prejudices of his slaveholding society. Blacks are just objects, not humans. When asked if a person was killed in a steamboat accident, Tom responds without hesitation, "No'm, killed a nigger."[6]

Joseph has been put to a test, and he does not have the ethical grounding that could lead to a different choice. When Julien denounces Joseph's collaboration, Joseph yells that the other boys are also at fault, others stole things, and Julien should stop being so pious. His final rationalization is, "There's a war going on." Still, Joseph has choices. Like the abbot in *Of Gods and Men* who is told he has no choice by the radical Muslim leader, Joseph does "have a choice." The abbot takes his Christianity seriously and it grounds his actions. After all, a war cannot excuse everything, even if it helps to explain certain behaviors. Joseph is not condemned to his final choice; it appears to be in line with his character.

The choices of Joseph, the betrayal of the religious sister, the German military assisting the boys, and the German officer's assistance to Julien's mom by throwing out the French collaborators—all of these moments highlight the contingent and murky nature of occupied life. With only slight changes, the outcomes could have been very different. So, is Malle like an ancient Greek author displaying how fate marches through our contingent lives to its terrible and unavoidable outcome? I do not think so. He

---

6. Twain, *Huckleberry Finn*, 306; On the way that we use words that dehumanize certain excluded or devalued groups by semantically comparing them to a disease, an animal, a waste product, a parasite, etc., see Brennan, *Dehumanizing the Vulnerable*, 6–7.

realizes the role of contingency, based on a variety of factors. One factor for which we do bear moral responsibility is the values guiding our choices. Other choices by Joseph and the sister betraying the student, or perhaps even Père Jean, might have led to a different outcome. And even if they did not, Catholic moral choices must be consistent with a recognition of our state of free will and capacity for discerning a moral path grounded in the human dignity of all people.

So, we enter the final scene of departure with mixed feelings. On the one hand, there is the courage of Père Jean and the innocence of the Jewish students. At the opposite end of the moral spectrum, there are the hideous and repulsive arguments of the Nazis who lecture the boys and the staff on the French nation's lack of discipline. France must be purified; the foreigners and Jews must be expelled.

Then, there is the middle ground of the students and staff representing the ambivalence of the French nation. One of the boys waiting in the courtyard in the final scene wonders if the students will be arrested and protests, "We didn't do anything." Indeed. The majority is often inactive when confronted by evil. Of course, silence is sometimes required; actions can betray. When the Gestapo inspector enters their classroom, it is Julien's glance back at Jean that gives him away. When Jean leaves the room, a monk tells them that three boys are Jewish, and that they were being hidden to protect them. Père Jean has been denounced. The boys recite the Lord's Prayer for the four.

Despite the error by Julien and the prayer, the Gestapo and by extension the German political and military forces have made reasonable moral choices very difficult. Jean comforts Julien in their last exchange by stating that, "They would have gotten me anyway." Perhaps we can forgive this innocent error of Julien, but can we forgive the free world that only resisted the flames of a pitiless hatred sweeping over the planet at the last second? It is the great failure of the civilized world that we witness in microcosm at the school.

Let me end where this chapter began. In the final scene, the boys refuse to answer whether there are other Jews. There is silence. A few students say goodbye to the departing priest. And he responds with, "*Au revoir les enfants,*" and utters a last hopeful phrase, "*à bientôt*". The French phrase *à bientôt* (see you soon) suggests that the parting is temporary, but the final gaze backward of Bonnet tells us that it will not be in this life. Eyes full of fear, Jean looks back one last time at Julien, who is stunned and waves

AU REVOIR LES ENFANTS (1987) (PG)

meekly. A guard then hustles Jean out a door and beyond our view. The camera then focuses on Julien's crestfallen face. His eyes seem on the verge of tears. Then we hear the last words of the narrator, Louis Malle: "More than forty years have passed, but I will remember every second of that January morning until the day I die." Thanks to this extraordinary film, we will not forget that morning either, and hopefully not its lessons for our humanity.

Questions

1) How does Julien's perception of Père Jean change during the course of the film? Why?

2) How does evil operate in the world of the film? Why is it insidious in warping our view of life and creating a distorted conscience? How does this empty perspective, this moral abyss exist in those who are otherwise normal human beings?

3) The taunting of the young man, Joseph, and his firing for black market activity contribute to his betrayal. How do you judge his decision to betray the headmaster? Is Joseph fully responsible for his actions or is he a victim of the distorted values of the society around him?

4) Have you ever witnessed bigotry and prejudice? Were you active in opposing it or were you a silent witness? Why is it difficult to oppose?

Resources

New, Elisa. "Good Bye Children; Good Bye, Mary, Mother of Sorrows: The Church and the Holocaust in the Art of Louis Malle." *Prooftexts* 22 1-2 (Winter/Spring 2002) 118-40.

Openshaw, Claire. "Memory's Progress, Ambiguity in Louis Malle's 'Au Revoir Les Enfants'." In *Through A Catholic Lens: Religious Perspectives of 19 Film Directors from Around the World*, edited by Peter Malone, 193-202. New York: Rowman and Littlefield, 2002.

Chapter 9

Dead Man Walking (1995) (R)

Director: Tim Robbins

Screenplay: Tim Robbins

Awards: Academy Award—Best Actress; Screen Actors Guild Awards—Best Actor and Best Actress

Values: mercy, unconditional love, fortitude, pilgrimage, conversion, redemption, justice, respect for life

Be mindful of prisoners as if sharing their imprisonment, and of the ill-treated as of yourselves ...

—HEB 13:3

The movie *Dead Man Walking* confronted an enormously difficult issue at a moment when support for the death penalty was peeking at 80 percent in the United States, in the mid-1990s.[1] Nonetheless, it was a success. The film critic Roger Ebert declared that *Dead Man Walking* "demonstrates how a movie can confront a grave and controversial issue in our society and portray it from all sides, not taking any shortcuts, and move the audience to a great emotional experience without unfair manipulation. What

---

1. Gallup, "Death Penalty."

Dead Man Walking (1995) (R)

is remarkable is that the film is also all the other things a movie should be: absorbing, technically superb and worth talking about for a long time afterward."[2]

The movie is the story of a woman—Sister Helen Prejean, SSJ—who is a guide for a death row prisoner to forgiveness, redemption, and unconditional love. I have had the honor of meeting Sister Helen twice. Based on the movie, I was expecting a version of Susan Sarandon, but I was in for a surprise.[3] Sister Helen was very diminutive, with circular hair and head on which she sported very large round glasses. Her unremarkable appearance masked a very remarkable personality. Down to earth with a quick wit, she embodied a kind of piercing energy. She is an engaging presence who impresses even the most skeptical of audiences[4]. At the core of her message is what she writes in her book when she autographs it: "Respect Life!"

Who is this Sister Helen Prejean that is such a force in the film and in real life? Her early life was not dramatic. Her father was an attorney who taught her to debate, and she learned compassion from her mother who was a nurse. She and her siblings prayed the rosary each night. She took long road trips with her family where she honed the art of storytelling. A student council president in high school, she became a religious sister at eighteen. She felt the need to give back the love that she had in her family. "I was hosed down with love by my parents. I was poured over with love and affirmation. If I don't give that back, then I'm really seriously defective. I see it as a matter of justice, not of charity. I've *got* to do this or—I'll explode or something."[5] It was this love that led her to join the Sisters of Saint Joseph of Medaille and to live in a housing project in New Orleans, where she received a letter from a death row inmate that opened a new chapter in her life.

Before proceeding into her death penalty odyssey, it is worth pausing for a moment to remember that it is a deeply committed religious who takes on this challenge. Sister Helen believes that "if you don't have communication with God in your life, there's not that dynamic relationship between drawing in and reaching out. I realize now that I really have that

---

2. Ebert, "Dead Man Walking."

3. Sister Helen has a cameo in the movie. She is one of the protestors praying with Susan Sarandon outside the prison.

4. I had her speak at a Catholic Business Persons Lunch that I am involved with in Atlanta. I was not sure how they would respond to her, but she was a wonderful speaker, waxing in turn humorous and prophetic. She received very high marks.

5. Feister, "Sister Helen Prejean, The Real Woman Behind Dead Man Walking."

combination within me. When I finish this work and I get on a plane, that plane is like my little cloister. I'm back to silence, back to my center, and I'm comfortable being quiet." She brought this spirituality to her death penalty journey. For her, God's presence "was very intense in the death house." In a dark place, there was a "circle of light" that encompassed her and the man about to be executed. "It was that deep center: 'You're here and I'm here and this is really hard, but it's going to be O.K.'"[6]

Operating in this world of pain and meaning, Sister Helen offers us a tough challenge about the limits of our compassion. In an interview about the movie *Dead Man Walking*, she wondered whether a human being who has been found guilty of causing inhuman suffering and "who appears without either remorse or conscience—who appears to lack even the minimal requisites of a human being—deserves to be treated like one."[7] This is not an easy question to answer. The horror of the crime contrasts with the warm colors used throughout the film. The director, Tim Robbins, changed this from the blues and greys used in his movie, *The Shawshank Redemption*. In *Dead Man Walking*, we enter a world not only of warm colors, but also of hope. The music in the opening sequence was written by a young Pakistani and is titled "The Face of Love." Sister Helen is driving and then walking around the Saint Thomas Housing Project, and the present is intercut with a grainy flashback to a young woman becoming a bride of Christ on the journey to becoming a nun. We also see young children playing hopscotch in the housing project. Sister Helen enters the busy and cheerful Hope House, a community organization program that helps their clients obtain housing, GEDs, and other services.

At Hope House, she receives a letter from a prisoner on death row, Matthew Poncelet.[8] The letter is designed to appeal to Sister Helen's sympathies. He outlines his life on death row, the endless hours in his six-by-eight cell where he spends twenty-three of twenty-four hours. The letter reveals a tortured state of mind. The food seems to be designed to fatten him like a sow before the slaughter. He mentions a dream that a guard with a chef's hat on was rolling him around in bread crumbs while "licking his chops." We then witness the first sign of his arrogance. He considers himself part of an "elite" at the prison because he will "fry." His lawyer and wife seem to

6. Ibid.

7. Hinson, "A Tale of Giving the Devil His Due."

8. Matthew Poncelet is a composite of two prisoners on death row, Robert Lee Willie and Patrick Sonnier.

Dead Man Walking (1995) (R)

have abandoned him. He wants legal help or at least a kind word. There is no mention of the crime, much less his fault.

After Sister Helen arrives at the infamous maximum security prison at Angola, Louisiana, there are searches and the sounds of buzzers and doors clanging followed by the staccato commands of the guards. "Woman on the tier!" We also become aware of why we are in this alien place. There are flashes of the brutal night of the rape and murder, a bloody knife moving downward. Hope Percy, the female victim, was stabbed seventeen times.

A world-weary priest who is a chaplain at Angola reprimands Sister Helen for not being in a habit and then presents the case for realism in such situations. He graphically tells Sister Helen of the nature of the killings and the rape and then questions her motives. "Do you know what you're getting into? So what is it sister? Morbid fascination? Bleeding heart sympathy? . . . Well, there's no romance here, sister. There's no Jimmy Cagney—I've been wrongly accused, if I only had someone believe in me nonsense. They are all con men and they will take advantage of you every way they can. You must be very, very careful."

In a later scene at a family dinner, Sister Helen's parents are also worried that Poncelet will take advantage of her. Sister Helen defends her actions, pleading that Poncelet grew up poor without a father. Poncelet's home is dingy. In contrast, Sister Helen's home is clean and inviting. Children are playing checkers in the background. Her home is a scene of familial comfort and calm. Sister Helen feels compelled to aid a man whose life was so different. She pleads, "The man's in trouble and for some reason I'm the only one he trusts." Her father notes that plenty of people have tough backgrounds and are not murderers. Also, he wonders why she doesn't help the victims' families. Her mother asks if this cause is the best use of her energies that could instead keep people out of prison and reminds her that "a full heart shouldn't follow an empty head." Her mother recalls that Helen was always bringing home strays as a child, and then she is the loving and worried mother: "Your heart is large, just take care."

At the first meeting, Sister Helen tells Poncelet that she is there and ready to listen. He calls her out. He senses that she comes from money and has never worked with a murderer. She seems "sincere," but she works with "niggers" who knock each other off like "beer cans on a fence." Sister Helen tries to turn this dismissal to her advantage. She notes that they share one thing in common, living with the poor. He has no reply except for lifting an eyebrow dismissively. Turning on a dime, he plays the pity card; his wife turned him in and gave their child to foster care. He shows Sister Helen a picture of his child.

Then, Poncelet discusses the crime. He is the victim of his partner who was in charge. They were drinking and on drugs including acid, and he was out of his head. Gazing directly at her, Poncelet pleads, "I didn't kill nobody. I swear to God I didn't." He needs a chance to prove his innocence with the Louisiana Board of Pardons and Parole or the United States Court of Appeals. Sister Helen is stunned by the request, but she takes his legal papers, vowing to help. There follows a montage of Sister Helen reading his papers, interspersed with shots of newspaper and television news coverage of the crimes. It includes Poncelet smirking after the jury verdict.

Sister Helen gets a lawyer, and the process of appeals begins. Now, the viewer is placed in the role of a juror on the life of Poncelet and judge of the death penalty system. There are no easy answers. As we slowly discern, Poncelet is a liar about his role. Moreover, behind his snarling presence and goatee, he is a manipulative and lethal killer seemingly devoid of any redeeming quality. We also know that we are dealing with a terrible absolute both in the crime and the punishment. The killing of a person takes away a life and all of its meanings. I am reminded of the western film, *Unforgiven*, and Clint Eastwood's character, Bill Munny, who is a hired assassin. Munny tells his companion, a remorseful young man who has killed his first human being, "It's a hell of a thing killing a man; you take away all he's got and all he's ever going to have."

So, should we constrain the criminal justice system from killing based on the intrinsic dignity of all persons or do we seek revenge for a terrible crime? The movie is a good example of director Tim Robbins's ability to value honesty and emotional ambiguity.[9] Whenever you begin to get comfortable with a view of the crime or the prisoner, he offers an opposing perspective. So when we begin to view Poncelet as human, *Dead Man Walking* pulls no punches in presenting how he abducted a young couple, killed both of them, and brutally raped the young woman. It is a horror beyond description. His lawyer tells Poncelet that his only choice with the Pardons Board is to convince them that he is not a monster but a human being. He does not want his "mama" at the hearing because he has his pride. Sister Helen gently tries to get him to understand how his mother should have the right to plead for him. He will not "kiss anybody's ass." Still, he agrees to think it over. His mother attends the hearing.

9. Baugh, *Imaging the Divine*, 151.

Dead Man Walking (1995) (R)

While the movie is about a specific instance, it also operates on a broader level to raise questions about the death penalty in general. The calculated taking of human life is not a normal choice. It seeks to offset one horror—a murder—by a second killing. It places the prisoner beyond forgiveness. Moreover, the abstract calculus of justice looks a little different at eye level. At the Board of Pardons and Parole hearing, Poncelet's attorney notes how human society has moved from decapitations and hangings to means that soothe our consciences, which suggests that we know there is something problematic about this process. The killing appears sterile only because the prisoner is numbed by an anesthetic before other drugs collapse his lungs and boil his internal organs. Still, the argument is not one-sided. Counsel for the state reminds the Board of the hideous murders annulling the hopes and dreams of the parents.

With the despicable facts of the crimes against Poncelet, it would appear to be an impossible task to present any reason for clemency. Yet, *Dead Man Walking* permits a modification of our view. How can it do this? I think the film succeeds in part by its honest and bracing portrayal of the reality of the crime and the punishment. Also, we are brought to a modification of our perspective in small and subtle steps. For example, in the first scene between Poncelet and Sister Helen, there is a visible mesh screen. As Poncelet lowers his guard, subsequent shots begin to modify and eventually eliminate this screen.

At the beginning, Sister Helen is unsure of how to proceed with such a diabolical soul. As the film proceeds, her encounters with Poncelet slowly remove the blinders from her eyes. She realizes that he is a calculating murderer and manipulator. Exhibiting persistence, she continues to be a spiritual counselor, urging him to admit his role and repent in order to seek forgiveness. Eventually we see that beneath the layers of bigotry, hatred, and violence, there is still a part of Poncelet that is human. For example, his mother shows Sister Helen pictures of Matthew as a child and Matthew shows Sister Helen a picture of his child.

The relationship between counselor and prisoner changes as Sister Helen probes Poncelet's poverty. Initially, Poncelet hides behind his bravado, racism, and dismissive answers. In television interviews, he claims to admire Hitler and support terrorism against the government. He denies the Holocaust. Sister Helen is exasperated by the crazy talk. She tells him he is "making it so easy for them to kill you." Poncelet's defenses are not easily removed. She confronts his tired macho cliches like "showing people" and "taking things like a man" and his racial bluster. He flirts. Sister Helen shoots reality right at him. "Death is breathing down your neck and you're playing your little man-on-the-make games."

For his part, Poncelet continues at times to refuse any spiritual help; he doesn't want any "loopholes" like the Bible. He continues his racist rants. She counters that he, of all people, should know that being the recipient of prejudice is not easy. People view death row inmates as "all monsters, disposable human waste, good for nuthin', suckin' up tax dollars." When she corners him on his prejudice, he changes the subject. She then shines a bright light on the hardest subject. Does he think about the kids or their families? He feigns indifference and notes their hatred for him. Once again, he avoids accountability.

Poncelet's life has drained away most of his humanity. Nonetheless, he slowly reveals to Sister Helen hints of humanity as he comes closer to the execution. The priest/chaplain notes that her job is to get Poncelet to accept the sacraments, "nothing more, nothing less." The salvation process is mechanical—just make him go through the motions. For his part, Poncelet also has a kind of mechanical view of faith. Jesus died for him, so he's bound for heaven. Sister Helen warns him, "Matt, redemption isn't some kind of free admission ticket that you get because Jesus paid the price. You've got to participate in your own redemption. You've got some work to do." She also rebukes him again for comparing himself to Jesus. He is nothing like Jesus. Jesus was about love, not killing.

The walls of Poncelet's ego begin to crumble as the final day approaches. After they measure him for a coffin, he admits to being scared and lonely. He also confesses, "I'm glad you're here." He is still worried about staying strong. I am not going to "let 'em break me." Nonetheless, he is thinking about redemption.

Poncelet leans heavily on Sister Helen on the last day; he needs company. He talks himself through the death process. He meets with his family. They reminisce and then there is a terrible quiet. There is so much pain that it seems to swallow the bare room. After the family leaves, Sister Helen wants to talk about the night of the murder. Poncelet lashes out at the victims and their families. She rejects his rationalizations when he blames drugs, his partner, the victims, the government—everybody, anybody but himself.

Time passes. He cries when his mother calls him. He admits that he loves her. He gives Sister Helen his Bible. The walls are falling faster. At last,

Dead Man Walking (1995) (R)

he confesses that he could have walked away, but he was trying to be as tough as his partner. Finally, he admits to killing the boy. Sister Helen says that although he did a terrible thing that with sincere repentance he can again be a "son of God." Poncelet hopes the parents will get some peace. He thanks her for loving him. Paradoxically, in death, he is finally finding life and love. She will be at his execution. "I can't bear the thought that you would die without seeing one loving face."

Then, there is the execution scene. The families are present. The chaplain is there. Matthew comes out screaming. Then he calms down. The ritual begins. Sister Helen says goodbye. "Christ is here . . . . Look, I want the last thing you see in this world to be the face of love. . . . You look at me. I will be the face of love for you." She puts her hand on his shoulder. The guards intone, "Dead man walking." As he walks, Sister Helen reads Scripture to him. Then she watches the process. He is strapped down. The needle goes in. He is lifted up, arms out like a person crucified. He speaks his last words. He asks for forgiveness and hopes the families get relief. He says to Sister Helen, "I love you." She reaches her hand out towards him. The machine is turned on. During this scene, there is haunting and agonizing music accompanying the watching. We flash back to the killing and then to Poncelet's death. Sister Helen sheds a tear. More flashbacks to a knife and the gun shots. His body shakes a little and he is gone. Poncelet's eyes open. From above, we see the murdered bodies, and then his lifeless body.

It would be easy to stop here. The transformation or conversion of a fallen soul is powerful, but what of the families of the victims? Sister Helen is jolted by her meetings with the families. At the Board of Pardons and Parole, Mr. Delacroix lashes out at her. How can she sit with a murderer and rapist while he, a good Catholic, sits without any spiritual aid and without his only son? The parents bear the daily pain of having lost all of the moments they could have shared and the joy of grandchildren. The Delacroix family name dies with the son. He accuses her of being duped. She offers him a card, but he dismisses her arrogance in presuming that he would call her.

Sister Helen bears the weight of considerable uncertainty. She too cannot escape judgment. There are constant flashback scenes to the killings reflecting what is streaming through her mind. The governor of the state defends the value of the death penalty. A fundamentalist preacher on the radio decries those who assist scum who kill. The preacher argues that the opponents of God's wrath cannot have the high ground. The children in the housing project walk out of her apartment when she comes in because she is defending a racist.

Despite these stinging rebukes, Sister Helen reaches out again to the victims' families. She travels to meet with Mr. Delacroix when he does not return her calls. It is not a coincidence that *de la croix* means "of the cross" in French. Mr. Delacroix has obviously been bearing a terrible cross. He is angry at her visit, but he also realizes that she is scared. He invites her into the house. Folks around his town are saying that she is a communist. His wife wants him to move on, but they are getting a divorce because he cannot. The murder is tearing him to pieces. He talks about the joy of his marriage and his son. He points out how his son connects to the furniture, for this is where he played and where he sat with Hope. "When you lose a child, all the memories get sealed in place, sealed like a shrine."

Sister Helen meets with the other family, the Percys. Hope Percy was to leave the day after the murder to join the military. She had come from work, and her mother put a safety pin in the loose hem of her skirt. There is a flash to the courtroom where the mother has to identify the skirt. That was her last discussion with her daughter. Here, we have the terrible juxtaposition of the ordinary followed by the horrific. She was discovered in the woods, spread eagle and naked. Poncelet taunts the father at the trial. The father wants to shoot him. Matthew Poncelet is "an animal"; he is "God's mistake." Sister Helen avers that she is following Jesus' example in believing that a person is more than their worst act. Mr. Percy throws the gauntlet down. "You can't have it both ways. You can't befriend that murderer and be our friend too."

The final scene of the movie is Sister Helen praying the rosary with Mr. Delacroix at a small church. For many years, Sister Helen would travel the first Friday of each month to pray with him. Meetings with the victims broadened her perspective. "To me, the image for the Church is to be on both arms of the cross," she told *St. Anthony Messenger* in 1991, "with the ones being executed and with the victims' families."[10]

In the end, Sister Helen refuses the logic of the cold-blooded killing of another human being because they killed someone. She declares in the film that "I just don't see the sense of killing people to say that killing people's wrong." The death penalty is a ghastly process that maims everyone involved and does not guarantee peace for the victim's families.[11] It is a long-standing

---

10. Feister, "Sister Helen Prejean."

11. I base this in part on personal experience. Many years ago, I was assisting counsel

Dead Man Walking (1995) (R)

principle of the Catholic Church that those guilty of terrible crimes deserve severe punishment, and society must be protected from them, but as Saint John Paul II recognized in his encyclical, *Evangelium Vitae*, punishment in places like the United States no longer requires death to insure justice and protection of the innocent.[12] "It is clear that, for these purposes to be achieved, the nature and extent of the punishment must be carefully evaluated and decided upon, and ought not go to the extreme of executing the offender except in cases of absolute necessity: in other words, when it would not be possible otherwise to defend society. Today however, as a result of steady improvements in the organization of the penal system, such cases are very rare, if not practically non-existent."[13] Similarly, the principle delineated in the new *Catechism of the Catholic Church* remains valid: "If bloodless means are sufficient to defend human lives against an aggressor and to protect public order and the safety of persons, public authority must limit itself to such means, because they better correspond to the concrete conditions of the common good and are more in conformity to the dignity of the human person."[14]

Pretermitting the issue of the innocently convicted, let us assume that those on death row have murdered and some are psychopaths. Still, if we insure their incarceration, what is the harm in giving them time to repent and seek forgiveness? Killing—especially a cold-blooded murder—is something that no human being or society should take lightly. We know this from the stories of Cain and Abel to *Dead Man Walking*. Still, God did not kill Cain and indeed put a mark on him so he would not be slain.[15] Poncelet's last words remind us what we are told in Genesis: "I just wanna say, killing is wrong, no matter who does it, whether it's me or y'all or your government."

---

on a death penalty case in Bremen, Georgia. You cannot really describe what it is like to have the responsibility for a life in your hands. We secured a plea deal for a life sentence thanks to the skill of my law partner and lead counsel, Matt Towery. When Matt was being interviewed by a reporter, I noticed something peculiar. His voice was fine, but his hand was trembling.

12. For a review of the Catholic Church's tradition of support for and recent revision of its position on the death penalty by John Paul II, see Thompson, "Augustine and the Death Penalty, Justice as the Balance of Mercy and Judgment," 181–203.

13. John Paul II, *Evangelium Vitae*, n. 56.

14. *Catechism of the Catholic Church*, n. 2267.

15. Gen 4:8–15.

Lights in the Darkness

Dead Man Walking is a wrenching movie. It tears at us from many angles. There is so much pain and darkness beginning with the vicious rape and murders of two innocent young people and ending with the cold-blooded killing of Matthew Poncelet. For the innocent victims, all their dreams and those of their parents are destroyed. Those who are still alive will never be the same. Amidst this agony, there is a ray of hope. A murderous, bigoted, manipulating man goes from blaming everyone to accepting his fault, asking for forgiveness, and accepting love. Is this just an example of Poncelet looking for a loophole? Perhaps. We can never be sure, but we have to admire Sister Helen's determination to find redemption in the worst of circumstances. Can we, like Sister Helen, accept that death cannot be the answer for death?

Dead Man Walking takes us to a dark edge of human experience. The movie explores very hard issues, and any answers we discern are subject to doubt. We are not allowed to easily dismiss the claims of the different perspectives raised in this movie. The movie cannot be boiled down to platitudes or bumper stickers. Perhaps we need to follow the example of Sister Helen and Mr. Delacroix praying in the church. They are seeking answers and some peace. As in the prison, Christ is there.

Questions

1) What are the arguments in the movie for judgment or mercy regarding Matthew Poncelet?

2) Does Poncelet have a real conversion or turning to accept his responsibility and to sincerely ask for forgiveness?

3) How do you feel about the process leading to the killing of Matthew Poncelet? Is it just? Humane? Cruel?

4) What is Sister Helen's objective in the movie? Does she succeed in obtaining this objective?

5) How do we feel about the families—the Poncelets, Delacroix, and Percys? Is there any balm for their pain?

Resources

Baugh, SJ, Lloyd. "The Woman as Christ Figure." In *Imaging the Divine: Jesus and Christ-Figures in Film*, 150–76. Franklin, WI: Sheed & Ward, 2000.

Dead Man Walking (1995) (R)

Leonard, SJ, Richard. "Dead Man Walking." In *Movies that Matter: Reading Film through the Lens of Faith*, 58–60. Chicago, IL: Loyola Press, 2006.

Prejean, Helen. *Dead Man Walking*. New York: Vintage, 1994.

Stone, Bryan P. "The Forgiveness of Sins." In *Faith and Film: Theological Themes at the Cinema*, 167–76. St. Louis: Chalice, 2000.

chapter 10

Entertaining Angels (1996) (PG-13)

Director: Michael Ray Rhodes

Screenplay: John Wells

Values: conversion, redemption, empathy, mercy, option for the poor, solidarity, common good, fortitude, justice

Do not neglect hospitality, for through it some have unknowingly entertained angels.

—HEB 13:2

On September 24, 2015, Pope Francis became the first pontiff to ever address the United States Congress. This was a historic moment for a church that was considered by many in the United States a century or so before as dangerous and antithetical to American democracy. His Holiness mentioned four Americans for their unique contributions to the United States and the world—Abraham Lincoln, Martin Luther King Jr., Thomas Merton, and Dorothy Day. He declared about Day that "In these times when social concerns are so important, I cannot fail to mention the Servant of God Dorothy Day, who founded the Catholic Worker Movement. Her social activism, her passion for justice and for the cause of the oppressed, were inspired by the Gospel, her faith, and the example of the saints."[1]

1. Pope Francis, "Address to the United States Congress." https://w2.vatican.

Entertaining Angels (1996) (PG-13)

Now, Dorothy Day is not only being lauded by the Pope, she has been declared by the Catholic Church a Servant of God, the first step of an official candidate for sainthood. During her lifetime, the Catholic social activist and writer Dorothy Day seemed an unlikely candidate for papal plaudits or sainthood. Her life was at times as volatile as the great San Francisco earthquake she witnessed as a child in 1906. As a young woman, she was a reporter, a socialist, an anarchist, and a suffragist. She went on a hunger strike in prison. She could drink most of her male colleagues under the table. She had an abortion. She divorced and then was the single mother of a child born out of wedlock. Even when she joined the Catholic Church, her path was unusual. A defiant pacifist, she opposed every war from the First World War through the Vietnam War. In her FBI file, she was accused of being a communist sympathizer. While bishops and cardinals often lived in mansions during the Great Depression, she sheltered and fed the poor in a dingy apartment. She started a newspaper, *The Catholic Worker*, devoted to helping workers and the destitute.[2]

Despite her controversial aspects, the United States Catholic Conference of Bishops unanimously approved Day's cause for sainthood in 2014. She now needs two confirmed miracles to be officially proclaimed a saint by the Church.[3] She has already been recognized as a model for Catholics living in the world. Pope Benedict XVI quoted from her writings and admired her tenacity, and observed that "The journey towards faith in such a secularized environment was particularly difficult, but Grace acts nonetheless ... God guided her to a conscious adherence to the church, in a lifetime spent dedicated to the underprivileged."[4]

The Catholic Church in the United States was intimately involved in developing and publicizing the movie. The movie was produced by Paulist Media, and the United States Catholic Conference contributed two hundred and twenty-five thousand dollars to its development. The Church's

---

va/content/francesco/en/speeches/2015/september/documents/papa-francesco_20150924_usa-us-congress.html.

2. *The Catholic Worker* newspaper is still being printed for one cent today. There are still over 240 Catholic Worker houses worldwide.

3. The goal of all Catholics is to be a saint, a person who is made holy in this life. The Church formally recognizes that certain persons were saints. There is a formal review process at the Vatican to ascertain if a person is a saint and had the requisite heroic virtue that is followed by two miracles attributed to their interventions. See *Catechism of the Catholic Church*, n. 2683.

4. Benedict XVI, "Pope: Pray for me, future Pope, the Lord will guide us!"

Campaign for Human Development annual appeal fundraising kit that was sent to 40,000 priests included a flyer about the movie. The National Conference of Catholic Bishops showed it to their staffers and Father Bruce Nieli, the conference's director of evangelization, gushed, "I would love every Catholic in the United States to see the movie." Catholic lay audiences seemed to approve as well. A Pax Christi audience stood and sang "Amazing Grace" at the end of the movie.[5] It has also received plenty of advice and some criticism from Catholic experts who were perhaps too knowledgeable of certain details of the life of Dorothy Day to approve of the movie.[6]

So, who was this woman who journeyed from being a libertine social radical to a pious if unconventional Catholic social justice advocate who is now awaiting a formal declaration of sainthood? The film, *Entertaining Angels*, exposes the critical years of her profound transformation. In the movie, we are not given much information on her earliest years that were, with the exception of the San Francisco earthquake, reasonably tame. Her parents were intelligent, middle class, and mildly religious. Her father was a sports reporter with expertise on horse racing. There were a few hints of her future path. She witnessed in the 1906 earthquake both the pain of a massive destruction and the solidarity of neighbors aiding one another. As a young girl, without much prompting, she regularly read the Bible and joined the Episcopal Church.[7] An avid reader, she was very fond of the social justice novel, *The Jungle*, by Upton Sinclair, about the horrific conditions of the Chicago stockyards. Day attended the University of Illinois at Champaign, where she supported herself, wore second-hand shoes, and read radical Christian writers. After only two years, she exited for New York.

Now, we can return to the movie. There is a short epigram from Dorothy Day. "I wanted the abundant life . . . I did not have the slightest idea how to find it." We are thus thrust into a journey devoted to discovering how to live a fully human life. We begin near the end. A young, screaming African American woman is dragged down a hallway in a prison in New York City in 1963. She is thrown into a jail cell. A grey-haired Day tries to calm her and offers a cigarette. The woman leans over Day and throws up on her shoes. As the film constantly reminds us, the full life can also be the messy

---

5. Finnigan, "Dorothy Day Hits the Big Screen in 'Entertaining Angels.'" Pax Christi is a Catholic organization that rejects war, preparation for war, and every form of violence.

6. Cf. Alleva, "Diminishing Dorothy Day," and Blake, "Converts."

7. Forest, *All is Grace*, 14–15.

Entertaining Angels (1996) (PG-13)

life. Day begins to softly sing "Amazing Grace" and caresses the fevered face of the young woman. "Amazing Grace, how sweet the sound that saved a wretch like me."

We are thus given a key question in the movie. How can grace operate in a world awash with distorted values and deep despair? How can the lost find a path? The prison scene dissolves in a flashback to a suffragist march. As a young woman, Day was attracted to controversial causes that sought to further humane ideals. The march ends in the women being attacked by the police and angry bystanders. There are punches thrown. Day lands a couple of solid blows. We next see her walking jauntily down a street in New York with her new friend Maggie from the march, pausing to buy a newspaper that has her front-page story.

In these days, we witness Day whirling through life in the streets of New York, at a newspaper office and at a bar. It is all very exciting and heady. In New York, Day wavered between socialist and anarchist beliefs. While working as a reporter, she was not only a vocal proponent of women's rights but also free love and birth control. In the barroom world of the literati and radical politics, we meet leading figures like the playwright Eugene O'Neill, who dwell in a swirl of wit, booze, and radical causes. The literati in-crowd thrives on cynicism, sexual banter, and pontificating. Day becomes aware that there has to be more than what one of her bohemian lovers, Lionel Moise, expounds in a bar. Moise declares that he will not commit himself "to any person, institution, or school of thought." Day toasts Moise as a "man without purpose, life without meaning." When Day leaves the bar, she tells O'Neill, "I'm restless, Gene. I have something to give but I don't know what it is, or whom I'm supposed to give it to. I know I want to live fully . . ." Day wants "more, much more."

Her search for that "more" is complicated by her alternating desire for social justice and personal pleasure. She continues to advocate for the poor, the evicted, and the homeless. Yet she is caught in a net of pleasurable despair, and it will take many trials and tribulations to discover a new path on her pilgrimage. It is not found in the bed of Lionel Moise, who listens to beautiful Italian operas but also gets her pregnant. She wants a commitment; he takes her to an abortionist. Day is scared and suffers through the procedure only to discover afterwards that he has abandoned her.

Day retreats to the relative calm of Staten Island, where she rents a cottage. Here, she walks before the timeless rolling of the waves that act as a balm for her troubled soul. The island will soon offer her two paths, both of which are appealing. The first is a new love interest. While searching for clams, she runs into Forster Batterham, an anarchist and biologist who comes regularly to the island. He is kind and honest. They fish and ride bicycles. Forster is smitten, but he accepts that she may not be ready for another relationship. Forster does not make demands or offer commitment. When she resists his advances, Forster states that, "whatever we'll have, we'll have. . . . No pressure, no expectations. Just us, the way we want to be." Day comes to deeply love Batterham. "I loved him for all he knew and pitied him for all he didn't know. I loved him for the odds and ends I had to fish out of his sweater pockets and for the sand and shells he brought in with his fishing. I loved his lean cold body as he got into bed smelling of the sea and I loved his integrity and stubborn pride."[8] The movie captures their joy and intimacy.

There was another path for her life. While biking with Forster, she almost runs over a religious sister, also on a bike. Later, she stops at a church. She walks in and meets this same Sister Aloysius, who introduces her to Lou, a homeless man whom she has seen on the beach and had scared her. Dorothy is uneasy among the poor people working on the dinner. She goes home.

Dorothy returns and assists at dinners at the church. Sister Aloysius laughs when Dorothy tells her that religion is the "opiate of the masses." She is handed a clam knife and is told, "You're no Marxist." Sister Aloysius chides her, "your ego is too big." In one of the sweeter moments of the film, Dorothy responds, "You're one to talk!" They both laugh. On another trip to the church, Dorothy confides that she believes that Gandhi was right that the problem with Christianity is that there are no real Christians; there is too much hypocrisy, escapism, and cowardice in the struggle for justice. Sister Aloysius counters that the Church is full of all kinds of people who find meaning there, not just the rich and the hypocritical.

The love of Forster and the love of Church are headed for a collision. At a beach party, Forster rails against the Catholic Church as part of the same political and social system that oppresses the working class. The Church also "sucks all the joy out of life." As a materialist, Forster trusts what he can "see, touch, feel." While he vows that he has no claims on Dorothy, he is obviously perturbed by her budding faith.

Then, there is the moment of truth. She is pregnant. Forster will not stop her pregnancy, but he is not exactly committed either. At the same

---

8. Ellsberg, "Dorothy in Love."

Entertaining Angels (1996) (PG-13)

time, God is calling her to a different kind of commitment. While praying by herself in church she proclaims, "You really sneak up on a person." Then, there is the confrontation with Forster. Day wants to have her child, Tamar, baptized; she refuses to again reject her instincts for a man unwilling to commit, even if she loves him. Forster proclaims that he will not be a hypocrite and attend the baptism. Religion is simply "mumbo jumbo." Day clings to her baby, and he takes off in a rowboat over the waves. The couple is indeed on rough waters; their worlds cannot remain together. In a later scene with Forster, after they had parted for a while, she demands a commitment, but Forster "will not be caged."[9] She has Tamar baptized with Lou and Sister Aloysius for her witnesses.

The next scene is Day returning to New York City in 1933. It is no longer the roaring twenties. Dorothy witnesses a scene of a family being evicted from a home. As a reporter, she is given a tour of poor areas; she is told there is little food and no jobs. There is plenty of dysentery, cholera, and even a flu epidemic. City services for the growing numbers of poor are limited. Day laments that "the city doesn't seem to care." She meets a mother with a dead child; Dorothy holds the dead child in her arms. She tells her editor that she wants to do something regarding the misery and the poverty, but "where do you start?" She wonders where the Catholics are in addressing the pain and suffering all around her.

Dorothy writes articles on what she witnesses, but it is not enough; she pleads to God, "Please show me how." These prayers are based on a true story of when she was at the National Shrine at Catholic University in Washington, DC.[10] She had just witnessed a homeless march in the capital. She returns to New York to find the man who will be her guide, Peter Maurin. He had been a French peasant, a Christian Brother teacher, and a homesteader in Canada. He is a ray of both joy and activism. He speaks incessantly, proclaiming his vision of the good news. His first words to Day are "You know what is wrong with the world? The people who act don't think and the people who think don't act." He continues to offer his homespun homilies until late in the evening. He focuses on the obligation of service. Real community is built through each person using their gifts as

---

9. In her autobiography *The Long Loneliness*, Day indicates that the parting was final at this point. With the recovery of some of Days letters, we have since learned that she pined for Forster for several more years. She was alternately loving and scolding in her letters. They remained in touch. Forster came to see her often in her final years. See Ellsberg, "Dearest Forster."

10. Day, *The Long Loneliness*, 166.

part of God's creation. The rich have resources to share and the poor share their gift of the feeling of neediness and their experience of God. Getting them together is part of a path to a holistic community. While Peter is still saying the prayer of Saint Francis, "Make Me an Instrument of Your Peace," Day gently guides him out of the apartment.

Maurin is on her stairs the next morning. He is the personification of pleasant persistence. He becomes her spiritual guide and reminds her that God is present among the poor, the sick, and the destitute. He is constantly preaching his gospel of service and hope. We observe him spending nights with the poor, regaling them with humorous anecdotes and spiritual stories in the alleys of New York. Maurin washes the sore feet of a poor man and gives him his shoes. When her brother and sister-in-law complain about Peter's presence, Day reminds them that he hears the voices of the poor, and she needs him to find her direction. He leads her to initiate the Catholic Worker houses of hospitality and a newspaper, *The Catholic Worker*.

Peter Maurin is impressive, but it is not easy living with a saint of the poor. He smells; he talks incessantly; he invites people into the apartment where Dorothy is living with her brother and sister-in-law to receive food. When Peter initiates the idea of Catholic Worker houses of hospitality and a newspaper, they do not know where they will get money for their newspaper. Dorothy spends rent money to start the paper. When Dorothy laments that they are fools, Peter adds, "Of course, fools for Christ."

And what of the Church? The Cardinal Archbishop of New York confides to Day that he is receiving many negative letters about her pacifism and social positions. Why does she refuse to support Franco and the Church in Spain? She is perceived by many to be a communist. Day retorts that just because communists are for it does not mean the Church has to be against it. She also observes that if you feed the poor you are a saint, but if you ask why there are poor, you are accused of being a communist. As for pacifism, she takes Jesus' Sermon on the Mount literally. Love your enemies. Turn the other cheek. The cardinal notes that she embarrasses the Church and threatens people by making them uncomfortable with their lives. Day wryly responds, "I am sorry to hear that." The cardinal threatens to take the word "Catholic" off of *The Catholic Worker*. She threatens to move her operation to Brooklyn, where the Church leadership is more hospitable. The chagrined cardinal concedes defeat.[11]

---

11. In real life her confrontation was with a chancery official, not a cardinal. Wintz, "Father Kieser's New Film."

Entertaining Angels (1996) (PG-13)

There are other issues. The strain of such a life is tough on her daughter, Tamar, who yearns for a more normal life with toys and play dates. The poor steal her food. Her father, Battingham, visits the young Tamar and wants to come back into their lives. Tamar is confused and often senses that she is secondary to her mother's many causes.[12]

In the midst of Day's many trials, Peter Maurin has a stroke and gets dementia, and she has to be a caregiver to her mentor. There are other challenges, and Day cannot right all wrongs. Dorothy takes in a woman who is a drug addict. She cuts herself with a razor and kills herself. There are fights; there are threats of eviction. Day lives a difficult and, at times, lonely life. She is there for everybody, but who is there for her?

Her staff rebels against her controlling ways. They confront her about the lack of money for the Catholic Worker newspaper. They accuse her of being dictatorial and egotistical. They are tired of dealing with drunks, bedbugs, and fights. They want to focus solely on the newspaper. That night, she goes to a church. She feels abandoned. She demands of God, "Where are you? Why don't you answer me? I need you. These brothers and sisters of yours are the ones you want me to love. Let me tell you something. They smell. They have lice and tuberculosis. Am I to find you in them? Well, you're ugly. You drink; you wet your pants, and you vomit. How could anyone ever love you? I need you, but you're not here. You've deserted me too, haven't you? I'm not who you thought I was. I'm sorry." This is the long night of the soul. Like Jesus wondering why God has forsaken him, she feels that the world has abandoned her. She has not made a difference. She cannot do it anymore; she is empty. She walks out of a darkened church where the candles have just been extinguished.

Perhaps, she is meant to abandon her quest for the marginalized. She visits a friend who is an editor and a communist. There is a storm outside. She confesses that she has not changed a thing. She has made young idealists who work for her hard and cynical. She thinks of leaving her social justice ministry and living a more normal life. She wants to come down off the cross. When she proclaims that she has nothing left to give, the editor reminds her that, unlike the communists, she feeds three thousand people a day and lets people who had nothing have something. She has made the world "a little more bearable."

---

12. For more on the life of Tamar Day Hennessey, see Patterson, "An Extraordinary Difficult Childhood."

Day returns to the Catholic Worker house where her friend Maggie, desperate for a drink, has stolen Day's money. Her friend is crazed and admits to being a slut, a drunk, and a thief. Dorothy tells her that she loves her and sees a light in her. Maggie pleads, "You can't. You are the only person who ever cared about me." Dorothy hugs her and responds, "We all care about you."

Dorothy then tells her comrades at the Catholic Worker house that she is sorry. She has been arrogant and self-righteous. She let her ego make her try and do it all by herself. She confesses to living a very lonely life, and she has wanted to fill the emptiness. That filling begins with those who are hurt, angry, and have nothing left to give. They are her meeting place with God. If she tries, God will give her the grace and love to be present for them. She realizes her faults, and their limitations as a group. She will understand if they leave. God will not judge them on their success in changing the world, but he will judge them in how faithful they are. When she awakens, they are still there.

Dorothy Day's source of strength is grace. Amidst chaos and infinite need, she seeks an infinite source of renewal. She regularly prays the rosary and attends daily mass. At one point in the movie, Day's sister-in-law speculates about Peter Maurin that, "You never know when you may be 'entertaining angels.'" This is part of the movie's charm—we are all called to be connected with one another and to be open to the angelic, to transcendent possibilities. As Thomas Merton observed, "Every moment and every event of every man's life on earth plants something in his soul. For just as the wind carries thousands of winged seeds, so each moment brings with it germs of spiritual vitality that come to rest imperceptibly in the minds and wills of men. Most of these unnumbered seeds perish and are lost, because men are not prepared to receive them."[13] This movie helps to demonstrate what can happen if we do notice and act on some of our spiritual possibilities. Grace will come to us. We can "entertain angels" and respond to the better angels of our nature.

Questions

1) How does the movie address the obligation of service to others?

---

13. Merton, *New Seeds of Contemplation*, 14.

Entertaining Angels (1996) (PG-13)

2) What is the source of Dorothy's conversion? Does God "sneak up on her"? If so, how does this happen?

3) What do you make of Peter Maurin's statement that "those who think do not act and those who act do not think"? Why is this the case?

4) In the movie, how do the poor provide a meeting place with God and for "entertaining angels"?

5) Why is it hard to do God's will like Day? What are your sources of renewal and inspiration?

Resources

Day, Dorothy. *The Long Loneliness*. San Francisco: Harper Collins. 1952.

Finnigan, David. "Dorothy Day Hits the Big Screen in 'Entertaining Angels.'" *National Catholic Register* (October 9, 1997). http://www.ncregister.com/site/article/dorothy_day_hits_the_big_screen_in_entertaining_angels.

Forest, Jim. *All is Grace: A Biography of Dorothy Day*. Maryknoll, NY: Orbis, 2011.

Keiser, Ellwood E. *The Spiritual Journey of a Showbusiness Priest*, 323–45. New York: Paulist, 1996, .

PART V

Prophetic Warnings

chapter 11

Decalogue 1 (1990)(NR)

Director: Krzysztof Kieslowski

Screenplay: Krzysztof Piesiewicz and Krzysztof Kieslowski

Awards: Bodil Award—Best European Award; Chicago Film Critics Award—Best Foreign Film; Venice Film Festival—FIPRESCI Award

Values: humility, balancing faith and reason, family, community, love, respect for life

You shall not have other Gods besides me.
—EXOD 20:3

Why would a director, who is not religious and living in communist Poland, want to produce a movie exploring the relevance of the Ten Commandments? In the late 1980s in the shadows of a fading communist regime, the formidable Polish director Krzysztof Kieslowski (1941–1996) observed that people were disoriented and suffering from moral anxiety. He wanted to explore this malaise, and the Ten Commandments provided a helpful framework. As he observed, "For 6,000 years, these rules have been unquestionably right. And yet we break them every day. People feel that something is wrong in life. There is some kind of atmosphere that makes people now turn to other values. They want to contemplate the basic questions of life, and that is probably the real reason for wanting to tell these stories."[1]

In the *Decalogue* movies, the Ten Commandments became a point of departure for examining difficult moral issues in a single apartment complex. Each commandment was explored in a separate film. There are many different ages, occupations, and types of relationships in this small world. The films gaze into the aspirations, struggles, and choices of the occupants. Kieslowski is alternately sardonic and compassionate as he explores the best and worst of humanity.

Familiarity with the Polish director's background will help viewers appreciate the development of the *Decalogue* films. His life was a combination of suffering, chance, and choice, and these elements are also exhibited in his films. In his adolescence, he traveled frequently in the aftermath of the Second World War in Poland seeking medical care for his sick father in various cities. His father died when he was a young man. His family lived on the edge of severe poverty; he lived a somewhat rootless life. He was separated at times from his family and placed in sanatoria for young children because his mother could not afford to raise him. He dropped out of fireman school after only a few months when he was sixteen. Lacking a college degree, he could not initially pursue his interest in a school for theater directors. Because his uncle directed the school, he entered the College for Theater Technicians, which continued his interest in the visual arts. This was pure chance. If he had an uncle who was the head of another kind of school, he might well have gone there and pursued another passion. Fortunately, this college sparked an interest in film. He eventually was accepted on the third try by the famed Lodz Film School. Fate, chance, and personal determination were thus intertwined in the arc of his professional life as they are in the lives of his film characters.[2] Such fortuitous connections are also associated with the discovery of his screenwriter. Kieslowski met Krzytzof Piesiewicz, who was a trial lawyer, when researching political trials for his movie, *No End*, in 1984. A chance meeting initiated an inspired collaboration over more than a decade.

In exploring suffering, chance, and choice in his films, Kieslowski employs an intense style of filmmaking. The films' intensity commands your attention and requires focused thought as they unpack the complex questions, paradoxes, and contradictions within our mortal coil. Kieslowski's

---

1. Facets, "The Decalogue."
2. Maurer, *Krzytzof Kieslowski*, 17–18.

Decalogue 1 (1990)(NR)

films assumed an intelligent and thoughtful audience as he did not suffer fools well either individually or collectively. For example, he thought the citizens of the United States rather superficial. Immersed with a Polish sense of tragedy and human limitation, he was surprised in America by "the pursuit of empty talk combined with a very high degree of self-satisfaction."[3]

Operating with a very small budget, Kieslowski produced an amazing array of stories within the apartment complex. For me, none is more profound than *Decalogue 1*. In the film, we are offered two competing worldviews. In Krzytzof, a computer science professor with the same first name as the director, we meet the man of science and technology who relies on objective reason, careful calculation, and utility. These material realities provide firm and controlled boundaries of human experience. There is nothing beyond what we can see, touch, feel, and smell. The senses provide data for the human capacity for reason to analyze and evaluate in order to increase pleasure and reduce pain. Employing this utilitarian calculus, each person must rely on their abilities within these constraints to advance themselves and the human condition. For Irena, Krzytzof's Catholic sister, there is no denial of reason, but there is more to life than utility and pleasure; there is the mystery of life, love, and time. In exploring these mysteries, the answers are not discerned through experiment and calculation. Life and death or the source and meaning of love raise very difficult questions that require imaginative reflection, not an empirical assessment or utilitarian calculus.

In the film, Krzysztof's son, Pawel, is an innocent foil for these two worldviews. Pawel wants to know how things work in the material world, but he is curious about Irena's views as well. The differences between Krzysztof and Irena become apparent in their dialogues with Pawel.

> **Pawel:** Why do people die?
>
> **Krzytzof:** It depends. Heart failure, cancer, accidents, old age . . .
>
> **Pawel:** I mean, what *is* death?
>
> **Krzytzof:** The heart stops pumping blood . . . it doesn't reach the brain, movement ceases, everything stops. It's the end.
>
> **Pawel:** So what's left?
>
> **Krzytzof:** What a person has achieved, the memory of that person. The memory's important. The memory that a person moved

3. Holden, "The Art of Film, via Brat and Brooder."

in a certain way, or that they were kind . . . you remember their face, their smile, that a tooth was missing. It's too early. What do you expect of me so early in the morning? . . .

Pawel: [**Reading a newspaper obituary**] "For the peace of her soul." You didn't mention a soul.

Krzytzof: It's a form of words of farewell; there is no soul.

Pawel: Auntie says there is.

Krzytzof: Some find it easier to live thinking that.

Pawel: And you?

Krzytzof [**shrugs**]**:** Me? Frankly, I don't know.

The final comment, "I don't know," indicates a kind of agnosticism that allows for the possibility for Krzytzof at the end of the movie, after the death of Pawel, to reconsider his position about transcendent possibilities. He is never fiercely locked into his materialist philosophy.

By contrast to the materialism of Krzytzof, his sister, Irena, is a devout Catholic. Her faith raises question for Pawel about his father's ideas. The contrast of worldviews is obvious when Irena tells Pawel that life is not merely matter and utility; it is a "gift." If life is a gift, this implies a creator, a giver of the gift. Irena then shows Pawel pictures of Saint John Paul II that initiates a discussion.

Pawel: Is he kind?

Irena: Yes.

Pawel: Clever?

Irena: Yes.

Pawel: Do you think he understands the meaning of life?

Irena: I think so.

Pawel: Dad told me we are living to make life easier . . . for those who come after us. But it doesn't always work out.

Irena: Not always. Your father is right. It's just . . . if you can do something for others, to help, to be there . . . even if it's only a little thing, you know you are needed . . . and life becomes brighter somehow. There are big and small things. Today, you liked the dumplings so that made me happy. One is alive and it's a present. A gift.

Decalogue 1 (1990)(NR)

Then, the issue between Irena and Pawel becomes why the brother believes in science and the sister in God and the Church. Here, we discover what is at the heart of the movie.

> **Irena:** Your father and I, we were brought up in a Catholic family. Your father noticed, even earlier than you . . . that many things could be measured. Later, he concluded that measurement could be applied to everything. . . . Your dad's way of life may seem more reasonable, but it doesn't rule out God. Even for your dad. Understand?
>
> **Pawel:** Not really.
>
> **Irena:** God is . . . very simple, if you have faith.
>
> **Pawel:** Do you believe in God?
>
> **Irena:** Yes.
>
> **Pawel:** So, who is he?
>
> [Irena hugs Pawel.]
>
> **Irena:** What do you feel now?
>
> **Pawel:** I love you.
>
> **Irena:** Exactly, that's where he is.[4]

There are a number of other moments highlighting the conflict of religion and a materialist philosophy. Religion is often near Krzytzof but he does not fully engage the issue until he is desperate at the end of the movie. Krzytzof accepts without resistance that Irena will take Pawel to religion classes and is indifferent when a junior colleague confides that he is speaking at a church about religion and science. Each time, Krzytzof permits the engagement just as long as he is not personally challenged or committed in the religious activity.

Krzytzof is involuntarily drawn into considering the possibility of a non-materialist reality by the shock of the death of Pawel. He learns that to be human is to be finite and this means our aspirations and capabilities

---

4. Cf. 1 John 4:7–8: "Beloved, let us love one another, because love is of God; everyone who loves is begotten by God and knows God. Whoever is without love does not know God, for God is love." See also 1 John 4:16: "We have come to know and to believe in the love God has for us. God is love, and whoever remains in love remains in God and God in him."

have limits whether we accept them or not. To say that Pawel's heart has stopped does not fully explain his experience of grief and loss.

The path to Pawel's death begins innocently. The father and son prepare calculations on the computer based on the ground temperature for the past several days to determine the density of the ice in the apartment complex pond. Krzytzof then admits what his son has suspected for a while; Pawel is getting a pair of ice skates. Confident of the calculations, Krzytzof gives Pawel permission to skate the next day. All appears well. Nonetheless, ominous signs indicate that all is not as it seems. A tea kettle bellows. A container of milk, a symbol of nurture and life, has soured. A bowl of ink spills on Krzytzof's work and stains it while Pawel is on the pond. The liquids seem almost malevolent.

When Krzytzof is working at home, he hears sirens. He has trouble locating Pawel. When he asks questions of neighbors and friends, all he receives are furtive looks, evasive answers, and doors swiftly closing. Why are they reluctant? Who wants to tell a father that his son is dead? What if they are wrong? Krzytzof gets progressively more frightened. He is irresistibly drawn to the pond. There is a crowd standing and staring at the firemen working on the lake. People drop to their knees and start praying. A small body, limp and lifeless, is lifted out of the water.

Krzytzof thus learns of his son's death. It is a tragedy that is the great fear of all parents. The father is left inconsolable, and the film does not provide a simple resolution for him or the viewers. In the film, we do not know why the calculations went wrong. In the original screenplay, there is a line about the dumping of warm water into the pond by a power station.[5] Either way, there is a mistake, a human failure. We cannot control all variables; this is the problem of relying solely on human autonomy, reason, and choice.

For Kieslowski, this is the fruit of an Old Testament God whose law has been broken. Krzytzof has turned his computer and belief in utility, calculation, and reason into idols, and idolatry begets punishment. Kieslowski explains his views of God in the Old Testament:

> The God of the Old Testament is a demanding, cruel God; a God who doesn't forgive, who ruthlessly demands obedience to the principles which He has laid down. . . . The God of the Old Testament leaves us a lot of freedom and responsibility, observes how we use it and then rewards or punishes, and there's no appeal

---

5. Kieslowski and Piesiewicz, *Decalogue*, 24.

Decalogue 1 (1990)(NR)

or forgiveness. It's something which is lasting, absolute, evident and is not relative. And that's what a point of reference must be, especially for people like me, who are weak, who are looking for something, who don't know.[6]

In the shocking conclusion to his film, we witness Kieslowski's interaction of fate, chance, and choice. Kieslowski declared that the exact reasons for this sacrifice, as in the story of Job, are not clearly revealed to the person suffering.[7]

In one of the final scenes, we are offered an enigmatic denouement. Krzytzof's materialism offers little consolation, and he yearns for an explanation, for relief from his suffering. He cannot accept his son's death as the elimination of oxygen from his body that causes the shutting down of bodily functions. This materialist explanation is simply not enough. Soon, it is nighttime and Krzytzof is alone in a half-completed church. There are a few candles on a makeshift altar. Behind the altar, there is the famous Polish icon, the Black Madonna of Częstochowa. He raises his fist and strikes at the temporary altar. The altar collapses and molten wax from a falling candle streams across the face of Mary in the icon and appear as tears. In pain, Krzytzof clutches a circle of frozen holy water and presses it against his forehead. This act has a resonance to his baptism. It is also an attempt to reconcile the holy in the water with the reasoning of the brain. Faith and reason seek a reconciliation, but to what end? Kieslowski wisely ends the movie at this point. His protagonist has gotten to the edge of religious possibility and words or visual imagery cannot capture what is beyond words—grace, God, etc. If we enter this realm, words or images will fail us. Remember what Bresson does when he gets to this point. He shows a cross and we hear the words "All is grace," but that is it. We cannot experience the grace in its fullness as it comes to the priest of Ambricourt or to Krzysztof.

The ending is frustrating in some ways, but a director has to know his limits. And to be honest, I believe Kieslowski, the agnostic, is not sure what is about to happen: is it revelation or the abyss? So we are left wondering, full of questions. Is there a God? If there is a God, why take the life of this innocent boy? For that matter, is there any meaning in death or life? What is the message that Krzysztof receives in the church, if any?

There are other peculiarities in the film that draw us into a deeper mystery. For example, there is a silent figure—the witness—who appears

---

6. Kieslowski, *Kieslowski on Kieslowski*, 149.
7. Kickasoola, *The Films of Krsysztof Kieslowski*, 168.

several times in the *Decalogue* films. This figure is a reminder of the fact that life is a gift that is both beautiful and fragile and often wasted. In *Decalogue 1*, he is across the pond by a fire. The warm fire and colors surrounding him contrasts with the bleak winter landscape. When Krzysztof goes to check the pond at night, the witness stares at him. Perhaps he represents a warning about human folly—or he may represent the director, who is posing difficult questions to the audience. Is he our conscience? Kieslowski stated that this figure "has no influence on the action, but he leads the characters to think about what they are doing. . . . His intense stare engenders self-examination."[8] At the time of the drowning, Krzysztof notices that the man has disappeared, and the fire is out.

There is another curious aspect of the film. Krzysztof's computer is a source of control and information. The computer can turn on lights and open doors and faucets. The computer can indicate where the missing mother is at a given time, but when asked it has no idea what she is dreaming. The interior life is beyond its database. Still, the computer almost seems to be a sentient entity. It turns itself on without a prompt and emits an eerie green light that is reflected on Pawel's face. The computer asks without any request, "Are you ready?" Pawel's computer asks the same question after his death. But, ready for what? To give a command? To accept death? Is the computer an oracle or demonic? Whatever the case, it is not a source of ultimate answers. In this sense, it is a void about the most important questions.

The limitations of the computer are made more obvious in the original screenplay, where there is a scene that did not make into the film, of a confrontation between Krzysztof and the computer. He asks for a sign. The computer cannot give a sign; it cannot detect the desperation of Krzysztof's request to offer him comfort. Rather, the computer defines the term "sign." Krzysztof tries asking the computer for "illumination" instead. This leads to other terms like "candle" and then to "church." Finally, he asks for a definition of "sense" and "hope." The computer states, "Terminology unrecognized." The computer cannot transcend its materialist database. It cannot make sense of the death or provide the father any hope.

This deleted scene provides quite a contrast with the icon of the Black Madonna of Częstochowa in the church in one of the final scenes. The Black Madonna has the title the Queen and Protector of Poland. The icon of the Madonna has two scars on the right cheek, allegedly from sword

---

8. Insdorf, *Double Lives, Second Chances*, 73.

Decalogue 1 (1990)(NR)

strikes by the Hussite heretics in the fifteenth century. So, the Madonna is both a protector of the Polish people but is scarred. Hence, an appeal in her presence has deep spiritual and historical resonance. The icon of the Black Madonna is a *hodegetria*, or a representation of the Madonna that "points the way." Mary is pointing to Jesus and Jesus is holding an open book of the Gospels. Jesus has one of his hands pointing to the viewer. Perhaps the Gospels hold the answer to Krzysztof's questions. It is not certain that Krzysztof will receive this message, but there are signs that he is coming closer to a source of hope and explanation. Perhaps he is ready to face the possibility of God or at least the prospect of a world that includes immaterial realities.

Is this analysis too optimistic, especially given Krzysztof's destruction of the altar in a rage? Or is he like Jacob wrestling with God? Anger here is directed at an antagonist; he is no longer passive and indifferent about religion. Kieslowski, referencing this moment, admitted that "In an act of rebellion we come to recognize that someone who did not seem to us to exist, in fact does exist. Rebellion is a manifestation of the faith that one denies.... [C]learly, he is rebelling against God."[9] Paradoxically, while Krzytzof seems to be on the verge of finding God, Irena wanders the streets crying after Pawel's death. Is she pushed into a moment of terrible doubt? Will she recover?

Decalogue 1 raises the complicated issue of Kieslowski's religious beliefs. He was not a confessing Christian—that much is clear. In one interview, he indicated that he had not been to a church in forty years. Despite his qualms about institutional religion, some of his comments suggested that he believed, or at least hoped, that there was something beyond our material reality. "The world is not only bright lights, this hectic pace, the Coca-Cola with a straw, the new car.... Another truth exists... a hereafter? Yes, surely. Good or bad, I don't know, but something else." At other times, he appears to straddle comfortably on the razor's edge of paradox. "I don't believe in God but I have a good relationship with him."[10]

Whatever the truth is about his spiritual beliefs, Kieslowski is an amazing interlocutor of religion, and certainly probes, with nuance and depth, profound issues and questions. He deals subtly with faith, grace, evil, and a host of other religious themes. He is certainly religious in the sense offered by the theologian Paul Tillich of examining "ultimate concerns."[11] Seeking

---

9. Baugh, "The Christian Moral Vision of a Believing Atheist," 158.
10. Ibid., 157; Tennant, "Heaven for a Terrorist."
11. Tillich, *Theology of Culture*, 8.

to make sense of human life, he has reflected deeply on religion and mined Catholicism for some insights into such ultimate concerns.

The tragedy in *Decalogue 1* places us on the boundary between despair and hope. The movie seeks meaning in what seems so meaningless, the death of an innocent child. Where is God in this time of despair? Are we ready to abandon hope or seek solace in a faith? The film shows at the beginning and at the end a video of Pawel slowly running and smiling in a video shot by a television news crew. He is frozen on film; he has become a memory. Joe Kickasoola, a professor of communications at Baylor University, observes that such an image on film is "rich, but it falls short of a real presence."[12] The video, like the computer, is not as real as a live human or human memory. And it certainly is not a soul. The death of Pawel and the final scene on the video reminds us that life can end swiftly, but as Irena tells Pawel, life is a gift—it is fragile and precious.

Questions

1) What do we learn from the film about life? Why is it a gift?
2) Does the character, Krzytzof, receive an answer about his son's death?
3) What is the role of the witness? What is the role of the computer?
4) What do we think about the issue of theodicy, God's justice in the world as depicted in this film?
5) What are the idols that replace God in this film? What are the idols of our world?

Resources

Baugh, Lloyd. "The Christian Moral Vision of a Believing Atheist: Krzysztof Kieslowski's *Decalogue* Films" In *Through a Catholic Lens: Religious Perspectives of 19 Film Directors from Around the World*, edited by Peter Malone, 157–72. Lanham, MD: Rowan and Littlefield, 2007.

Insdorf, Annette. *Double Lives, Second Chances: The Cinema of Krzysztof Kieslowski*. New York: Hyperion, 1999.

Kieslowski, Krzytzof, and Krzytzof Piesiewicz. *Decalogue: The Ten Commandments*. Translated by Phil Cavendish and Susannah Bluh. London: Faber and Faber, 1991.

Kieslowski, Krzytzof. *Kieslowski on Kieslowski*. New York: Faber and Faber, 1995.

---

12. Kickasoola, *The Films of Krzytzof Kieslowski*, 168.

chapter 12

GATTACA (1997)(PG-13)

Director: Andrew Niccol

Screenplay: Andrew Niccol

Award: Academy Award—Best Art Direction; Golden Globe Award—Best Original Score; London Critics Circle Film Festival—ALFS Award

Values: fortitude, faith, hope, reverence for life, compassion, sacrifice, pilgrimage

I praise you, because I am wonderfully made; wonderful are your works!
My very self you know.
—PS 139:14

We used to think our fate was in our stars. Now we know, in large measure, our fate is in our genes.
—JAMES WATSON, NOBEL PRIZE-WINNING GENETICIST

If *Decalogue 1* in the previous chapter examined how current computing powers combined with a worldview dominated by materialism are problematic, the film, *GATTACA*, invites us into an even more troubling future. This prophetic movie takes as its basis current biotechnologies related to genetics, assumes reasonable advances in the coming decades, and then prophetically explores the resulting ethical dilemmas. In calling the film prophetic, I mean that it presents a perspective that invites viewers to explore and critique the assumptions of this future society in order to make better choices. In *GATTACA,* the central concerns pertain to human development in a world where humanity arguably becomes dehumanized by excessive use of and reliance on technology. We enter a world of voluntary eugenics and genetic determinism that accelerates human evolution by improving our genome.[1] In *GATTACA,* genes have become destiny.

GATTACA is set in a time in the near future where genetics has advanced to the point that a parent can select a child's physical and mental qualities. These options are premised on genetic determinism—the presumption that our genes definitively and exclusively determine our personality, behavior, and physical appearance. The movie's genetic determinism might seem farfetched, because there are other important factors such as environmental and social influences. Nonetheless, genetic determinism has impressive advocates. Dean Hamer, who was until 2011 the Chief of Gene Structure and Regulation at the National Cancer Institute's Laboratory of Biochemistry, asserts that everyone's "core personality is hardwired into our bodies since birth, a genetic legacy from their parents as surely as the color of their eyes."[2] If we accept this assertion, it becomes reasonable to posit that there is a chain of genetic determinants running from the gene to the individual to the broader society.[3] This is the fundamental assumption of *GATTACA*.

The exploration of genetics as an aspect of social policy is not a new idea, but the sources and methods have changed. In the early twentieth century, genetic manipulation by involuntary sterilization to eliminate the "unfit" was led by elite scientists, medical institutes, and governmental officials who engaged in public relations efforts and legislative initiatives to back their eugenic plans. The American experience of eugenics in the twentieth century was thus centered on statutory provisions for sterilization that were implemented by public medical institutions. Concerns for individual rights and freedoms were easier to ignore in such an age thanks to broad public support and loose judicial oversight. There was sporadic opposition

---

1. A genome is the complete set of genetic material present in an organism.
2. Hamer, *Living with Our Genes,* 6.
3. Lewontin et al., *Not in Our Genes,* 6.

GATTACA (1997)(PG-13)

from the Catholic Church. There were also dystopian novels like Aldous Huxley's *Brave New World* in 1931.

When *GATTACA* was released in 1997, the technologies it depicts and their ethical problems were somewhat distant from the realm of possibility. The technologies and challenges seem a lot closer today. We can regularly read headlines about advanced technologies like "Altered Gene points to longer life span," "The Plug and Play Brain," or "Scientists' experiment 'melds' minds."[4] Despite the profound benefits of many future medical advances that will help to restore health, the biotechnological revolution will raise unprecedented ethical issues in part because they may alter what it means to be human. For example, we may be able to read thoughts with brain imaging and erase memories by blocking them with a chemical that inhibits the proteins essential to retrieving certain memories. Most relevant to *GATTACA*, there is the possibility of gene editing with precision in systems like CRISPR–Cas9. Eventually, these technologies will be able to change our germ (egg and sperm) line or long-term genome. We will be able to select for a wide variety of physical and mental traits by genetic technologies.

At this moment when we need careful reflection on genetic advances and the resulting ethical quandaries, cautionary novels and movies can stimulate the moral imagination to thoughtfully consider the future of our species and planet. Religions need this moral stimulation as well. After all, the assumption in the Abrahamic faiths is that God created the world and it was good. We are stewards of creation, not owners. How do we wisely draw the lines between acceptable modifications to achieve better health and radical efforts to perfect our natures? The problem with seeking a eugenic regime of perfect births and natures is twofold as demonstrated in *GATTACA*. First, what is the perfection of human beings that is sought? The parents in the movie, the Freemans, initially agreed to allow for some imperfections, but they are told by the genetic expert to give him all the perfection that can be genetically programmed into him. Deferring to the expert, they give in. This goal of seeking human perfection makes two highly questionable assumptions. One assumption is that our current natures are imperfect. A second assumption is that we can agree on a definition of the perfect replacement for our current biology. Such a quest, as

---

4. Marcus and Koch, "The Plug and Play Brain," C1; Winslow, "Altered Gene Points to Longer Life Span," A3; Doughton, "Scientists' experiment 'melds' of a Believing Atheist 2 minds," A10.

we see in *GATTACA*, is also likely to have unintended consequences such as class differences and the false and self-fulfilling expectations of failure based on a person's genetics.

Genetic manipulation in *GATTACA* is a societal choice determined by available resources and preferences. It is a market-based form of eugenics that seems a much more likely scenario in the United States than a government-imposed eugenics. Indeed, viewers may notice similarities between the world of *GATTACA* and elective medical procedures in present-day America. A viable market niche for genetic enhancement already exists through which people respond to the urge to perfect themselves and their children. This is why we have accent reduction clinics, an explosion of plastic surgeries, steroids, and selective embryo reduction.[5] The business of self-enhancement is popular and profitable for corporations. Given our current cultural predilection for self-improvement, it is not too much of a leap to say that genetic technologies directed towards physical enhancement offer the prospect of a profitable return on investment.[6]

GATTACA explores a family living in this paradigm. The ironically named Freemans are a couple who decided to have one "natural" or "faith birth" child—a child conceived without genetic engineering—and one "valid" or a genetically improved child. Their first child, Vincent, is a "natural" or "invalid," while his younger brother, Anton, is genetically engineered and therefore a "valid." When Vincent is born, the genetic testing indicates a substantial possibility of manic depression and attention deficit disorder, and a 99 percent chance of heart failure and death by the time he is thirty. With these discouraging results, Vincent's father refuses to give him the name originally planned for the baby, Anthony, at birth.

In deciding the traits of Jerome's younger brother Anton, the Freemans have a discussion with a genetic consultant who appeals to every parent's desire to offer their child the best chance in life:

> **Geneticist:** You have specified hazel eyes, dark hair, and fair skin. I have taken the liberty of eradicating any potentially prejudicial conditions: premature baldness, myopia, alcoholism, and addictive susceptibility, propensity for violence, obesity, etc.

---

5. For an excellent study of our insatiable desire to modify ourselves beyond a return to a normal state of health, see Elliot, *Better Than Well*.

6. Revenues for biotechnology companies has grown in just a few decades to more than ninety billion dollars worldwide. Innovation capital alone increased by 36 percent from 2012 to 2013. Ernst and Young, "Beyond Borders."

GATTACA (1997)(PG-13)

Marie Freeman: We didn't want ... I mean diseases yes, but ...

Antonio Freeman: Right, we were just wondering if it would be good to leave a few things to chance.

Geneticist: You want to give your child the best possible start. Believe me, we have enough imperfection built in already. Your child doesn't need any additional burdens. And, keep in mind this child is still you, simply the best of you.

Over the years, the differences in the natural and modified brother become all too clear. The differences are both real and in part a matter of expectation. The brothers become distant as they do not exactly share the same genetic heritage. The father is proud that his younger son, Anton, is tall, taller than his older brother Vincent. Anton does not want to share Vincent's blood when it is offered to him as part of a blood brothers' pact at the beach. As a child, Anton can also swim further out into the ocean. When Vincent is young, the doors are already closing to him. A school refuses to enroll Vincent because his insurance costs are too high. Literally and figuratively, the gate slams in his face. He is excluded and walled out from many opportunities throughout his life. Later, as a janitor, he peers through the glass separating him from the workers inside the GATTACA Aerospace Corporation, a private space agency. We soon learn that determination and the human spirit cannot be measured or instilled by genetic tests or engineering. Vincent has dreams of becoming an astronaut, but his parents counsel realism. The father dismisses Vincent's dreams with, "The only way you will see the inside of a spaceship is if you are cleaning it."

Vincent moves away and disconnects from his family to pursue these dreams on his own. Genetic discrimination, or "genoism," is illegal, but the law is easily circumvented. Genetic samples of skin, saliva, blood, or urine are required from prospective employees. Vincent is a janitor at GATTACA. On the basis of his genome, he is labeled an "invalid" or a "de-generate." Genetic tests determine your fate. Vincent realizes that his world has "discrimination down to a science." He is painfully close to his objective at GATTACA and yet so far away from it. Vincent continues to physically train and to study the relevant subjects for space travel. The problem is that his DNA will always betray him.

Vincent discovers that there is a difficult and illegal path into space. The market decides who can be genetically modified, but a black market offers "naturals" a chance to play a "false hand," and use somebody else's DNA to circumvent the GATTACA testing. He finds on the black market a donor, Jerome Eugene Morrow. Jerome Eugene has finely tuned genetics, as his middle name suggests. Eu-gene means "good genes." Yet in spite of his good genes, he is not happy. Jerome obtained a silver medal at the Olympics, but this is not good enough for him. Convinced that he was not designed for second place, Jerome tried to commit suicide by stepping in front of a car. When Vincent meets him he is paralyzed from the waist down. Vincent finds a black marketer who can secure bodily materials from Jerome for a steep fee, including his hair, skin, and blood. Vincent has to change his hairstyle, wear contacts, and go through an excruciating surgery and recovery to add several inches to his height to match Jerome's profile.

Having secured Morrow's blood, skin, and hair samples, Vincent is able to trick the system. Vincent is admitted to work at GATTACA solely on the basis of the superior DNA in the urine and blood that he has borrowed from Jerome. Vincent becomes a star at GATTACA and is selected for a one-year mission to the moon, Titan, that orbits Saturn. Vincent's scheme is always perilously close to being exposed. He must constantly scrub his skin and shave to avoid leaving any sample of his real DNA at work. He has heart palpitations during his exercises at the agency that are almost discovered. This hiding of genetic identity is complicated by a murder at GATTACA that brings in the police including Jerome's brother, Anton, who is now a detective. As the police sweep GATTACA for samples of bodily materials, the detectives secure an eyelash of the real Vincent. The police now suspect an invalid has penetrated GATTACA.

Vincent's brother, Anton, and his girlfriend, Irene, pose challenges because they gradually realize that Vincent has assumed Jerome's identity. Vincent leaves one of Jerome's hairs on his desk. Irene takes one of the hairs that is really Jerome's and has it analyzed. The test confirms Jerome's genetic perfection, although in reality both Jerome and Irene share a common problem, a weak heart. Irene judges herself as unworthy of Jerome and is paralyzed by her sense that genetics is destiny. Jerome eventually confronts her assumption that she is severely limited by her genetics. "You are the authority on what is not possible, aren't you, Irene? They have got you looking so hard for any flaw that after a while that is all that you see. For whatever it is worth, I am here to tell you that it is possible. It is possible."

Anton becomes increasingly aware that "Jerome Morrow" at GATTACA is actually Vincent posing as Jerome. Vincent is a DNA fraud, a "borrowed ladder." Anton eventually confronts Vincent and calls his brother a criminal but offers to rescue him. Vincent reminds his brother that he,

GATTACA (1997)(PG-13)

Vincent, once saved Anton in the ocean when they were swimming to see how far out each could go. For Vincent, this realization of his capabilities in saving his brother was the "moment that made everything else possible." The brothers decide to reenact the swim in the ocean. In the swells of the ocean, with a haunting music in the background, they keep going further and further. Vincent refuses to quit, and Anton reluctantly turns back. The invalid has won again. As Anton begins to drown, Vincent saves him again. Later, Vincent reveals his secret in the race; he saved nothing for the swim back.

In the end, Vincent makes it into space. His brother stays quiet, and Irene supports his quest. On his way to the spaceship, Vincent is given a surprise urine test. Vincent has none of Jerome's urine available to him. Vincent appears doomed. Surprisingly, the doctor doing the test validates his urine sample. The doctor has a son who has not measured up to his genetic profile, but he admires what Vincent has done and remains hopeful for his son, confiding to Vincent, "Who knows what he could do?"

Vincent has made it at last. He has defied every objection, prediction, and calculation. He has soared into space where he can discard genetic expectations. He has found love and purpose. The head of GATTACA states at one point about his astronauts that "no one exceeds his potential." The director determines potential by a genetic calculus. Vincent exceeded the limits of genetic expectations because of his persistence and courage. These elements of the human person are not testable and are not reflected in a DNA sequence.

GATTACA raises many complex ethical questions. How far should we go with our attempts to control nature, especially human nature? At the beginning of the movie, we see a quote from Ecclesiastes 7:13: "Consider God's handiwork: who can straighten what He hath made crooked?" This is followed by a quote from the bioethicist Willard Gaylin: "I not only think we will tamper with mother-nature, I think mother wants us to." The truth is that we have tampered with nature from our first days as a species. Our earliest tool building to improve our quality of life was a form of tampering with nature. A host of subsequent technologies have made a dramatic impact on the planet. With all due respect to Willard Gaylin, tampering is not inherently good. For example, we have been responsible for the destruction of many animal and plant species. We appear to be responsible for global warming. We can eliminate all life with a nuclear war.

So, the question with genetic engineering is whether or not we should tamper and, if so, how far we should tamper with our natures. When genetic engineering seeks to return a human being to a state of normal health, there is no problem. But when does genetic enhancement begin to tamper with our very essence or nature as a species? Perhaps, seeking genetically engineered offspring that are perfect is a problematic tampering. Children would no longer be a gift, but an act of production since we would be able select for a wide range of physical and mental capabilities. Moreover, are we comfortable that economics may determine our choices? Many people may not be able to afford genetic engineering. Potentially, a class hierarchy will develop based on genetically manufactured qualities. We may divide society into valids and invalids.

Paradoxically, the Freeman family is not freed by their genetic choices. Their choices result in one of the most primordial of struggles of a brother against a brother. The Bible is replete with these struggles—Cain and Abel, Jacob and Esau. The normal filial bonds of Vincent and Anton are strained because of their different forms of birth. They become competitors who are desperate to prove their superiority as demonstrated in their ocean competitions. Then, there is that biblical motif of the lost child. The father and mother fail to support Vincent. Vincent casts away his family; his parents went to their grave believing that he had died.

Anton and Vincent are not the only ones who must struggle with their heritage. Irene analyzes everything through the lens of her genetics. Her flawed heart haunts her until Vincent liberates her by demonstrating that a human life is not solely determined by genetics. Towards the end of the movie, when offered a sample of his hair by Vincent so she can verify he is an invalid, Irene follows his lead and drops the hair so it cannot be tested. She is no longer bound by genetic judgments. Sadly, the actual Jerome Morrow is dominated and then destroyed by a sense of meaninglessness because his genes failed him at the Olympics. We are reminded of this perspective when the movie displays him in his wheelchair beneath a ladder that looks like a DNA helix. He is crushed by his hopes and failures, which all hinge on his genetics. Jerome helps Vincent but then Jerome ends his life in a blazing furnace. He cannot accept his disability just like he could not accept his failure at the Olympics. He feels as if he is worthless refuse and burns himself to ashes.

GATTACA presents a society distorted by the imperatives of a genetic determinism. Vincent is initially captured by this fundamental assumption.

GATTACA (1997)(PG-13)

He must learn to reject the idea that "from an early age, I came to think of myself as others thought of me—a chronic invalid."[7] The genetic imperative makes such a world claustrophobic and paranoid. In the initial award-winning sequence, we witness the actors' names appearing on screen with the letters of the four DNA bases, guanosine, adenosine, thymine, and cytosine, G-A-T-C, emphasized in their names and also the basis for the movie's name, *GATTACA*. There are close-ups of fingernail clippings crashing down, hair follicles thumping against a surface, and a rain of grating skin. Blood and urine from Vincent are constantly being tested. Vincent is a human pincushion, from his foot as a baby to his urine test before departing for space. We are never far from Vincent scrubbing himself clean to prevent any bit of his body falling off and revealing his secret. Vincent worries about the hairs he has left on Irene's bed after spending the night at her place. Vincent then scrubs himself on a freezing cold beach with stones to remove any skin cells that might reveal his identity.

Vincent's genetics must be manipulated by disguising his reality. His genetic deceit is part of a broader set of genetic assumptions and judgments that are revealed throughout the movie. Women get samples of human hair or saliva to test prospective mates. Dating, conception, education, and employment are tied to genetic markers. The result is a rigid caste system based on genetics. Everyone must comply with the genetic determinism. The atmospherics in the movie confirm this reality. At GATTACA, there are rows of employees in dark suits and outfits that are reminiscent of 1940s fashions as people move in measured distances through turnstiles that test their blood. They work in rows of monochrome cubicles looking at uniform-sized screens. The buildings are largely linear and concrete with occasional uniform curves. The common colors in fashion and architecture are blacks, greys, and blues. The environment is sterile and pristine like living in a "cold, relentless machine."[8] There are a few exceptions. When the Freemans make love in their car to conceive their "God child," Vincent, we are suddenly surrounded by natural colors with a variety of vibrant greens. The same is true at Vincent's birth, with his mother clutching a rosary. Natural life and natural births are denoted by warm colors.

---

7. Expectations can foster self-fulfilling results. As an example in education see Wildhagen, "How Teachers and Schools Contribute to Racial Differences in the Realization of Academic Potential," 1–27.

8. Kaufmann, "Intriguers," 26.

GATTACA garnered praise from notable members of the scientific community at the time of the film's release. Sony Pictures screened the movie with the Society for Mammalian Biologists. The society members present approved of the movie, even the original ending that showed pictures of famous people such as Albert Einstein, Abraham Lincoln, and others who lived with hereditary medical conditions and made remarkable contributions to their times and places that might have been eliminated in the GATTACA era because of inherited afflictions. The movie was to close with the words, "Of course, the other birth that would surely have never taken place is your own." This ending was pulled because test audiences found it heavy-handed.

Subsequent reviews of the film by scientific journalists were often hostile. The editor of *Scientific American*, Phillip Yam, denounced it as a tale of "science bashing" related with "punchless storytelling and flat characterizations."[9] Kevin Davies in *Nature* declared the movie a "pedestrian affair" that has a "moral in there somewhere." Davies cites the geneticist James Watson as validation for the notion that we should give a child "superior character" if we can.[10] But, what is "superior character"? It is not self-evident and is a point about which reasonable people can disagree.

Genetic determinism at GATTACA has become a kind of unchallengeable assumption. The holy scripture of this world is the human genome that explains the natural and moral order. More specifically, our DNA can explain our history, social relationships, behavior, and morality.[11] Our genes are our fate. Instead of a soul, we are made eternal by passing on our genetic material in what the scientist Richard Dawkins refers to as the imperative of our genetic heritage. If we pass on our genes to the next generation, we in a sense survive indefinitely. This is the goal of our "selfish genes."[12] The ultimate trajectory and objective of this new faith is the refining of our genome to create the strongest, healthiest, most intelligent, and most emotionally balanced possible human beings through genetic refinements. Guided by this new prime directive, the society in *GATTACA* relies on and promotes the values of efficiency, utility, conformity, and hierarchy.

9. Yam, "Clean Genes."
10. Davies, "Discrimination Down to a Science," 33.
11. Green and Donovan, "Genetics as Religion," 123.
12. Dawkins has subsequently regretted he didn't title his book *The Selfish Gene*, the "Immortal Gene." The term selfish implies some kind of human intent whereas the imperative to survival is impersonal. Dawkins, "It's All in the Genes."

GATTACA (1997)(PG-13)

The results are dehumanizing. The movie suggests that human nature and choices are complex and cannot be easily regulated or determined because we are the result of a complex blend of nature and nurture. For example, Vincent's challenges help to develop his strength and perseverance.

The Catholic Church assumes a very different teleology and moral anthropology with that assumed in *GATTACA*. In Catholic theology, human beings are part of a fallen humanity within a good creation. In this good creation, we are given our current biological structure and mental capacities. We are certainly allowed to fully use the gift of our minds to restore our health. Once we cross the line from restoration or the full use of our current physiology or mind, we easily glide onto the path of eugenics, the attempted perfecting of our species. Even if we develop advanced genetic technologies, we are fallen and morally deficient creatures whose ability to choose is imperfect. It is not certain that we are capable of handling such a power over ourselves. We have the historical example of how problematic our choices in eugenics can be in the horror of involuntary sterilizations on the "unfit" initiated in the United States at the beginning of the twentieth century and then by the Nazi regime in Germany.[13] The possibility that the eugenics of the future would be voluntary does not make it less problematic, as *GATTACA* makes abundantly clear.

In modern debates about genetics, the movie *GATTACA* has already entered as a reference point for important bioethical discussions. A current area of genetic advancement is the transfer of mitochondrial DNA of one person into the egg of another person to encourage fertility or to prevent genetic diseases. The mitochondria in our cells help to provide the energy essential to cell life. These scientific procedures were the subject of a Food and Drug Administration (FDA) conference in February of 2014. One technique combines the nuclear DNA of one person with all of the mitochondria of another. The procedures have raised numerous objections to genetic sharing by three persons. Objections arose from scientific and ethical communities. Stuart Newman, a professor of cell biology at New York Medical College, observed that the moving of a cell nucleus into a hollowed-out egg would create massive genetic modification. Enola Aird, from Mothers for a Human Future, noted that "Allowing the creation of children with genetic material from three or more parents would open the door to the alteration of the human species, and the creation of 'GATTACA'-like

---

13. On this issue see the excellent book Lombardo, *Three Generations, No Imbeciles*.

classes of human beings and the dissolution of our common humanity."[14] To be fair, Aird's comments may be a bit premature; these experiments are not genetic modifications seeking to go beyond the restoration of health. Nonetheless, this example reminds us that we are entering an age of genetic engineering, and the public policy debate has begun with *GATTACA* as an important reference point. Aird's use of the *GATTACA* analogy suggests the movie's impact and our need to use such films carefully. The message is that much good can come from advances in genetic technology, but the technology can be used for good or ill. Fallible human beings are easily tempted by false idols, and these temptations may lead us away from a fully human life. Hence, we need to think deeply and imaginatively in order to discover the right path, and *GATTACA* poses difficult questions regarding our biotechnological future that will help us to make better choices.

Questions

1) Vincent, Jerome, and Irene all suffer from the expectations associated with their genetic inheritances. How does each of them handle this expectation? How do expectations of parents, teachers, and society impact how they perform or act? What about such expectations in our world?

2) How is improvement for genetically engineered children defined in the movie? Can we define a desired perfection for human beings? What is perfection? Do we sometimes benefit from our mental or physical challenges, our imperfections?

3) How much control should parents have over the genetic makeup of their children? Where do we draw any limits on parental control of their children's future? Do we prefer conception as a gift or should we desire to produce our children?

4) Is there such a thing as a human nature? If such a nature exits, what justifies modifying it and what does not?

14. Tingley, "One Child, Three Parents," 26–31, 38.

GATTACA (1997)(PG-13)

Resources

Barnes, Elizabeth. "Gattaca and A.I.: Artificial intelligence: Views of salvation in an age of genetic engineering." *Review & Expositor* 99:1 (Winter 2002) 59–70.

Frame, Tom. "Gattaca and the Challenge to Christian Anthropology." *St. Mark's Review* 178 (1998) 27–34.

Green, Ronald, and Aine Donovan. "Genetics as Religion: Gattaca's Disquieting Vision." In *The Human Genome Project in College Curriculum: Ethical Issues and Practical Strategies*, edited by Aine Donovan and Ronald Green, 122–31. Hanover, NH: Dartmouth University Press, 2008.

Kirby, David A. "The New Eugenics in Cinema: Genetic Determinism and Gene Therapy in GATTACA." *Science Fiction Studies* 27:2 (2000) 193–215.

PART VI

The Problems with Jesus Movies

Chapter 13

The Challenges of a Jesus Movie

I am with you always, even unto the end of time.
—MATT 28:20

In a book titled *Lights in the Darkness*, written by a Christian about movies, it would be reasonable to ask: why has there not been a discussion of a single movie about Jesus to this point? After all, there have been many Jesus films over the past century, and many of them have considerable merit. From a religious standpoint, Christians should relish the opportunity to have an artistic avenue for exploring the heart of their faith, but there is an intractable problem. I agree with the Catholic theologian Romano Guardini, who confessed to a "systematic lack of confidence in the possibility of representing Jesus through an actor."[1] This lack of confidence is partly grounded in the difficulty of presenting a person with fully human and a fully divine natures. In addition, the scarcity of scriptural biography, the diverse tradition of Jesus interpretation, and the difficulty of defining the roles of the Jews and Romans in the life of Jesus further complicate the adequate rendering of the life of Jesus.

---

1. Siciliano, *Pasolino*, 273.

Challenge #1—Fully Human and Fully God

A fundamental and thorny issue is how to portray a person with two natures—one fully human and one fully divine. As Bryan Stone has observed in *Faith and Film*, "Go too far in one direction and the film will be viewed as disrespectful and blasphemous; go too far in the other direction and Jesus becomes a mythical figure, far removed from our own concrete life situations."[2]

The choice to lean towards the divinity or humanity of Jesus is most often revealed by which of the four Gospels are chosen as primary for the screenplay. The Synoptic Gospels (Matthew, Mark, and Luke) focus more on his teachings for the mortal life and are coyer about Jesus' divinity, while the Gospel according to John concentrates more on his divinity and cosmic mission. How do these theological questions impact a movie? Well, a director has to determine, for example, when Jesus becomes aware of his divinity? In *The Greatest Story Ever Told*, which relies heavily on the Gospel of John, Jesus knows he is God's Son from the beginning. In other movies, the moment of his awareness is not always clear. In *Jesus of Nazareth*, Jesus' meeting with John the Baptist is transformative, but we are not sure why. In *The Last Temptation of Christ*, the entire movie depicts Jesus' exploration of his relationship to God. His divine mission is not fully revealed until the very end.

An artistic rendering of a human life relies on personal experience or on human experiences related by other people. So, how do filmmakers imagine the life of someone whose nature is both fully human and fully divine? Do they make him very human as in *The Last Temptation of Christ*, with Jesus wondering what it would have been like to live a more normal life with a family? Do they see him as a proto-socialist activist as in Pasolini's neorealist film, the *Gospel According to Saint Matthew*? Do they see Jesus as detached, all too aware of his divinity as in *The Greatest Story Ever Told*? Or is he the suffering servant of *The King of Kings* and *The Passion of the Christ*? A director can depict Jesus as a more-than-human figure who is constantly violating the laws of nature by walking on water and healing the dead and is usually accompanied by ethereal soundtracks. Jesus radiates a kind of eternal glow on his visage. As an aspect of his human nature, is Jesus afraid of death and reluctant to die through torture? Does he feel himself abandoned, or is this part of the plan that he realizes is necessary

---

2. Stone, *Faith and Film*, 69.

The Challenges of a Jesus Movie

for his divine mission? This issue makes his relationship with Judas highly problematic.

In giving filmmakers due credit for the difficulty of their efforts to portray Jesus, we should remember that the issue of who Jesus was occupied the minds of the Church Fathers for the first few centuries after his death. These groups make a wide array of assertions about whether Jesus was divine or human. Let us look at just a few examples. Some claimed that he was separate from and begotten by God (Arianism); some claimed that he was born human and adopted by God (Adoptionism); and others claimed that his mind was divine and his lower body emotions were human (Appolinarism). The orthodox position that was eventually expressed in the Nicene-Constantinopolitan Creed and accepted by most Christians was that Jesus was a single person with two wills corresponding to his two natures. Hence, the director of a Jesus movie must attempt to present this unique duality and unity.

Challenge #2—Jesus and His Gaps

Another problem in writing a screenplay for a Jesus movie is that there are large parts of his life for which there is little or no information. We have retellings of his birth and related stories, followed by a brief vignette at the temple. The Gospels then fast forward to Jesus receiving adult baptism and the beginning of his brief ministry. Such gaps present problems in depicting his life. The Scriptures present illuminative spiritual vignettes, but they are not an exhaustive autobiography, listing every event in Jesus' life in exact chronological order. Filmmakers must decide what to do. As examples of opposite extremes, the filmmaker can try to adhere closely to a Gospel like Pier Pasolini's the *Gospel According to Matthew* or engage in wild speculations like *The Last Temptation of Christ*. Either way, there are difficulties, gaps, and a huge potential for distortion because there is much we do not know about Jesus' life.

If a director hews too closely to the original Scripture with almost no deviations or additions, they have to make a major portion of the movie into a long series of lectures about his teachings with a sprinkling of miracles. In *The Gospel According to Saint Matthew*, this is exactly the problem. There is a sequence of shots with Jesus delivering a series of parables and words of wisdom. He is often delivering these as he walks briskly, and his disciples are trying to keep up with him. This approach can become more of a moving lecture than a stirring narrative.

If filmmakers choose to fill in the gaps, they must decide what to add and how to fill in the small talk and tasks of daily living. How do we depict Jesus or the disciples eating, sleeping, or laughing? Trudging long distances in Judea and Galilee, relying on the generosity or lack of generosity of strangers, would make for a rough outdoor life. Should the disciples, like normal people, complain a bit, or do you have them steel themselves for sacrifice? How should they look after all of this difficult travel? They were probably gaunt, dirty, and sweaty. In some of the films, Jesus and the disciples as in the *King of Kings* look remarkably clean and well dressed, as if they are in a play.

What are the roles of minor characters like Mary Magdalene, Satan, Judas, and Mary, the mother of Jesus? The importance and interpretation of their roles can be a key to discerning the direction of the film, but there are difficult thickets of interpretation. For example, is Mary Magdalene a prostitute? There is not a shred of biblical evidence for this proposition, but unfortunately there is a very long tradition of portraying her this way in Christianity. It is interesting that many of the earliest movies such as *La Vie et La Passion de Jesus* (1902) and *Satana; overro; il Drama dell'Umanita* (1912) did not present Mary Magdalene as a fallen woman.[3] Nevertheless, most of the Jesus movies from the 1927 version of *King of Kings* through *The Last Temptation of Christ* (1988) depict her this way because the portrayal offers a seductive whiff of scandal, reinforces that Jesus engaged public sinners, and secures a compelling plot line of a sinner becoming a saint. However, it seems even more compelling that she was the first to view the risen Christ, and the Gospels offer solid testimony for this claim.

Filmmakers sift through evidence and interpretation to choose how to portray historical characters. The question of how to portray Satan requires additional theological considerations from filmmakers. What is the essence of a personification of evil? Satan appears in a human form like the worldly portrayal of Donald Pleasance in *The Greatest Story Ever Told*. Other films portray him as a flame, or a cobra, or a deceptive young girl in *The Last Temptation of Christ*, or as an androgynous demon in *The Passion of the Christ*. He does not appear at all in *The Son of God*.[4] If he appears more than

---

3. Haskins, *Mary Magdalen*, 377.

4. In *The Son of God*, complaints were made that the devil looked like Barack Obama so he was dropped from the script.

The Challenges of a Jesus Movie

in the desert, then the movie strays beyond the Gospels. Do multiple appearances indicate a cosmic battle of good and evil as in *The Greatest Story Ever Told* or *The Passion of the Christ*?

Judas is also a subject of much speculation. The rather sparse verses of the New Testament beg for a more complete explanation. He is definitely an intriguing figure who clarifies the mission and end of Jesus' human life. It is generally agreed that he betrays Christ for money to the authorities. The relationship between Jesus and Judas, however, is not entirely clear. Is Judas a zealot who ultimately disagrees with Christ's peaceful reproach of the Romans as in *The King of Kings*? In that film, Judas tries to force Jesus into a violent response by turning him over to the authorities. Judas expects Jesus to "call down hosts to destroy the fortress of Pilate," so he is shocked, angry, and upset when Jesus does not respond to his efforts but instead accepts capture. Or is Judas both a zealot and a close childhood friend of Jesus who assists him to complete his mission, as in *The Last Temptation of Christ*? In *Jesus of Nazareth*, there is a creative role for Judas; he is a victim fooled by the evil Zerah, a leader of the Sanhedrin. In the end, filmmakers must ask the question: is Judas a force for evil or is he essential to fulfilling Jesus' ultimate mission, or both?

The portrayal of Mary, the mother of Jesus, can also be very revealing. The larger the role of Mary, the more likely a Catholic or at least a person operating in the Catholic tradition is making the film. A good place to discover whether this perspective is operational or not is if we are taken back to her earliest biblical roots as a young woman betrothed to Joseph. In this context, she is told by an angel of her role as "the handmaiden of the Lord" who is "full of grace" and "blessed among women."[5] In this revelation, the choice of angel can be as diverse as a beam of light in *Jesus of Nazareth* or a young woman figure in *The Gospel According to St. Matthew*. In any event, does Mary continue to be involved in the life of Jesus as in *The Greatest Story Ever Told*, where she seems to know what is coming? What is her role regarding his crucifixion? In *The Passion of Christ*, there are a number of scenes demonstrating her pain and love for her son. She is the sorrowful and grieving Mary.

So in the end, any director must confront the Jesus gaps. Is there any other way to deal with the gaps? In their book *Film and Religion*, Paul Flesher and Robert Torry claim that one vehicle for presenting Jesus accurately is

---

5. Those familiar with the rosary prayer will note its connection to Mary in Luke 1:28, 42.

the use of targum. In Jewish tradition, targums are expansions and explanations of a text. The primary rules of targum require that when presenting an original text, one should do so exactly; and, when adding material to the text, one should integrate it smoothly into the translation.[6] These and other additional rules allow an interpreter to add to a text but without grossly violating its integrity or meaning. Hence, the Sermon on the Mount in the movie *King of Kings* is not one long lecture. It becomes a series of questions and answers about halfway into the sermon. The question-and-answer format does not alter the words spoken, but it does arrange them a bit differently. This approach offers the audience a more dynamic exchange that allows for the use of different camera angles. The question-and-answer format constitutes a successful and appropriate use of targum.

Challenge #3—Which Jesus?

We have already discussed the challenge of depicting the human and divine natures in the person of Jesus accurately without sacrificing artistic forms of expression. Directors must also contend with a whole host of existing cultural interpretations and expectations about Jesus. Most audience members already have preconceptions about what Jesus looked like and how he dressed because two millennia of paintings, iconography, poetry, fiction, book illustrations, and other films have all informed their views. These cultural artifacts have created cultural expectations for Americans about what Jesus should look like. In America it is common to see representations of Jesus in which he looks rather European, with a beard and long hair. He might in fact have been short, and his beard would have been trimmed according to Jewish law. Long hair was considered effeminate and inappropriate in the Jewish culture of the time.[7] He also might have the darker coloring of his Semitic heritage. Filmmakers must decide whether to meet expectations or attempt a more historically accurate portrayal.

Such choices are fraught with complications. Portrayals of Jesus that are too familiar to audiences feel flat, uninspired, or overly preachy. However, if Jesus does not look or act at least somewhat like audiences expect him to, then audiences might feel alienated from a film and might disregard its message completely. In general, people expect portrayals of Jesus to match

---

6. Flesher and Torry, *Film and Religion*, 20.

7. Joan Taylor, "What Did Jesus Look Like?" BBC News. (December, 2015). http://www.bbc.com/news/magazine-35120965.

their expectations, and they are less inclined to expand their imaginations on the person they consider the savior of the world. Thus, Jesus movies may reveal more about the current culture of the audiences than the historical reality of Jesus.

Filmmakers have two millennia of reflections to choose from as they develop their films. In different movies Jesus is a social activist, apocalyptic prophet, king, cosmic Christ, teaching rabbi, liberator, the prince of peace, the sacrificial lamb, the suffering soul, or the prophet of the kingdom of God, and all of these perspectives have some basis in Scripture.[8] These reflections allow a rich diversity of approaches that can frame the narratives of the films, but they cannot provide completely comprehensive representations of Jesus' identity. Furthermore, audiences who already know who they think Jesus is may find themselves mentally critiquing a narrative or dialogue. These viewers may be restricted by their mental preconceptions of Jesus and less captivated by the one they see onscreen. Filmmakers must think about historical accuracy, audience expectations, and cultural emphases when they create their versions of Jesus.

Challenge #4—Fault Lines: The Role of Jews and Romans

The issue of the portrayal of Jewish people in Jesus films has been a significant issue given the long and shameful history of Christians oppressing Jews because of their role in crucifying Jesus. The justification for this prejudice is often the trial before the high priest of the Sanhedrin, Caiaphas, and the role of the Jewish mob before Pilate who demand his death and cry out in the Gospel of Matthew, "His blood be upon us and our children."[9] From such specific biblical moments, there has arisen at times in the history of Christianity a condemnation of all Jewish people for all time. Any Jesus film must account for this historical distortion and its consequences. A film can opt to limit almost any discussion of Jesus and his Jewishness or the role of the Jewish people, as in *King of Kings*. Unfortunately, this avoidance also denies a sense of Jesus' Jewish context. Similarly, in *The Last Temptation of Christ*, there is avoidance of Jewish responsibility. There is no trial before Jewish authorities or any claim of the Jewish crowd that Jesus' blood is on their heads. Pontius Pilate and the Romans are to blame. Another option is

---

8. A good book to look at the different portrayals of Jesus is Pelikan, *Jesus Through the Centuries*.

9. Matt 27:25.

to have the devil fomenting the decisions of Roman and Jewish leaders as in *The Greatest Story Ever Told*. The devil made them do it.

A balanced approach to the vexing Jewish question is to provide an historical perspective on the role of the Jewish people. To this end, Franco Zefferelli before filming *Jesus of Nazareth* went to the Vatican library and read the following passage in the Second Vatican Council declaration, *Nostra Aetate*:

> True, the Jewish authorities and those who followed their lead pressed for the death of Christ; still, what happened in His passion cannot be charged against all the Jews, without distinction, then alive, nor against the Jews of today. Although the Church is the new people of God, the Jews should not be presented as rejected or accursed by God, as if this followed from the Holy Scriptures. . . . Furthermore, in her rejection of every persecution against any man, the Church, mindful of the patrimony she shares with the Jews and moved not by political reasons but by the Gospel's spiritual love, decries hatred, persecutions, displays of anti-Semitism, directed against Jews at any time and by anyone.[10]

In this spirit, Zefferelli declared his intent to portray Jesus as a Jew who was no enemy to his people, past or present. In *Jesus of Nazareth*, there are numerous positive scenes of Jewish life including synagogues, the marriage of Mary and Joseph, and the flight to Egypt. The viewer never doubts Jesus' Jewishness. There are positive portrayals of Nicodemus, who counsels with Jesus, and Joseph of Arimathea, who arranges for his burial. They are both members of the Sanhedrin. The debates in the Sanhedrin raise, in an intelligent way, important issues for Jewish leaders about the teachings of Jesus as the Son of God. These reasonable portrayals reveal that the Jewish community was diverse and thoughtful in its opinions and responses to Jesus.

By way of contrast, director Mel Gibson's *The Passion of the Christ* (2004) elicited a very stormy response. The Anti-Defamation League in the United States described *The Passion of the Christ* as offering an "unambiguous portrayal of Jews as being responsible for the death of Jesus. There is no question in this film about who is responsible. At every single opportunity, Mr. Gibson's film reinforces the notion that the Jewish authorities and the Jewish mob are the ones ultimately responsible for the Crucifixion."[11] It was not just Jewish people who found the film problematic. At the behest of the

---

10. Second Vatican Council, *Nostra Aetate* (1965), n4.
11. Anti-Defamation League, "ADL and Mel Gibson's 'The Passion of the Christ.'"

The Challenges of a Jesus Movie

United States Catholic Conference, a panel of three Jewish and six Catholic scholars reviewed a draft of the screenplay. The panel concluded that the movie was anti-Semitic and inaccurate. A panel member, Sister Mary C. Boys, a professor at Union Theological Seminary, commented, "All the way through, the Jews are portrayed as bloodthirsty." The Jewish leaders are portrayed like a brood of snarling vipers with long noses and leering expressions.[12]

In the Catholic film community, Sister Rose Pacatte of the Paulist Media Center noted that Gibson violates *Nostra Aetate*, which emphatically rejected any portrayal of Jews in the trial of Jesus that places guilt upon all Jews for the death of Christ.[13] Furthermore, she observed that the movie seems to violate the United States Council of Catholic Bishops document "Criteria for the Evaluation of Dramatizations of the Passion." This document makes clear that Passion enactments should strengthen the bonds between Christian and Jews and refrain from presentations that make the Jews look evil or avaricious, fail to reflect the diverse opinions of the Jewish community at the time, or suggest Jesus was in rebellion against his Jewish identity.[14]

Some in the Catholic hierarchy praised *The Passion of the Christ*.[15] Some traditional Catholic commentators preferred to talk about the movie's Marian aspects and the moving depictions of suffering for human sins. These commentaries generally ignored or deflected allegations that the film might be perceived as anti-Semitic. There was some defensiveness regarding any criticism. The Catholic League published a list of "incendiary" remarks directed at the movie. It is quite a long and diverse list, but the Catholic League did not address aspects of the film that might suggest a problem with the movie. Why not counter the specific criticisms with specific defenses? Instead, the Catholic League called the attacks against Gibson and the movie "unseemly" and they initiated a counteroffensive against his detractors.[16] The term *unseemly* is curious because this word does not necessarily suggest that such perspectives are untrue. "Unseemly" events or words are events or words that are not in good taste or are inconvenient.

---

12. Orlet, "*Mel Gibson vs. 'The Jews.'*"

13. Pacatte, "A decade later, 'The Passion' still raises questions of anti-Semitism."

14. Unites States Catholic Conference Bishops' Committee, "Criteria for Evaluation of Dramatizations of the Passion."

15. Donohue, "What Catholics Have Said About the Passion of the Christ."

16. Ibid.

One wonders why the league did not directly declare that the movie's detractors were wrong.

Another unusual twist in *The Passion of the Christ* is the portrayal of Pontius Pilate as a reluctant persecutor. In this film the Roman governor is seeking again and again to exonerate Jesus because of a dream of his wife warning him not to kill Jesus. This spousal warning is an interesting plot twist based on Matthew 27:19. It is unlikely, however, that Pilate was as reluctant to kill Jesus as *The Passion of the Christ* suggests. Pilate routinely crucified Jews without trials. Eventually, Pilate was recalled to Rome for his excessive violence.[17] Even among the extremely violent Romans, he was considered too violent.

After *The Passion of the Christ* was primarily considered to be an unnecessarily negative depiction of the Jewish people, the subsequent movie, *Son of God*, received a positive reception for its portrayal of Jews and Judaism. Abraham Foxman, the head of the Anti-Defamation League, observed that "the *Son of God* is the most sensitive, caring depiction of the story of Jesus that I have ever seen. The producers have done everything possible to put the events into historical, political and psychological context."[18]

An Impossible Task

The making of the perfect Jesus movie is probably an almost impossible task. This chapter discusses many of the difficulties encountered when producing a Jesus movie. It is worth remembering the special moments in these movies as well where we gain new insight on his life and mission. Moreover, these movies raise important if difficult questions about Jesus in his time, his relevance for our time, and the role of his followers. They also reveal much about our own understanding of Jesus, so let us hope that these efforts will continue in future years. Each Jesus film begins another dialogue about the nature of our Christian faith and allows us once again to bear witness to the fecundity of Jesus as a source of inspiration in film and in the arts. My professor at the University of Chicago, David Tracy, observed that a work is considered a "classic" if it has many layers and possibilities that cannot be exhausted. In an analogous way, Jesus will never be

---

17. United States Catholic Conference Bishops' Committee, "Criteria for Evaluation of Dramatizations of the Passion," 2(b).

18. Cunningham, "'Son of God.'"

exhausted as a subject matter for the arts. He will continue in movies and other artistic venues to offer new angles on the infinite and the human.[19]

Questions for a Jesus Movie

1) Is Jesus portrayed as more human or divine in this film? What makes you think he is more human or divine in the movie? At what time, and how, do you know of his divinity?

2) What is the role of the apostles? Are they more than an audience for Jesus? How so? Do they seem realistic to you?

3) What is the role of the Jewish people or Romans in the death of Jesus? Who is primarily responsible?

4) What is the role of characters like Barabbas, Judas, Mary Magdalene, Satan, Mary and Martha, Pontius Pilate or other Romans? Why are their roles significant?

5) Is the crucifixion or the resurrection more significant in a film? Why is this important in evaluating the film?

Resources

Baugh, SJ, Lloyd. *Imaging the Divine: Jesus and Christ-Figures in Film*. Franklin, WI: Sheed and Ward, 2000.
Flesher, Paul V. M. "Filming Jesus." In *Film and Religion: An Introduction*, 97–157. Nashville: Abingdon, 2007.
Peilikan, Jaroslav. *Jesus Through the Centuries: His Place in the History of Culture*. New Haven, CT: Yale University Press, 1999.
Tatum, W. Barnes. *Jesus at the Movies*. Salem, OR: Polebridge, 1997.
Walsh, Richard. *Reading the Gospels in the Dark: Portrayals of Jesus in Film*. Harrisburg, PA: Trinity, 2003.

---

19. Tracy, *The Analogical Imagination*, 68.

PART VII

Director's Cut

chapter 14

Exploring the Lights

The Church which is so full of youthful vigor and is constantly renewed by the breath of the Holy Spirit is willing at all times to recognize, welcome, and even assimilate anything that redounds to the honor of the human mind and heart.

—SAINT JOHN XXIII, *PRINCEPS PASTORUM*

Since the beginning of the twentieth century, movies have informed and been informed by our religious understandings as a culture. This connection is important because film is a powerful artistic medium. Movies are part of how our culture shapes our views and sometimes even inspires our destinies. I have met several attorneys who have told me that they knew they wanted to be a lawyer when they saw *To Kill a Mockingbird*. The film still has this impact.[1]

In an insightful book on movies, Richard Blake, SJ, uses the psychological term "afterimage" to describe the impact of a movie. An afterimage is "an image or sensation that remains or returns after the external stimulus has been removed."[2] Oftentimes it remains, in the words of the French novelist, Marcel Proust, an "involuntary memory." In one of Proust's novels, *In Remembrance of Things Past*, the taste of a pastry, a madeleine dipped in tea,

---

1. Papantonio, *In Search of Atticus Finch*; Markaj, "A Changed View of 'To Kill a Mockingbird.'"
2. Blake, *Afterimage*, xii.

involuntarily ignites a long novel's worth of memories. A visual memory can also be prompted and retrieved by a variety of stimuli. We retain information best if it is conveyed with a combination of visual and oral methods, as one finds in movies. Hence, a screen image with sound can be an especially powerful medium for presenting and retaining information.[3]

Our visual memories particularly shape the current screen-dominated age. The average adult American spends more than ten hours in front of a screen.[4] There is an enormous growth of diverse screen opportunities. However, the advent of cell phones, iPads, laptop and personal computers, has not rendered movie theaters, much less movies, obsolete. On the contrary, tickets sales for movies have doubled over the last couple of decades.[5]

Because the many movies we watch leave an impression on us, those who wish to make films with religious themes in the current screen age must discern how to effectively communicate in this medium with the faithful and the curious without abandoning or grossly simplifying their intellectual and spiritual traditions. False opportunities and paths will readily present themselves. One pastor in Colorado allows kids to play *Halo* before receiving their Bible lesson.[6] Massive online killing precedes discussions of the prince of peace. Surely, the problem here is self-evident. In the realm of film, Director Mel Gibson's *The Passion of the Christ* applies many of the techniques of extreme violence and bizarre images found in modern horror films. Think of the bulging eyes of the children surrounding Judas, the crow pecking the eyes out of the "bad thief" on the cross, and the androgynous Satan with the clinging demon child.[7] Religious films that try to compete with the contemporary trend to ever-greater violence, noise, speed, and horror on the screen risk becoming a sorcerer's apprentice in the process.

Let me suggest another path for the contemporary pilgrimage in the screen age. Hopefully this book has been an application of John Paul II's term "critical openness" towards the phenomena of film. We must be open to the spiritual and ethical lessons in film and yet also not abandon our critical capacities in assessing their merits. In this book, there has been no

---

3. Butcher, "Learning from text with diagrams," 182–197; Mayer and Moreno, "A split-attention effect in multimedia learning," 312–320.
4. Bauder, "Media Use in America Up a Full Hour Over Just Last Year."
5. Box Office Mojo. "Yearly Box Office." http://www.boxofficemojo.com/yearly/.
6. Richtel, "Thou Shalt Not Kill Except in a Game at Church."
7. Pacatte, "The Passion of the Christ, A Female Critic's Perspective."

automatic presumption that secular films are unworthy or that all religious films have merit.

All of the movies in this book raise serious questions and invite self-examination. Can we love and sacrifice like the women in *Babette's Feast* and *The Spitfire Grill*? Can we appreciate and learn about religious conscience and spiritual integrity in the life and death choices of *A Man for All Seasons* and *The Mission*. Thinking of justice, are we prepared to engage the displaced and marginalized like the homeless in *Entertaining Angels*, the leper in *The Flowers of Saint Francis*, Jews in *Au Revoir les Enfants*, and the despised on death row in *Dead Man Walking*? Can we imitate the spiritual courage in *Of Gods and Men* or confront indifference and pettiness as the priest does in *Diary of a Country Priest*? These movies present challenges of the past and present, but what of the future and its new technologies? In the years ahead, we must be careful to avoid new idolatries (*Decalogue 1*) and the goal of perfection through the seductive claims of eugenics (*GATTACA*).

There are lessons in the Jesus movies, but the efficacy of the films is diminished by a peculiar difficulty. The perfect Jesus movie has not yet been made and I suspect will not be made, because of the impossible task of presenting a person that is fully human and fully divine. There is also the formidable task of parsing Scriptures that have many different details and emphases and sorting through two millennia of interpretation of these stories. The questions range from the sublime such as, do I make Jesus appear more human or more divine in my characterization of him to what is the right look for Jesus?

In addition to Jesus films, I have mentioned in the preface and introduction some of my criteria that eliminate from my consideration worthy films. I was not looking for light and entertaining fare such as *The Sound of Music*. There is one more category that I excluded—there are no films that relate to the priest pedophilia issue or other Church scandals. My focus has been on Catholic themes and so these films were not the best choices for my purposes. They often reveal severe failures to abide by the key Catholic themes I am highlighting. I do not say this to deny their merits, but to offer an explanation why they are not central to my project. Nonetheless, these movies have many merits and do touch on important issues of justice, compassion, and reconciliation. I commend the trinity of movies *Doubt*, *Spotlight*, and *Calvary* that highlight the sources, cover-ups, and consequences associated with the priest pedophilia scandal.

Lights in the Darkness

Returning to the twelve movies at the heart of this book, I believe that they all have considerable depth and nuance. After I presented a lecture on movies for Catholics at a parish someone asked me why I did not select happier movies like *The Bells of Saint Mary's*. This is a fair question because eight of the twelve movies discussed in this book end with a death, and these deaths are certainly tragic from a human perspective. As I thought about how to answer this question, however, I remembered the speculation of the English writer and Catholic apologist, Malcolm Muggeridge, who imagined an elderly woman dying and going to heaven, where she approaches Shakespeare and complains about the brutality of what was done to King Lear. Shakespeare responds, "I could have arranged for him to take a sedative at the end of Act I, but then madam there would have been no play."[8] Drama is often centered on a tragedy and no subject is more tragic than death. Of course, for Christians, death is not the end of life. An incarnational faith centered on a resurrection offers another possibility. Jesus reveals to the good thief on the cross that they will be together in heaven. This is why the curé in *Diary of a Country Priest* can end his suffering with the words "All is grace." This is also why the abbot Christian de Chergé in *Of Gods and Men* can forgive his killer and look forward to their being reunited in heaven.

The tragedies and painful realities in the movies discussed in this book are not designed to dampen the human spirit. Quite the contrary. Rather, the movies celebrate the immense complexity and fecundity of the human experience despite the terrible losses that challenge our faith. The church father, Cyril of Jerusalem, warned his catechumens that "The dragon is at the side of the road watching those who pass. Take care lest he devour you. You are going to the Father of souls, but it is necessary to pass by the dragon."[9] This dealing with the dragons of sin, pain, and despair can make for rich, multivalent, and compelling drama. *The Bells of Saint Mary's* is entertaining, breezy, and happy. There is nothing wrong with such a charming movie, but it is not going to adequately probe the sublime operation of divine grace in this world with the same nuance and depth as the movies in this book. Some passages on the dragon's path are dramatic and terrible such as a death, but some are less obvious and are, for example, the

---

8. Buckley and Muggeridge, "How Does One Find Faith?"

9. I plucked this quote from the Flannery O'Connor lecture of William Sessions at Emory University. Sessions, "Flannery O'Connor and Freud, the Meaning of Life in Death."

result of innumerable small rejections like that experienced by the curé in *Diary of a Country Priest* or the consignment to maid status of the famous cook, Babette Hersant. Our persistence in confronting and overcoming our dragons is an important aspect of the selected movies. Such stories reveal our deepest connections to one another because we inherently possess human dignity. We may learn to celebrate this dignity in a true community in *Babette's Feast* or a community of love and giving as in *The Flowers of Saint Francis*.

Human choices often go astray, however, as we adopt false idols in the place of the living God. The excuses for such behaviors include religious fundamentalism (*Of Gods and Men*), political ideology (*Au Revoir les Enfants* and *Dead Man Walking*), a social and scientific ideology (*GATTACA*), imperialism and racism (*The Mission*), selfishness, fear, and insularity (*Diary of a Country Priest* and *The Spitfire Grill*), power and glory (*A Man for All Seasons*), and economic dislocations (*Entertaining Angels*). The vices of humanity become the dragon and the result: despair, hatred, and indifference reign. Even in these circumstances, such vices are countered by fortitude, charity, and justice. We see these virtues at work in many of the key characters in these movies. The characters stand as testimony to the fact that the light of hope and faith will never die in the world. Whether our society's challenges are dramatic or quotidian, we must renew our spirits. Films can offer new possibilities and vistas for this renewal.

As we watch films that renew our spirits, we can remember that Jesus is present wherever we witness grace, insight, and truth. A deep and nuanced reflection on life in a film will present us with grace if the director discovers what Flannery O'Connor described as that "peculiar crossroads where time and place and eternity somehow meet." Many of these films explore grace acting in the hearts of characters in order to help grace function in the lives of audiences. Grace is demonstrated in the integrity of Thomas More in *A Man for All Seasons*, or in the possibility of the just society created by the Jesuits in Latin America in *The Mission*. Grace can operate even on death row in the conversion and the possibility of forgiveness in *Dead Man Walking* or in the recollection of the sovereignty of God in *Decalogue 1*.

Profound films will continue to present opportunities and challenges. As this book is prepared for printing, the movie, "Silence" had just entered theaters. Based on a novel by the Catholic convert, Shūsaku Endō, it is directed by Martin Scorcese. "Silence" is set in 17th century Japan where the Christian faith is being persecuted. Two Jesuit missionaries land in Japan to serve the remaining Christians. They are captured and are forced to watch the horrible torture and killing of Christians. If they recant their faith, the killing will stop. Finally, Jesus breaks his silence and tells a priest that he can recant and step on his image. Jesus came into the world to share the suffering of humanity so he allows this act. Peter C. Phan, a Catholic theologian at Georgetown, analyzes the moral dilemma this way, "The question is this: Are we allowed to do an essentially evil act to obtain a good result? If it is done to save himself, then the answer is no. But the novel is so complex because he does it for his followers, for the good end of saving his flock. He will go to hell—but he will go to hell for their sake." Thus, the movie is for Scorcese part of an ongoing pilgrimage of faith, seeking to explore its depths, anguish, and glory.[10]

Like the movie, *Silence*, my selected movies present many possibilities. We can be Christian pilgrims with the restless spiritual heart of Saint Augustine, exemplified by the professor in *Decalogue 1*, who is desperately seeking an answer for his son's death. We can lose our way in the modern forest of visual images that is often populated with superficial narratives and glitzy baubles appealing to our worst motives. In these cases, the visual flashes blind rather than illuminate. Nonetheless, we can still recognize in many films a "religious sensibility" that lives "on the limit of the possible, in hope for and in expectation of the impossible".[11] I believe that we can choose films that carefully explore the special gift of the complexity of human life. Movies at their best can illuminate this journey when they provide a light that "shines through the darkness"[12] and help us to find "a pearl of great price."[13]

---

10. James Martin, S.J., "Full Transcript: Interview with Martin Scorcese" *America* (December 9, 2016) http://www.americamagazine.org/print/224370; Paul Elie, "The Passion of Martin Scorcese" *New York Times*. http://www.nytimes.com/2016/11/27/magazine/the-passion-of-martin-scorsese.html. (November 21, 2016).

11. Caputo, *On Religion*, 67.

12. Ps 112:4.

13. Matt 13:46.

Appendix

The following are lists to provide additional movies for consideration by the reader. The movies in bold are analyzed in this book.

Vatican—Pontifical Council for Social Communications
For the 100th Anniversary of Cinema (1995)

Religion
Andrei Rublev * Andrei Tarkowsky (1969, USSR)
The Mission * Roland Joffé (1986, UK)
La passion de Jeanne d'Arc (The Passion of Joan of Arc) * Carl T. Dreyer (1928, France)
La vie et la passion de Jésus Christ (Life and Passion of Christ) * Ferdinand Zecca and Lucien Nonguet (1905, France) *Identified on the Vatican film list as* La Passion Pathé
Francesco, giullare di Dio (The Flowers of St. Francis / Francis, God's Jester) * Roberto Rossellini (1950, Italy)
Il Evangelo secondo Matteo (The Gospel According to Matthew) * Pier Paolo Pasolini (1964, France/Italy)
Thérèse * Alain Cavalier (1986, France)
Ordet (The Word) * Carl T. Dreyer (1955, Denmark)
Offret — Sacrificatio (The Sacrifice) * Andrei Tarkowsky (1986, Sweden/UK/France)
Francesco * Liliana Cavani (1989, Italy/Germany)
Ben-Hur [A Tale of the Christ] * William Wyler (1959, USA)
Babettes gæstebud (Babette's Feast) * Gabriel Axel (1987, Denmark)
Nazarín * Luis Buñuel (1958, Mexico)
Monsieur Vincent * Maurice Cloche (1947, France)
A Man for All Seasons * Fred Zinnemann (1966, UK)

Appendix

Values
Gandhi * Richard Attenborough (1982, UK/USA/India)
Intolerance * D. W. Griffith (1916, USA)
Dekalog (The Decalogue) * Krzysztof Kieslowski (1987, Poland) Identified on the Vatican film list as **Il Decalogo**
Au Revoir, Les Enfants (Goodbye, Children) * Louis Malle (1987, France)
Dersu Uzala * Akira Kurosawa (1974, Japan)
L'albero degli zoccoli (The Tree of the Wooden Clogs) * Ermanno Olmi (1978, Italy/France)
Roma, città aperta (Open City) * Roberto Rossellini (1946, Italy)
Smultronstället (Wild Strawberries) * Ingmar Bergman (1957, Sweden)
Det sjunde inseglet (The Seventh Seal) * Ingmar Bergman (1957, Sweden)
Chariots of Fire * Hugh Hudson (1981, UK)
Ladri di biciclette (The Bicycle Thief) * Vittorio de Sica (1948, Italy)
It's a Wonderful Life * Frank Capra (1946, USA)
Schindler's List * Steven Spielberg (1993, USA)
On the Waterfront * Elia Kazan (1954, USA)
Biruma No Tategoto (The Burmese Harp) * Kon Ichikawa (1956, Japan)

Art
2001: A Space Odyssey * Stanley Kubrick (1968, UK/USA)
La Strada * Federico Fellini (1954, Italy)
Citizen Kane * Orson Welles (1941, USA)
Metropolis * Fritz Lang (1927, Germany)
Modern Times * Charlie Chaplin (1936, USA)
Napoléon * Abel Gance (1927, Italy)
8½ * Federico Fellini (1963, Italy)
La grande illusion (Grand Illusion) * Jean Renoir (1937, France)
Nosferatu * F. W. Murnau (1922, Germany)
Stagecoach * John Ford (1939, USA)
Il Gattopardo (The Leopard) * Luchino Visconti (1963, Italy/France)
Fantasia * (1940, USA)
The Wizard of Oz * Victor Fleming (1939, USA)
The Lavender Hill Mob * Charles Crichton (1951, UK)
Little Women * George Cukor (1933, USA)

APPENDIX

Richard Leonard, S.J., author of *Movies That Matter*

Groundhog Day
The Mission
A Man for All Seasons
Places in the Heart
Witness
Hannah and Her Sisters
Babette's Feast
The Name of the Rose
Gandhi
Dead Poet's Society
Romero
JFK
Unforgiven
Schindler's List
Shadowlands
Philadelphia
Three Colors Trilogy: Red, White, Blue
The Shawshank Redemption
Dead Man Walking
Life is Beautiful
The Godfather
Men with Guns
Chariots of Fire
The Road Home
The Passion of the Christ

The Apostle
The Truman Show
The Insider
The Exorcist
Billy Elliot
Erin Brockovich
Gladiator
Chocolat
The Lord of the Rings
Glory
Bowling for Columbine
In America
Vera Drake
The Third Miracle
Italian for Beginners
Whale Rider
The Hurricane
The Crime of Father Amaro
Finding Nemo
Bruce Almighty
City of God
Gallipoli
Tender Mercies
The Magdalene Sisters

National Catholic Register Top 100 Pro-Catholic Movies

In 2004, the National Catholic Register and *Faith and Family* magazine gathered online nominations for films that best celebrate Catholic life.

1. The Passion of the Christ (2004)
2. The Sound of Music (1965)
3. A Man For All Seasons (1966)
4. The Song of Bernadette (1943)

Appendix

5. It's a Wonderful Life (1946)
6. The Ten Commandments (1956)
7. The Scarlet and the Black (1983)
8. Jesus of Nazareth (1977)
9. Schindler's List (1993)
10. The Bells of St Mary's (1945)
11. Thérèse (2004)
12. Braveheart (1995)
13. The Miracle of Our Lady of Fatima
14. **The Mission (1986)**
15. Lilies of the Field (1963)
16. The Miracle of Marcelino (1955)
17. Les Miserables (1998)
18. The Quiet Man (1952)
19. Ben Hur (1959)
20. Rudy (1993) *
21. The Robe (1953)
22. Return to Me (2000)
23. We Were Soldiers (2002)
24. Becket (1964)
25. Going My Way (1944)
26. Romero (1989)
27. Sister Act (1992)
28. Pope John Paul II (1984)
29. Jonah: a Veggie Tales Movie (2002)
30. Shoes of the Fisherman (1986)
31. Brideshead Revisited (1981)
32. The Keys of the Kingdom (1944)
33. On the Waterfront (1954)
34. I Confess (1953)
35. Boys Town (1938)
36. Molokai: the Story of Father Damien (1999)
37. Quo Vadis (1951)
38. The Trouble With Angels (1956)
39. **Babette's Feast (1987)**
40. The Rookie (2002)
41. The Reluctant Saint (1962)
42. One Man's Hero (1999)

Appendix

43. Brother Sun, Sister Moon (1972)
44. The Exorcist (1973)
45. Dead Man Walking (1995)
46. Joan of Arc (1948)
47. The Agony and the Ecstasy (1965)
48. The Passion of Joan of Arc (1928)
49. Angels In the Outfield (1951)
50. Moonstruck (1987) *
51. The Miracle Maker: the Story of Jesus (2000)
52. Henry V (1989) *
53. Heaven Knows, Mr. Allison (1957)
54. Entertaining Angels: The Dorothy Day Story (1996)
55. Knute Rockne: All American (1940)
56. The Greatest Story Ever Told (1965)
57. The Singing Nun (1966)
58. Marty (1955)
59. Monsieur Vincent (1948)
60. The Assisi Underground (1985)
61. Au Revoir Les Enfants (1987)
62. Come to the Stable (1949)
63. Diary of a Country Priest (1951)
64. In This House of Brede (1975)
65. The Jeweller's Shop (1988)
66. The Miracle of the Bells (1948)
67. The Fighting Sullivans (1944)
68. The Fourth Wiseman (1985)
69. The Juggler of Notre Dame (1970)
70. Barabbas (1962)
71. King of Kings (1961)
72. Francis of Assisi (1961)
73. The Adventures of Robin Hood (1937)
74. The Decalogue (1987)
75. The Gospel According to Saint Matthew (1966)
76. Angels With Dirty Faces (1938)
77. The Fugitive (1947)
78. The Longest Day (1962)
79. Thérèse (1986)
80. The Gospel of John (2003)

Appendix

81. A.D. (1985)
82. Faustyna (1995)
83. The Son (2002)
84. Francesco (1989)
85. The Flowers of St. Francis (1950)
86. Brother Orchid (1940)
87. Demetrius and the Gladiators
88. Nazarin (1958)
89. The Silver Chalice (1954)
90. When In Rome (1952)
91. Not of This World (1999)
92. Open City (1945)
93. 3 Godfathers (1948)
94. Don Bosco (1988)
95. Abraham (1994)
96. The Detective (1954)
97. The Hoodlum Saint (1946)
98. The Sign of the Cross (1932)
99. The Wrong Man (1956)
100. Padre On Horseback (1977)

Bibliography

Alleva, Richard. "Diminishing Dorothy Day." *Commonweal* 123 (October 25, 1996) 18.
Anker, Roy. *Catching Light, Looking for God in the Movies*. Grand Rapids: Eerdmans, 2004.
Anti-Defamation League. "ADL and Mel Gibson's "The Passion of the Christ." http://www.adl.org/education-outreach/interfaith-affairs/c/adl-and-mel-gibsons-the-passion.html.
Aquinas, Thomas. *Commentary on the Metaphysics of Aristotle*. New York: Henry Regnery, 1961.
———. *Summa Theologica*. New York: Benziger Brothers, 1947.
Avila, Wanda. "*Diary of a Country Priest*: The Transcendent on Film." *Journal of Religion and Film* 10 (October 2006). http://www.unomaha.edu/jrf/Vol10No2/Avila_CountryPriest.htm.
Baker, Elizabeth Gaylynn. "Rediscovering Community Care of the Spitfire Grill." *Body Mind Spirit Magazine* 15 (September, 1996) 54–55.
Barbour, Ian. *Religion in an Age of Science*. San Francisco: Harper Collins, 1990.
Barkley, Elizabeth F. "The Mission: The Film and Its Music." Center for History and New Media. http://chnm.gmu.edu/worldhistorysources/d/268/whm.html.
Bauder, David. "Media use in America up a full hour over just last year." *Associated Press* (June 29, 2016). http://bigstory.ap.org/article/ce2d9d9a7a0d4bc1821e3bf097b1b3d4/media-use-america-full-hour-over-just-last-year.
Baugh, Lloyd. "The Christian Moral Vision of a Believing Atheist: Krzysztof Kieslowski's *Decalogue* Films." In *Through a Catholic Lens*, edited by Peter Malone, 157–72. Lanham, MD: Rowan and Littlefield, 2007.
———. *Imaging the Divine: Jesus and Christ Figures in Film*. Franklin, WI: Sheed and Ward, 2000.
Baum, Gregory. *Man Becoming: God in Secular Experience*. New York: Seabury, 1979.
Bazin, Andre. *What is Cinema?* Vols 1–2, translated by Hugh Gray. Berkeley: University of California Press, 2005.
Beaty, Katelyn. "Of Gods and Men: A quiet, profound meditation on martyrdom, based on a true story of Trappist monks." *Christianity Today* (February 25, 2011). http://www.christianitytoday.com/ct/2011/februaryweb-only/godsandmen.html.
Benedict XVI. "Pope: Pray for me, future Pope, the Lord will guide us!" Vatican Radio (February 13, 2013). http://en.radiovaticana.va/storico/2013/02/13/pope_pray_for_me,_future_pope,_the_lord_will_guide_us!/en1-664501.
Black, Gregory D. *The Catholic Crusade Against Movies 1940–1975*. Cambridge: Cambridge University Press, 1997.

Bibliography

Blake, Richard A. *AfterImage: The Indelible Imagination of Six Catholic Filmmakers.* Chicago: Loyola University Press, 2000.

———. "Converts." *America* (September 28, 1996) 32–33.

Brennan, William. *Dehumanizing the Vulnerable.* Chicago: Loyola University Press, 1995.

Brunette, Peter. *Roberto Rossellini.* Berkeley: University of California Press, 1986.

Buckley, William F., Jr., and Malcolm Muggeridge. "How Does One Find Faith?" Firing Line (1980). http://www.malcolmmuggeridge.org/pr/faith.pdf.

Butcher, K. "Learning from text with diagrams: Promoting mental model development and inference generation." *Journal of Educational Psychology* 98 (2006) 182–97.

Caputo, John. *On Religion.* New York: Routledge, 2001.

Catechism of the Catholic Church: Revised in Accordance with the Official Latin Text Promulgated by Pope John Paul II. Vatican City: Libreria Editrice Vaticana, 1997.

Chesterton, G. K. *The Fame of Blessed Thomas More, Being Addresses Being Delivered in His Honour in Chelsea, July, 1929.* London: Sheed and Ward, 1929.

Church of England. "Holy Days." https://www.churchofengland.org/prayer-worship/worship/texts/the-calendar/holydays.aspx.

Clark, John Scott, and John Price Odell. *A Study of American and English Writers*, vol. 3. New York: Row Peterson, 1916.

Cornwell, John. *Hitler's Pope.* New York: Penguin, 1999.

Criterion Collection. "The Gospel According to Saint Matthew." http://www.classicartfilms.com/gospel-according-to-st-matthew-the-1964.

Crowther, Bosley. "A Sturdy Conscience, a Steadfast Heart: 'A Man for All Seasons' Opens at Fine Arts Paul Scofield Excels in Film by Zinnemann." *The New York Times* (December 13, 1966). http://www.nytimes.com/movie/review?res=9B02EED8153CE43BBC4B52DFB467838D679EDE&module=Search&mabReward=relbias%3Ar%2C%7B%221%22%3A%22RI%3A8%22%7D.

Cunningham, Lawrence. *The Catholic Heritage.* Eugene, OR: Cascade, 2002.

Cunningham, Todd. "'Son of God': Jewish Leader Hopes Bible Film Will Be 'Antidote' to 'Passion of the Christ.'" *The Wrap* (February 25, 2014). Online: http://www.thewrap.com/jewish-leader-hopes-son-god-will-antidote-passion-christ/.

Davies, Kevin. "Discrimination Down to a Science." *Nature* 390 (1997) 33.

Dawkins, Richard. "It's All in the Genes." *The Sunday Times* (March 12, 2006). http://web.archive.org/web/20110615135027/http://entertainment.timesonline.co.uk/tol/arts_and_entertainment/books/article738678.ece.

Day, Dorothy. *The Long Loneliness.* San Francisco: Harper Collins, 1952.

Doebler, Peter L. "Jest in Time: The Problems and Promises of the Holy Fool in Francesco, giullare di Dio, Ordet, and Ikiru." *Journal of Religion & Film* 17 (2013). http://digitalcommons.unomaha.edu/jrf/vol17/iss1/35.

Donohue, William. "The Passion of the Christ." The Catholic League (December 31, 2003). http://www.catholicleague.org/the-passion-of-the-christ-2/.

———. "What Catholics Have Said About the Passion of the Christ." The Catholic League (December 23, 2004). http://www.catholicleague.org/what-catholics-have-said-about-the-passion-of-the-christ/.

Doughton, Sandl. "Scientists' experiment 'melds' 2 minds." *Atlanta Journal and Constitution* (September 1, 2013) A10.

Ebert, Roger. "Dead Man Walking." (January 12, 1996.) http://www.rogerebert.com/reviews/dead-man-walking-1996.

Bibliography

———. "Diary of a Country Priest." (April 13, 2011.) http://www.rogerebert.com/reviews/great-movie-diary-of-a-country-priest-1951.

———. "Of Gods and Men." (March 10, 2011.) http://www.rogerebert.com/reviews/of-gods-and-men-2011.

Elliot, Carl. *Better Than Well*. New York: Norton, 2004.

Ellsberg, Robert. "Dearest Forster." *America* (November 15, 2010). http://americamagazine.org/issue/755/ideas/dearest-forster.

———. "Dorothy in Love." (November 25, 2010). http://americamagazine.org/issue/755/ideas/dorothy-love.

Ernst and Young. "Beyond Borders: Unlocking Value, Global Biotechnology Report 2014." http://www.ey.com/GL/en/Industries/Life-Sciences/EY-beyond-borders-unlocking-value-financing.

Facets. "The Decalogue: A Synopsis." http://www.facets.org/decalogue/synopsis.html.

Farago, Jason. "What does Pope Francis's taste in art, music and film say about him?" *The Guardian* (September 19, 2013). https://www.theguardian.com/world/2013/sep/19/pope-francis-jesuit-journal-interview-art.

Father Leo, Father Angelo, and Father Rufino. *Legend of Three Companions: Life of Saint Francis of Assisi*. Charleston: Nabu, 2012.

Feister, John Brooker. "Sister Helen Prejean, The Real Woman Behind Dead Man Walking." http://www.americancatholic.org/Messenger/Apr1996/feature1.asp.

Finnigan, David. "Dorothy Day Hits the Big Screen in 'Entertaining Angels.'" *National Catholic Register* (October 9, 1997). http://www.ncregister.com/site/article/dorothy_day_hits_the_big_screen_in_entertaining_angels.

Flesher, Paul V. M., and Robert Torry. *Film and Religion: An Introduction*. Nashville: Abingdon, 2007.

Forest, Jim. *All is Grace: A Biography of Dorothy Day*. Maryknoll, NY: Orbis, 2011.

Francis. "Address to the United States Congress." (September 24, 2015.) http://www.usccb.org/about/leadership/holy-see/francis/papal-visit-2015/media-resources/upload/11-EN-congressional-address.pdf.

Gaffney, Edward McGlynn, Jr. "Principled Resignation of Thomas More." *Loyola Los Angeles Law Review* 31 (1997–1998) 63–78.

Gallagher, Tag. *The Adventures of Roberto Rossellini*. Cambridge, MA: Da Capo, 1989.

Gallup. "Death Penalty." (June, 2014.) http://www.gallup.com/poll/1606/Death-Penalty.aspx.

Ganson, Barnara. *The Guarani Under Spanish Rule in the Rio De La Plata*. Stanford, CA: Stanford University Press, 2005.

Glatz, Carol. "Homebody, soccer fan, tango-lover—some papal pastimes revealed." *Catholic News Service* (April 3, 2013). http://www.catholicnews.com/data/stories/cns/1301503.htm.

Green, Ronald, and Aine Donovan. "Genetics as Religion: Gattaca's Disquieting Vision." In *The Human Genome Project in College Curriculum: Ethical Issues and Practical Strategies*, edited by Aine Donovan and Ronald Green, 122–31. Hanover, NH: Dartmouth University Press, 2008.

Greydanus, Steven D. "Is Hollywood Anti-Catholic?" *Christianity Today* (May 12, 2009). http://www.christianitytoday.com/ct/2009/mayweb-only/ishollywoodanticatholic.html.

Hagelstein, Roman. *Explaining the Violence Pattern of the Algerian Civil War*. University of Suffolk: Institute of Development Studies, 2008.

Bibliography

Hamer, Dean. *Living with Our Genes*. New York: Doubleday, 1998.
Haskins, Susan. *Mary Magdalen: Myth and Metaphor*. New York: Harcourt and Brace, 1993.
Haught, John. *Science and Religion, From Conflict to Conversation*. New York: Paulist, 1995.
Hayward, Susan. *French National Cinema*. London: Routledge, 1993.
Henry VIII. *The Supremacy Act 1534*. http://law2.umkc.edu/faculty/projects/ftrials/more/moreacts2.html#The_Supremacy_Act_1534.
Higher Education Research Institute at UCLA. *The American Freshman: National Norms for Fall 2003*.
———. "The American Freshman: National Norms for Fall 2015."
Hinson, Hal. "A Tale of Giving the Devil His Due." *Washington Post* (January 12, 1995). http://www.washingtonpost.com/wpsrv/style/longterm/movies/videos/deadmanwalking.htm#hinson.
Holden, Stephen. "The Art of Film, via Brat and Brooder." *The New York Times* (August 5, 1998). http://www.nytimes.com/movie/review?res=9B05E1D9173BF936A3575BC0A96E958260.
Insdorf, Annette. *Double Lives, Second Chances: The Cinema of Krzysztof Kieslowski*. New York: Hyperion, 1999.
Jewett, Garth S. "'A Capacity for Evil': The 1915 Supreme Court Decision." *Historical Journal of Film, Radio, and Television* 9:1 (1989) 59–78.
Joffe, Roland. "*The Mission* Audio Commentary." https://wn.com/Roland_Joffe/video-details.
John Paul II. *Evangelium Vitae*. Boston: Pauline, 1995.
———. *Fides et Ratio*. Boston: Pauline, 1998.
———. "Letter to George V. Coyne." http://www.vatican.va/holy_father/john_paul_ii/letters/1988/documents/hf_jp-ii_let_19880601_padre-coyne_en.html.
———. *Proclaiming Saint Thomas More Patron Saint of Statesmen and Politicians*. (October 31, 2001), n4. http://w2.vatican.va/content/john-paul-ii/en/motu_proprio/documents/hf_jp-ii_motu-proprio_20001031_thomas-more.html.
John XXIII. *Mater et Magistra*. New York: Paulist, 1963.
Kaufmann, Stanley. "Intriguers." *The New Republic* (November 17, 1997) 26.
Keegan, John E. "Robert Bresson's 'The Diary of a Country Priest': The Experience of God as Grace." *Sewanee Theological Review* 54 (Christmas 2010) 47–59.
Kickasoola, Joe. *The Films of Krzytzof Kieslowski*. New York: Continuum, 2004.
Kieslowski, Krzytzof. *Kieslowski on Kieslowski*. New York: Faber and Faber, 1995.
Kieslowski, Krzytzof, and Krzytzof Piesiewicz. *Decalogue: The Ten Commandments*. Translated by Phil Cavendish and Susannah Bluh. London: Faber and Faber, 1991.
Kirby, David A. "The New Eugenics in Cinema: Genetic Determinism and Gene Therapy in GATTACA." *Science Fiction Studies* 27:2 (2000) 193–215.
Kiser, John W. *The Monks of Tibhirine: Faith, Love, and Terror in Algeria*. New York: St. Martins, 2000.
Lane, Anthony. "Brothers: 'Cedar Rapids' and 'Of Gods and Men.'" *The New Yorker* (February 28, 2011) 80–81.
Lawrence, D. H. *Late Essays and Articles*. Edited by James T. Boulton. London: Cambridge University Press, 2004.
Lawson, Lewis A., and Victor A. Kramer, eds. *More Conversations with Walker Percy*. Jackson, MI: University of Mississippi Press, 1984.

BIBLIOGRAPHY

Leary, Robin. "Surviving His Own Bad Habits: An Interview with Walker Percy." In *More Conversations with Walker Percy*, edited by Lewis Lawson and Victor Kramer, 59–65. Jackson, MS: University of Mississippi Press, 1993.

Leonard, Richard. *Movies That Matter: Reading Film through the Lens of Faith.* Chicago: Loyola Press, 2006.

Lewontin, Richard, et al. *Not in Our Genes.* New York: Pantheon, 1984.

Lombardo, Paul. *Three Generations, No Imbeciles: Eugenics, the Supreme Court, and Buck v. Bell.* Baltimore: John Hopkins University Press, 2010.

Magliano, Tony. "Vatican Conference Urges Church to Abandon Just War Theory." *National Catholic Reporter* (April 25, 2016). http://ncronline.org/blogs/making-difference/vatican-conference-urges-church-abandon-just-war-theory.

Marcus, Gary, and Christof Koch. "The Plug and Play Brain." *The Wall Street Journal* (March 15–16, 2014) C1.

Markaj, Ornela. "A Changed View of 'To Kill a Mockingbird.'" *TSJ* (March 5, 2014). http://thestudentlawyer.com/2014/03/05/a-changed-view-of-to-kill-a-mockingbird/.

Martin, James. "A Profound Work of Art." *America* (February 27, 2011). http://americamagazine.org/content/all-things/profound-work-art.

Martin, Joel, and Conrad E. Ostwalt Jr. *Screening the Sacred: Religion, Myth, and Ideology in Modern American Film.* Boulder, CO: Westview, 1995.

Maurer, Monika. *Krzytzof Kieslowski.* Hapenden: Pocket Essentials, 2000.

Mayer, R., and R. Moreno. "A split-attention effect in multimedia learning: Evidence for dual processing systems in working memory." *Journal of Educational Psychology* 90 (1998) 312–20.

McNaspy, C. J. *Lost Cities of Paraguay.* Chicago: Loyola University Press, 1986.

Merton, Thomas. *Conjectures of a Guilty Bystander.* New York: Doubleday, 1966.

———. "Letter to Mr. L. Dickson." In *Witness to Freedom*, edited by William M. Shannon, 168–69. New York: Harcourt Brace, 1994.

———. *New Seeds of Contemplation.* New York: New Directions, 1961.

Miles, Margaret R. *Seeing and Believing: Religion and Values in Film.* Boston: Beacon, 1996.

Nagy, Zoltan Abadi. "Walker Percy, The Art of Fiction No. 97." *Paris Review* 103 (Summer, 1987). http://www.theparisreview.org/interviews/2643/the-art-of-fiction-no-97-walker-percy.

New, Elisa. "Good Bye Children; Good Bye, Mary, Mother of Sorrows: The Church and the Holocaust in the Art of Louis Malle." *Prooftexts* 22:1–2 (2002) 118–40.

Niebuhr, Gustav. "Spiritual Values Are in But Please no Sermonizing." *The New York Times* (September 1, 1996) 7, 14.

Nielsen, "Content is King, But Viewing Habits Vary by Demographic." (December 3, 2014). http://www.nielsen.com/us/en/insights/news/2014/content-is-king-but-viewing-habits-vary-by-demographic.html.

Nouwen, Henri J. M. *Bread for the Journey: A Daybook of Wisdom and Faith.* New York: Harper Collins, 2006.

The Numbers. "Domestic Movie Theatrical Market Summary 1995 to 2016." http://www.the-numbers.com/market/.

O'Connor, Flannery. *Mystery and Manners.* New York: Farrar, Strauss and Giroux, 1969.

Orden, Erica. "Hollywood's New Bible Stories." *Wall Street Journal* (September 28, 2012) D1–D2.

BIBLIOGRAPHY

Orlet, Christiopher. "Mel Gibson vs. 'The Jews'." *Salon* (August 14, 2003). http://www.salon.com/2003/08/14/gibson_6/.

Ortiz, Gaye Williams. "Women, Theology and Film." In *Teaching Religion and Film*, edited by Gregory J. Watkins, 165–76. Oxford: Oxford University Press, 2008.

Pacatte, Rose. "A decade later, 'The Passion' still raises questions of anti-Semitism." *National Catholic Reporter* (February 22, 2014). http://ncronline.org/news/art-media/decade-later-passion-still-raises-questions-anti-semitism.

———. "'Exodus: Gods and Kings' is stunning but barely concedes the miraculous." *National Catholic Reporter* (December 12, 2014). http://ncronline.org/blogs/ncr-today/exodus-gods-and-kings-stunning-barely-concedes-miraculous.

———. "The Passion of the Christ, A Female Critic's Perspective." http://www.marianist.com/articles/passion-of-the-christ-nun.pdf.

Papantonio, Mike. *In Search of Atticus Finch*. Pensacola, FL: Seville, 1996.

Parham, Thomas. "Why Do Heathens Make the Best Films?" In *Behind the Screen: Hollywood Insiders on Faith, Film, and Culture*, edited by Spencer Lewerenz and Barbara Nicolosi, 53–64. Grand Rapids: Baker, 2005.

Patterson, Margot. "An Extraordinary Difficult Childhood." *National Catholic Reporter* (March 7, 2003). http://natcath.org/NCR_Online/archives/030703/030703k.htm.

Pelikan, Jarolsav. *Jesus Through the Centuries: His Place in the History of Culture*. New Haven, CT: Yale University Press, 1999.

Percy, Walker. *The Moviegoer*. New York: Vintage, 1998.

Pew Research, Religion and Public Life Project. "Nones on the Rise." (2012). http://www.pewforum.org/2012/10/09/nones-on-the-rise/.

Pipolo, Tony. *Robert Bresson, A Passion for Film*. New York: Oxford University Press, 2009.

Pius XI. "On the Occasion of the Papal Mass in St. Peter's for the Canonization of St. Thomas More." (1935). http://www.catholictradition.org/Papacy/piusxi-masterpiece.htm.

———. *Vigilanti Cura*. National Catholic Welfare Conference: Washington, DC, 1936.

Pius XII. "Technical Advances and the Power of Movies." In *Pius XII and Technology*, edited by Leo J. Hagerty, 232–36. Milwaukee: Bruce, 1962.

Plate, Brent S. *Religion and Film: Cinema and the Recreation of the World*. New York: Wallflower, 2008.

Polk, Bryan. Review of Peter Dans, *Christians in the Movies: A Century of Sinners and Saints*. *Journal of Religion & Film* 17 (2013). http://digitalcommons.unomaha.edu/jrf/vol17/iss2/2.

Ponder, Justin. "O Great God, Humility and Camera Movement in Roberto Rossellini's 'The Flowers of St. Francis.'" *Journal of Religion and Film* 17 (April, 2013) 1–32.

Prejean, Helen. *Dead Man Walking*. New York: Vintage, 1994.

Radcliffe, Timothy. "The Christian Imagination and the Contemporary Search for Wisdom." (2012) http://www.bing.com/videos/search?q=youtube+aquinas+center&qpvt=youtube+aquinas+center&FORM=VDRE#view=detail&mid=35D49380DDF907EA855A35D49380DDF907EA855A.

Reed, Annette. "Who Gets to Decide if Noah is Biblical?" (April 1, 2014.) http://www.religiondispatches.org/archive/atheologies/7741/who_gets_to_decide_if_noah_is_biblical/.

Renoux, Christine. "The Origin of the Peace Prayer of Saint Francis." (2011.) http://www.franciscan-archive.org/franciscana/peace.html.

Richtel, Matt. "Thou Shalt Not Kill Except in a Game at Church." *The New York Times* (October 7, 2007) A1, A20.

BIBLIOGRAPHY

Rossellini, Roberto. *My Method: Writings and Interviews*. Padua: Marsilio, 1995.
Rychlak, Ronald J. *Hitler, the War and the Pope*. Huntington, IN: Our Sunday Visitor, 2000.
Saeger, James Schofield. "The Mission and Historical Missions: Film and the Writing of History." *The Americas* 51 (1995) 393–415.
Sartre, Jean-Paul. *No Exit and Three Other Plays*. New York: Vintage, 1949.
Schrader, Paul. *Transcendental Style in Film: Ozu, Bresson, Dreyer*. Berkeley: University of California Press, 1972.
Scorsese, Martin. "A Personal Appreciation." (2005). http://eurekavideo.co.uk/moc/catalogue/francesco-giullare-di-dio/essay.
Second Vatican Council. *Nostra Aetate*. http://www.vatican.va/archive/hist_councils/ii_vatican_council/documents/vat-ii_decl_19651028_nostra-aetate_en.html.
———. *Pastoral Constitution on the Church in the Modern World: Gaudium et Spes*. Boston: Pauline, 1966.
Seitz, Matt Zoller. "Noah." (2014.) http://www.rogerebert.com/reviews/noah-2014.
Sessions, William. "Flannery O'Connor and Freud, the Meaning of Life in Death." https://www.youtube.com/watch?v=ReXP1W-pm8w.
Siciliano, Enzo. *Pasolino*. Translated by John Shepley. New York: Random House, 1982.
Stelter, Brian. "8 Hours a Day Spent on TV." *The New York Times* (March 26, 2009). http://www.nytimes.com/2009/03/27/business/media/27adco.html?_r=0.
Stok, Danusia, ed. *Kieslowski on Kieslowski*. London: Faber and Faber, 1993.
Stone, Bryan. *Faith and Film*. Saint Louis: Chalice, 2000.
Teilhard de Chardin, Pierre. *Hymn of the Universe*. New York: Harper and Row, 1964.
Telford, William R. "Religion, theology and the Bible in recent films (1993–2004)." In *Cinéma Divinité*, edited by Eric Christianson, et al., 347–51. London: SCM, 2005.
Tennant, Agnieszka. "Heaven for a Terrorist." *Books and Culture, A Christian Review* (March 2003). http://www.booksandculture.com/articles/2003/marapr/4.19.html.
Thompson, Phillip. "Augustine and the Death Penalty: Justice as the Balance of Mercy and Judgment." *Augustinian Studies* 40:2 (2009) 181–203.
———. *Returning to Reality, Thomas Merton's Wisdom for a Technological World*. Eugene, OR: Cascade, 2012.
Tillich, Paul. "The Lost Dimension in Religion." *Saturday Evening Post* 230 (June 14, 1958) 29, 76–79.
———. *Theology of Culture*. Edited by Robert C. Kimball. New York: Oxford University Press, 1964.
Tingley, Kim. "One Child, Three Parents." *The New York Times Magazine* (June 29, 2014) 26–31, 38.
Tolkien, J. R. R. "Leaf by Niggle." *The Dublin Review* 432 (January 1945) 46–61.
Tracy, David. *The Analogical Imagination*. New York: Crossroad, 1998.
Twain, Mark. *Huckleberry Finn*. New York: Harper and Brother, 1912.
United States Conference of Catholic Bishops. "Liturgy of the Hours." http://www.usccb.org/prayer-and-worship/liturgy-of-the-hours/.
United States Conference of Catholic Bishops' Committee for Ecumenical and Interreligious Affairs. "Criteria for Evaluation of Dramatizations of the Passion." Washington, DC: 1988.
Vogel, Gretchen. "From Science Fiction to Ethical Quandary." *Science* 277 (1997) 1753–54.
Walsh, Frank. *Sin and Censorship*. New Haven, CT: Yale University Press, 1996.
Ware, Kallistos. "Holy Fool as Prophet and Apostle." *Sobernost* 6:2 (1984) 6–28.

BIBLIOGRAPHY

Weinstein, Harvey. "In Memoriam—Krzysztof Kieslowski." http://www.petey.com/kk/docs/smkedrnk.txt.

Wildhagen, Tina. "How Teachers and Schools Contribute to Racial Differences in the Realization of Academic Potential." *Teachers College Record* 114:7 (2012) 1–27.

Winslow, Ron. "Altered Gene Points to Longer Life Span." *The Wall Street Journal* (August 30, 2013) A3.

Wintz, Jack. "Father Kieser's New Film." *Catholic Messenger* (September 1996). http://www.americancatholic.org/Messenger/Sep1996/Feature1.asp.

Wolf, Kenneth Baxter. *The Poverty of Riches: St. Francis of Assisi Reconsidered*. Oxford: Oxford University Press, 2003.

Wright, Melanie J. *Religion and Film: An Introduction*. New York: Palgrave MacMillan, 2008.

Yam, Phillip. "Clean Genes." *Scientific American* (October, 1997) 153–154.

Zupan, Katherine A. A. *Philosophy for Breakfast*. Lulu.com, 2012.

Index/Subject Index

A
A Man for All Seasons, 10–13, 19–28, 38, 165
Alleva, Richard, 112
 "Diminishing Dorothy Day", 112n6
Anker, Roy, 74
 Catching Light, Looking for God in the Movies, 74n10, 74n11
Aquinas, Thomas, xiii–xiv, 8, 57n9
Au Revoir Les Enfants, 9, 13–14, 89–97, 165
Axel, Gabriel, 71–72

B
Babette's Feast, 6, 9, 13, 71–78, 165
Baker, Elizabeth Gaylynn, 85
 "Rediscovering Community Care of the Spitfire Grill", 85n8
Barbour, Ian, xiv
 Science in an Age of Religion, xivn17
Batterham, Forster, 114
Bauder, David, xi
 "Media use in America up a full hour over just last year", xin4
Baugh, Lloyd, 102
 Imaging the Divine, 102n9
 "The Christian Moral Vision of a Believing Atheist", 131n9, 131n10
Baum, Gregory, 52
 Man Becoming: God in Secular Experience, 52n4
Bazin, Andre, 30, 133

"What is Cinema?", 30n2, 133n12
Beaty, Katelyn, 62
 "Of Gods and Men", 62n7
Beauvois, Xavier, 60
Benedict XVI, 111
 "Pope: Pray for me, future Pope, the Lord will guide us!", 111n2
Bergman, Ingrid, 36
Bernanos, Georges, 52, 52n5
Berrigan, Daniel, 43n12
Black, Gregory D., xii
 The Catholic Crusade Against Movies, xiiin10
Black Madonna of Częstochowa, 130–31
Blake, Richard A., xvi, 163
 Afterimage, The Indelible Imagination of Six Catholic Filmmakers, xvin24
 "Converts", 84n5, 163n2
Blixen, Karen, 72, 72n4
Bock, Jonathan, xv
Bolt, Robert, 19, 19n1, 38
Bond, James, 3
Bresson, Robert, 51–53
Brother Sun, Sister Moon, 4–5
Brunette, Peter, 31
 Roberto Rossellini, 31n6

C
Cain, 42n10
Calvary, 165
Caputo, John, 167
 On Religion, 167n11

183

Index/Subject Index

Catechism of the Catholic Church, 107n14
Catholic
   directors, xvin24
   eugenics, 143
   Legion of Decency, xi
   No proselytizing, 84
Catholic League, 157
Catholic Worker, 110–19
censorship, xi-xiii
Chesterton, G.K., 19–20
   The Fame of Blessed Thomas More, 20n3
Clark, John Clark and Odell, John Price, 20
   A Study of American and English Writers, 20n4
Clement XIV, 41
college students, xv
   religious affiliation, xv
Comar, Etienne, 60
common good, 9, 13, 73–80, 83–86
community, 83–85, 166
compassion, 1–2, 35, 65, 94, 100–101, 103–4
Connery, Sean, 3
conscience, 10, 27, 42, 45, 105
conversion, 7, 42–43, 55–56, 61, 76–77, 80, 85, 103–8
Coyne, George, xiv
Crowther, Bosley, 20n5
Cunningham, Lawrence, 29
   The Catholic Heritage, 29
Cyril of Jerusalem, 165

D
Davies, Kevin, 142
   "Discrimination Down to a Science", 142n10
Dawkins, Richard, 142
   "It's All in the Genes", 142n12
Day, Dorothy, 110–19
Day, Tamar, 117
Dead Man Walking, 10, 14, 98–109, 165
death penalty, ix

Decalogue 1—I am the Lord Your God, 11, 14, 123–32, 165
Decalogue 5—You Shall Not Kill, ix
De Niro, Robert, 7
Derrickson, Scott, x
Diary of a Country Priest, 7, 13, 51–59, 165
Diogenes, 57, 57n10
Dirty Harry, 2
Dogma, x
Donohue, William, 157
   "The Passion of the Christ", 157n15, 157n16
Donovan, Aine, 142
   "Genetics as Religion", 142n12
Doubt, 165
Dreyer, Theodore, 73n6
Dr. Zhivago, 3, 47

E
Eastwood, Clint, 2
Ebert, Roger, 58, 65, 98–99
   "Of Gods and Men", 65n10
   "Dead Man Walking", 99
Elie, Paul, 167n10
Eliot, Carl, 136
   Better Than Well, 136n5
Ellsberg, Robert, 114
   "Dorothy in Love", 114n8
Elshtain, Jean Bethke, v, xix
Endo, Shusaku, 167
Entertaining Angels, 14, 110–19
Erasmus, 19
eucharist, 74–75
eugenics, 133–144
Exodus, xv

F
faith, 117, 125–32
faith and reason, 10
Feister, John Booker, 99
   "Sister Helen Prejean, The Real Woman Behind Dead Man Walking", 99n5, 100n6
Fellini, Frederico, 29, 31
Finnigan, David, 112

Index/Subject Index

"Dorothy Day Hits the Big Screen in 'Entertaining Angels'", 112n5
Flesher, Paul and Robert Torry, 153
  Film and Religion, 154n6
Forest, Jim, 112
  All is Grace, 112n7
forgiveness, 68, 76
fortitude, 7–8, 22–26, 52, 55, 58, 66, 137–39

G
Gallagher, Tag, 32
  The Adventures of Roberto Rossellini, 32n8
Ganson, Barbara, 40
  The Guarani Under Spanish Rule, 40n2
GATTACA, 8, 10–11, 15–16, 133–45, 165
Gaudium et Spes, 10, 10n12
Gaylin, Wilard, 139
Gibson, Mel, 156, 156n11
Glatz, Carol, 71
  "Homebody, soccer fan, tango-lover--some papal pastimes revealed", 71n2
grace, 5, 7–8, 52–53, 56–58, 74, 118
Greydanus, Steven D., x
  "Is Hollywood Anti-Catholic?", xn3
Guardini, Romano, 149

H
Hagelstein, Roman, *Explaining the Violence Pattern of the Algerian Civil War*, 62n5
Hamer, Dean, 134
  Living with Our Genes, 134n2
Haught, John, xiv
  Science in an Age of Religion, xivn17
healing, 79–86
Henry VIII, 20–21, 23
Heyward, Susan, 93
  French National Cinema, 93n3
Hinson, Hal, 100

"A Tale of Giving the Devil His Due", 100n7
Holden, Stephen, 125
  "The Art of Film, via Brat and Brooder", 125n3
Holocaust, 89–97
Homer, 73
  Odyssey, 73
hope, 107
hospitality, 74
Huckleberry Finn, 95, 95n6
humility, 31–33
Huxley, Aldous, 135

I
idolatry, 11
information technology, 164
Innocent III, 30
Insdorf, Annette, 130
  Double Lives, Second Chances, 130n8
integrity, 22–24
Irons, Jeremy, 7

J
Jansenism, 51n1
Jesuits, 38–40, 42
Jesus, 11, 14, 74, 81, 84, 104, 131, 149–159, 165
Jesus of Nazareth, 150, 153, 156
Jewett, Garth S., xii
  "A Capacity for Evil, The 1915 Supreme Court Decision", xiin8
Joffe, Roland, 38
John XXIII, xiv, 9, 163
  Mater et Magistra, 9n11
  Princeps Pastorum, 163
John Paul II, xiii–xiv, 10, 27, 107, 126
  critical openness, xiii–xiv, 164–65
  death penalty, 107n12
  Evangelium Vitae, 107n13
  Fides et Ratio, 10, 10n13
  "Letter to George Coyne", xivn16
  "Proclaiming Saint Thomas More Patron Saint of Statesmen and Politicians", 27, 27n11

Index/Subject Index

Judas, 152–53, 164
justice, ix, 13–14, 24, 107–8
just war, 3, 45

K
Kauffman, Stanley, 141
   "Intriguers", 141n8
kenosis, 77
Kickasoola, Joe, 129, 131
   The Films of Krzysztof Kieslowski, 129n7, 131n12
Kieslowski, Krzysztof, ix, 3, 123–25, 127–29, 131
   Kieslowski on Kieslowski, 129n6
Kiser, John W., 60–61, 61n3
   The Monks of Tibhirine, Faith, Love, and Terror in Algeria, 61n3, 62n4

L
Lane, Anthony, 63
   "Brothers: 'Cedar Rapids' and 'Of Gods and Men'", 63n8
Lascaux caves, x
Lawrence, D.H., 77
   "Late Essays and Articles", 77n16
Laydu, Claude, 58n11
Leary, Robin, xi
   "Surviving His Own Bad Habits", xin4
Leo X, 20
Leonard, Richard, xvii
Liberius, Pope. 30n1
Lombardo, Paul, 143
   Three Generations, No Imbeciles, 143n13

M
Magliano, Tony, 3
   "Vatican Conference Urges Church to Abandon Just War Theory", 3n5, 45n14
Malle, Louis, 89
Martin, James, 60–61
   "A Profound Work of Art", 61n1

"Full Transcript Interview with Martin Scorsese", 167n10
Maurer, Monika, 124
   Krzysztof Kieslowski, 124n2
Markaj, Ornela, 163
   "A Changed View of to 'Kill a Mockingbird'", 163n1
Mary Magdalene, 152, 152n3, 153
Mary, mother of Jesus, 152
Mary Poppins, 2
Maurin, Peter, 115–116
McNaspy, C.J., 40
   Lost Cities of Paraguay, 40n4
Merton, Thomas, xi
   Conjectures of a Guilty Bystander, xin5
   New Seeds of Contemplation, 118n13
Miles, Margaret, x
   Seeing and Believing, Religion and Values in the Movies, xn2, 40n5, 41n7
Montesquieu, 40
   Esprit des Lois, 40
More, Thomas, 10–11, 19–28, 44, 51
Motion Picture Production Code, xii
Muggeridge, Malcolm, 165, 165n8
Mutual Film Corporation v. Industrial Commission of Ohio (1915), xiin8

N
National Catholic Register, xvii
nature, 35, 47, 84, 139–40
New, Elisa, 93
   "Good Bye Children; Good Bye, Mary, Mother of Sorrows", 93n4
Niccol, Andrew, 133
Niebuhr, Gustav, 85
   "Spiritual Values are in But Please no Sermonizing", 85n7
Nieli, Bruce, 112
neorealism, 30–31
Noah, xiv–xv
Nostra Aetate, 156, 156n10, 157

Index/Subject Index

Nouwen, Henri, 82–83
  Bread for the Journey, 83n4

O

O'Connor, Flannery, xvii
  Mystery and Manners, xviin26
Odyssey, 80
Of Gods and Men, 1–2, 9, 13, 60–68, 89, 95, 165
O'Neill, Eugene, 113
Ora et labora, 62
Orden, Erica, xv
  "Hollywood's New Bible Stories", xvn20
Orlet, Christopher, 157n12
Ortiz, Gaye Williams, 5
  "Women, Theology and Film", 5

P

Pacatte, Rose, 157, 157n13, 164n7
pacifism, 45n14, 46, 111
Papantonio, Mike, 163
  In Search of Atticus Finch, 163n1
Parham, Thomas, xvi
  Why Do Heathens Make the Best Films, xviin25
Pasolini, Pier, xiv
Patterson, Margot, 117
  "An Extraordinary Difficult Childhood", 117n12
Pax Christi, 112, 112n5
Pelikan, Jaroslav, 155n8
  Jesus Through the Centuries, 155n8
penance, 42–43
Percy, Walker, xi, 53, 53n7
Phan, Peter, 168
Piesiewicz, Krzysztof, 123–24
Pilate, 153, 155, 158
pilgrimage, 8, 55, 63–67, 113, 139
Pius XI, xii, 21, 27–28
  Vigilanti Cura, xiin12
  "On the Occasion of the Papal Mass in St. Peter's for the Canonization of St. Thomas More", 28n13
Pius XII, xii, xiii, 93

"Technical Advances and the Power of Movies", xiiin13
holocaust 93
Pleasance, Donald, 152
Polk, Bryan, xvi
  "Review of *Christians in the Movies*", xvin23
Ponder, Justin, 31
  "O Great God, Humility and Camera Movement in Roberto Rossellini's 'The Flowers of St. Francis.'", 31n5
Pope Francis, 71, 110–11
  "Address to the United States Congress", 110n1
poverty, 35–36, 113–18
Prejean, Helen, 99–108
pride, 32, 55
priest, pedophilia scandal, 165
Proust, Marcel, 163–64
  In Remembrance of Things Past, 163–64

R

Radcliffe, Timothy, 1–2
  "The Christian Imagination and the Contemporary Search for Wisdom", 2n1
reason and faith, 23–24, 129
redemption, 7–8
Rhodes, Michael Ray, 110
Robbins, Tim, 98, 100
Rossellini, Roberto, 29–32, 37, 30n4
Rousseau, Jean Jacques, 40
  Discourse on the Origin and Foundation of the Inequality Amongst Men, 40

S

sacramentality, 6, 8, 56–57, 67, 73–75, 129
sacrifice 80
Saeger, James Schofield, 41
  "The Mission and Historical Missions, Film and the Writing of History", 41n6
Saint Francis, 4–6, 29–37, 51

San Francisco Earthquake, 110
Sartre, Jean Paul, 52
 No Exit, 52, 52n3
Satan, 152, 156
Saving Mr. Banks, 2n2
Scorsese, Martin, 34, 36, 168
 "A Personal Appreciation", 34n11, 36, n12
Seitz, Matt Zoller, xv
 Noah, xvn9
servant leader, 46
Sessions, William, 166
Shakespeare, 165
Siciliano, Enzo, 149n1
 Pasolino, 149
Silence, 167–168
Sinclair, Upton, 112
 The Jungle, 112
Sisyphus, 42
solidarity, 65
Song of Bernadette, 6
Spitfire Grill, 11, 13, 79–86
Spotlight, 165
Stok, Danusia, 3
 Kieslowski on Kieslowski, 3
Stone, Bryan, 43, 150
 Faith and Film, 43n11, 150n2
suffering, 53
suffragist, 113
Swift, Jonathan, 20

T
targum, 154
Taylor, Joan, 154n7
Teilhard de Chardin, Pierre, 6
 Hymn of the Universe, 6n7
Tennant, Agniezcka, 131
 "Heaven for a Terrorist, 131n10
The Bells of Saint Mary, 166
The Deer Hunter, 4
The Exorcism of Emily Rose, x
The Flowers of Saint Francis, 5–6, 10, 29–37, 165
The Gospel According to Saint Matthew, 150–51, 153
The Greatest Story Ever Told, 150, 152–53, 156

The Incredible Hulk, xi
The King of Kings, 150, 152–155
The Kiss, xi
The Last Temptation of Christ, 150–153, 155
The Mission, 7, 9, 12, 38–48, 51, 165
The Others, x
The Passion of the Christ, 150, 152–153, 156–57, 157n13, 157, n15, 157n16, 158
The Son of God, 152, 152n4, 158
The Sound of Music, 165
The Widow Jones, xi
Thompson, Phillip, 107
 "Augustine and the Death Penalty, Justice as the Balance of Mercy and Judgment", 107n12
Tillich, Paul, xiii, 131
 "The Lost Dimension in Religion", xiiin14
 Theology of Culture, 131n11
Tingley, Kim, 144
 "One Child, Three Parents", 144n14
To Kill a Mockingbird, 3–4, 81n3, 163
Tolkien, J.R.R., 75
 "Leaf by Niggle", 75n12
Tracy, David, 158, 159
 The Analogical Imagination, 159n19
Transformers, xiv

U
Unforgiven, 102
United States Catholic Conference, 111, 157, 157n14
Urban VIII, 41n8

V
V for Vendetta, x
Vatican Office of Social Communications, xvii
Vietnam War, 4

W
Walsh, Frank, xi-xii
 Sin and Censorship, xin7, xiin9

Index/Subject Index

Ware, Kallistos, 31
  "Holy Fool as Prophet and
    Apostle", 31n7
Watson, James, 133
Wells, John, 110
Wildhagen, Tina, 141
  "How Teachers and Schools
    Contribute to Racial
    Differences in the Realization
    of Academic Potential", 141n7
Wintz, Jack, 116
  "Father Kieser's New Film, 116
wisdom, 11
  biblical, 123–24
  discernment, 63–64, 66–67,
    105–6
  genetic determinism, 135–36
  life as gift, 141, 143
  in humility, 34, 77, 129
  in realizing error, 80
  life as gift, 126, 128–29
  self-examination, 130
  servant leader, 46–47
  spiritual guidance, 55–56
  through education, 24–26
Wolf, Kenneth Baxter, 34
  *The Poverty of Riches: St Francis of
    Assisi Reconsidered*, 34n10
Wright, Melanie, x
  *Religion and Film: An
    Introduction*, xn1

X
xenia, 73

Y
Yam, Phillip, 142
  "Clean Genes", 142n9

Z
Zefferelli, Franco, 156
Zinnemann, Fred, 19, 19n1
Zlotoff, David Lee, 79, 81, 84–85
Zupan, Katherine, 19
  Philosophy for Breakfast 19

Scripture Index

OLD TESTAMENT

Deuteronomy

25:5	20n6

Ecclesiastes

3:1–2	11, 75
7:13	139

Exodus

20:13	11

Genesis

4:8–15	107
4:14	42n10
6:4	xivn18
19:1–3	73n7
20:3	123
24:22–25	73n8
31:21–55	80

Isaiah

9:2	vi

Jeremiah

8:21–22	80
8:22	79

Job

6:11	89

Leviticus

20:21	20n6

Nahum

1	80

Psalm

85	76
112:4	168
139:14	133

1 Samuel

1	80n1

2 Samuel

17:22–29	80

Wisdom

7:28–29	1

Scripture Index

NEW TESTAMENT

1 Corinthians
1:27–29	29
13:2–13	43

Galatians
3:28	47

Hebrews
13:2	110
13:3	98

1 John
4:7–8	127n4
4:16	60

John
1:5	47
4:1–3	77n15
6:51	74, 74n9
11:14	51
13:35	71

Luke
1:28, 42	153
5:29	74n9
23:24	67n12

Mark
8:36	19

Matthew
4:16	vi
8:13	5
8:20	149
10:16	11
11:15	76
13:46	168
27:19	158

Romans
2:14–15	7n9

2 Timothy
4:7	59n13

www.ingramcontent.com/pod-product-compliance
Lightning Source LLC
Chambersburg PA
CBHW021730220426
43662CB00008B/781